TOXIC FRIENDSHIPS

TOXIC FRIENDSHIPS

Knowing the Rules and Dealing with the Friends Who Break Them

Suzanne Degges-White and Judy Pochel Van Tieghem

ROWMAN & LITTLEFIELD
Lanham • Boulder • New York • London

Published by Rowman & Littlefield
A wholly owned subsidiary of The Rowman & Littlefield Publishing Group, Inc.
4501 Forbes Boulevard, Suite 200, Lanham, Maryland 20706
www.rowman.com

Unit A, Whitacre Mews, 26-34 Stannary Street, London SE11 4AB

British Library Cataloguing in Publication Information Available

Library of Congress Cataloging-in-Publication Data

Degges-White, Suzanne.
Toxic friendships : knowing the rules and dealing with the friends who break them / Suzanne
Degges-White and Judy Pochel Van Tieghem.
pages cm
Includes bibliographical references and index.
ISBN 978-1-4422-3997-5 (cloth : alk. paper) — ISBN 978-1-4422-3998-2 (electronic)
1. Friendship. 2. Friendship in women. I. Van Tieghem, Judy Pochel, 1960– II. Title.
BF575.F66D443 2015
158.2'5082—dc23
2014046225

∞™ The paper used in this publication meets the minimum requirements of
American National Standard for Information Sciences Permanence of Paper for
Printed Library Materials, ANSI/NISO Z39.48-1992.

Printed in the United States of America

CONTENTS

Acknowledgments   vii

Preface   ix

PART I: UNDERSTANDING THE NEED FOR SOCIAL CONNECTION   I

1 The Need for Community   3

2 Friendship Patterns from Girlhood through Older Adulthood   13

PART II: THE RULES OF FRIENDSHIP AND THEIR ROLE IN RELATIONSHIPS   25

3 It's a Matter of Trust   27

4 Just the Way You Are   37

5 Any Friend of Hers Is a Friend of Mine   51

6 Being There with Emotional Support   63

7 A Friend in Need   77

8 Keep the "Friendship Favors" Balance in Check   87

9 Defending Your Honor   97

10 Bring Joy to Your Friends   109

11 Criticism Is Not Okay   119

12 Jealousy Is Not Okay   129

13 A Rule-by-Rule Guide for Parents   139

PART III: TOXIC ENVIRONMENTS OUTSIDE THE HOME   155

14 Soccer Moms and Carpool Divas   157

15 Church and Civic Group Friends   167

16 Down the Street and on the Job: Getting Along with
Neighbors and Coworkers   175

PART IV: TAKING STOCK AND CUTTING BACK   187

17 Playing by the Rules   189

18 Writing Your Own Rules of Relationship   203

19 Taking Stock and Letting Go   221

Notes   237

Bibliography   253

Index   261

About the Authors   265

ACKNOWLEDGMENTS

Thank you so much to all of the women who willingly shared their stories when invited to speak about past friendship conflicts and their difficult friends. Many of these women had learned beneficial lessons through these incidents, and they expressed hope that their own experiences might play a role in preparing readers to deal more effectively with any friendship conflicts they may face. The time and energy these women spent in sharing their stories is deeply appreciated.

We also would like to acknowledge the enthusiastic support of our editor, Suzanne Staszak-Silva. Her continued belief in our work is greatly appreciated. Lastly, we thank Lucy Parker and Jamie Colbert for their willingness to read even very rough drafts and provide constructive feedback, which definitely enhanced the final product.

S.E.D. & J.P.V.

PREFACE

While everyone needs a good friend, most of us have experienced a falling out with a friend or had a friendship fail at some point in our lives. A friend may have violated our trust, turned cold and distant, become too needy, refused to return a favor, or committed any one of a hundred other acts that bring the purpose and the value of the friendship into question. *Toxic* is a word frequently used to describe behaviors that poison or fracture relationships, and when we asked women to share their experiences with toxic friends, almost everyone had a story to tell.

Friendships and social networks are essential to our well-being throughout our lives. While many Western cultures (particularly that of the United States) may be much more individualistically focused than Eastern cultures, building networks to meet personal needs happens in every sphere of our lives, including social networks, neighborhood networks, professional networks, and so on. Most people learn how to build these relationships through trial and error. We model our relationships on a "give and take" social exchange framework. Within this framework, most of us recognize that we must invest in the friendship to be able to enjoy benefits from the relationship. Unfortunately, friends sometimes shortchange you or, perhaps, leave you feeling cheated. When this happens, it can produce a range of responses including anger, confusion, heartache, and feelings of betrayal. You may feel unsure of how to proceed. In this book, we share suggestions for assessment, evaluation, and responses to toxic incidents. Due to the complex composition of any relationship, there is seldom a "one size fits all" solution to any relationship conflict. However, we provide new perspectives and suggest areas for personal exploration to help you choose the solution that is right for you when faced with a toxic challenge.

ORGANIZATION OF THE BOOK

Within this book are the shared stories of composite clients and women who have experienced and dealt with friendships that have been marred by toxic behaviors. Out of respect for confidentiality, no real names have been used. Some stories provide hope that a fractured friendship can be mended and that some unfit friendships can be detoxified and restored to a healthy footing. Other tales underscore the irreparable damage that can be done to a relationship through just one toxic act. Through the course of this book, we explore the need for friendships, the unspoken rules of friendship, and suggestions for responding to those friends who break these rules. Although the focus of this book is women's friendships, much of the content is applicable to men as well.

Understanding the Need for Social Connection

The first section of the book is titled "Understanding the Need for Social Connection." The first chapter of this section explores the depth and breadth of the innate need for social connection, and the second chapter provides a life stage review of the role of friendships across the life span. For the purposes of this book, the life span has been segmented into the following six groups: "Young Girls and Almost Teens," "Teens and New Adults," "The Twenties and Thirties," "Mom-to-Mom Networks," "Midlife Connections," and "Older Adults." The first two groups cover young women from toddlerhood up through their very early twenties. The next group, "The Twenties and Thirties," covers women in adulthood as they establish and maintain their adult identities. The "Mom-to-Mom Networks" section addresses the complex social networking activities of mothers and their children. "Midlife Connections" covers women in the middle third of adulthood, from around age forty through around age sixty. The eponymous "Older Adults" section is focused on older adult women in the final third of adulthood from their early sixties onward.

The Rules of Friendship and Their Role in Relationships

The second section of the book is titled "The Rules of Friendship and Their Role in Relationships," and it includes eleven chapters. These chapters address ten unspoken, but universally understood, rules related to healthy relationships. Included in this group are "Being" rules; these rules describe the essential "ways of being" that we should demonstrate within relationships. These include being trusting and trustworthy, being empathetic to our friends, and being accepting of the other friends whom our friends will invariably possess. The next set of rules are the "Doing" rules; these describe the behaviors that are expected in friendships. The "doing" behaviors covered include providing emotional support, giving instrumental support, repaying favors without being asked, and standing up for your friends when they are not there to defend themselves. The last set consists of the "Refraining" rules, which describe behaviors that friends should avoid within the relationship. These include refraining from being a negative force or a nag to your friends, not criticizing your friends in the presence of others, and avoiding the expression of jealousy over your friends' other relationships.

Putting the Rule into Practice

Within each chapter addressing a specific rule, we present an overview of the importance of the rule and how the breaking of that rule may play out based on life stage. At the end of every chapter is a section called "Finding the Solution That Works," in which a variety of relevant points of reflection are presented. Not every toxic incident warrants dissolution of the relationship, but some breaches permanently dissolve the trust or positive regard essential to an enduring friendship. We offer suggestions for using the *severity* of the breach as a gauge to govern the appropriate level of response. We end this section with a chapter written just for parents of daughters who are involved in rule-breaking friendship exchanges.

Toxic Environments Outside the Home

The third section of the book is "Toxic Environments Outside the Home." In this section are three chapters that each address a potentially, and often unexpectedly, toxic environment. These include child-related networks such as athletic teams and carpool groups; church and civic organizations; and neighborhoods and workplaces. In each of these chapters, we share composite "types" of toxic individuals who may appear in these relational networks. Some of the toxic types may seem a bit extreme, but each is based on real people who have shown up and significantly affected interviewees' network-specific experiences. Suggestions for responding to these different types of difficult individuals are provided. These suggestions were developed based on the knowledge that many of these relationships must be preserved due to the setting in which they are found. Quitting your job, moving out of your home, changing affiliations or memberships, or removing your child from a team roster or convenient carpool group are seldom ideal solutions. Thus, learning how to detoxify your own responses and reactions to toxic situations may be the preferred way to cope with some of the "frenemies" you encounter outside the friendship and family relationship boundaries.

Taking Stock and Cutting Back

The final section of the book is "Taking Stock and Cutting Back." It includes three chapters that explore the process of determining which toxic relationships are worth efforts at repair and which friendships are ripe for elimination. In the chapter titled "Playing by the Rules," the essential personality traits necessary for participating in healthy friendships are described. In the following chapter, "Writing Your Own Rules of Relationship," we provide several self-reflection exercises that can help you recognize the vulnerable spots in your relationships as well as help you develop the rules you need to maintain healthy boundaries and healthy friendships. In the final chapter, "Taking Stock and Letting Go," reminders and guidelines related to the process of ending toxic relationships are presented. Choosing to end a relationship is often less difficult than actually letting go of the relationship. This chapter provides support to readers as they move from the planning stage to the doing stage of ending friendships that no longer serve a purpose in their lives.

CONCLUSION

Healthy friendships are vital to your overall well-being, but when they are disrupted by the toxic behaviors of a friend, you can be negatively affected in a variety of ways. Learning how to handle the most frequently experienced conflicts will provide you with the foundation necessary to respond to other unexpected friendship setbacks. In the following chapters, we explore the value of healthy social connections, the unspoken expectations of behavior, and guidelines for intentional self-exploration and relational decision-making. We hope that you enjoy reading this book and that it provides relevant information and helpful suggestions for refining and strengthening your friendscape.

Part I

Understanding the Need
for Social Connection

I

THE NEED FOR COMMUNITY

What's the first thing you tend to do each morning after you've fed the dogs, poured your coffee, and sat down at the table or desk or on the train? A decade or two ago, women would likely have mentioned something about opening the newspaper or checking out the *Today* show or *Good Morning America*. The current answer for many of us is probably "checking out the news on my phone," "catching up on e-mail," or "taking a look at Facebook." No longer are we tied to landlines, corded or cordless phones, or inflexible network television programming schedules. We can consume just about any form of media at any time that works for us. What hasn't changed is our need to stay connected to our friends and our social communities.

When Mark Zuckerberg created Facebook for its original limited purpose, he struck social gold and unintentionally found the perfect solution to meet the primal need for social connection. The latest statistics from the Pew Research Center[1] indicated that half of adult Facebook users have over two hundred friends in their networks. Clearly, we are a society that likes to connect. We are "friending" people we knew in middle school as well as people we just met this morning.

Growing our networks virtually, however, might not be the same at all as growing our networks in real time. The latter social circle may be the true measure of your social capital. Not all of us might feel comfortable calling on every one of those two hundred and some "friends" for some of the more demanding aspects of friendship. Most of us have a limited number of people we could reasonably expect to lend us a few hundred dollars, pick us up on the highway if our car has broken down, or let us whine about work for hours at a clip.

Women enjoy Facebook for reasons somewhat different from men's.[2] We like to see the photos and videos that are posted—it helps us feel more connected than e-mail and saves the time of a phone call when schedules are tight. We also like to connect with a lot of people at one time—uploading a single photo can share exciting news with all of our friends in one click—whether it's the photo of the new graduate, the brand-new grandbaby, the blushing bride, or a new SUV. Whether we have good news or bad news, we enjoy contact with our friends to help us celebrate or commiserate the significant and insignificant moments in our lives.

WITH A LITTLE HELP FROM OUR FRIENDS

A sentiment musically phrased by the Beatles[3] five decades ago provided a clear summation of what we all need most in life—good friends to help us get through it as easily as possible. People are driven to connect and build interpersonal ties with others for the purposes of comfort, security, and belonging.[4] In fact, social engagement can enhance our self-esteem[5] and leave us feeling better about the world and ourselves. Not only do we enjoy intrinsic rewards from social interaction, we also rely on our ability to build communities in order to advance civilization; today, these include online and virtual communities. Throughout history, social organizations have grown increasingly complex as our ability to "tame the world" has increased. Historically, community collaboration allowed people to enjoy benefits and reap rewards that individuals or even families could not generate on their own. We have learned to rely on others to produce the goods that we cannot produce ourselves—whether it's vegetables from a garden, wool from a sheep, an engine for our car, or healing for our hearts. This mutual reliance speaks to the faith we have in others' ability to help us meet our needs.

ANCIENT CHINESE SECRET?

Although complicated trade rules, taxes, and bartering agreements are in place for dealing with others around the globe, these are simply formal extensions of the inherent social exchange rules that bubble up within any culture that has the potential to sustain itself and thrive. In ancient China, Confucius used naming as a tool to promote and protect social order.[6] He would assign names to citizens to reward and inspire positive and productive behaviors as well as remove and reassign names when the named virtue was absent. The success of this system relied on the value individuals placed on their position in the social order and their willingness to uphold the value of their literal and metaphorical *good name*. This form of leadership actually served as the tool to provide oversight of the peaceful societal structure that Confucius believed would encourage compassion and justice. These values were accurately perceived as essential to societal strength and longevity. Values, such as those encouraged by Confucius, continue to serve as the foundation for healthy friendships.

CARE AND COMPASSION NEVER GO OUT OF STYLE

Compassion and justice require that individuals are able to understand and appreciate others' perspectives. These are akin to empathy, which is the ability to see the world as if you were in another person's shoes. This is another skill that allows humans to be supportive of their neighbors. In fact, research shows that we appreciate and follow social rules even when doing so goes against pure reason and logic.[7] It's as if we are programmed to make choices that are in the best interest of the community even if they do not support our own personal gain. Sci-fi fans may even recall a classic exchange between Spock and Captain Kirk from the 1982 *Star Trek* film, *Wrath of Khan*. Spock proclaimed, "Logic clearly dictates that the needs of the many outweigh the needs of the few." Captain Kirk affirmed, "Or the one." We are hardwired to both rely on and support our communities, and when we develop friendships with others, it makes our communities nicer places to be.

As new relationships develop, we take into account a trust-influenced "time perspective" in our relational decisions.[8] As you get to know a new friend more intimately through increasingly personal interaction, you are able to assess your friend's levels of commitment and investment in the developing relationship. Early on, just like in new love, you need evidence of a new friend's reliability to invest in the relationship at the level that you are investing. Many people seem to have a mental scorecard on which they keep a running tally of social credits and debits. After a friendship has matured, you no longer need the scorecard because your history with the friend provides all the evidence you need of her commitment.[9]

TIME WILL TELL

In interviews with women about friendship, almost every woman answers one question in a similar way: *What makes your relationship with your best friend special or different?* The responses uniformly reveal appreciation that she and her best friend can be out of contact for a day, a week, a month, or a year or more, and pick up right where they left off. It is as if no time at all has passed, and the lack of recent interaction or exchange is immaterial—the scorecard no longer exists, and no one worries about who made the last call or who gave the pricier birthday gift. The relationship is built on history and trust—and I bet your own answer about your own best friendship is probably a variation on this theme. Your relationships with friends grow in direct proportion to the level of mutual trust and mutual commitment you bring to them. However, your earliest relationships may influence every subsequent social relationship, for good or for bad.

FAMILY PATTERNS AFFECT SOCIAL CONNECTIONS

Before you first step outside your own yard to make friends with other kids on the block, your early attachment experiences with your mother or father may have already created firm expectations about social relationships. Even as tiny babies, we are picking up cues about the infant-caregiver relationship in terms of the social exchange system in place as well as learning about trust and dependability. When a friend assumes that she will always get her way in the friendship, you might think to yourself that she was probably spoiled as a child. On the other hand, parentified children, those who have to step into an adult role as children due to economic or environmental circumstances, [10] might grow to be friends who caretake and assume responsibility for their friends. Early attachment experiences have been shown to predict the patterns of attachment that we experience as adults. [11] The foundational attachment theory suggests that there are four separate attachment styles: secure, disorganized, anxious-avoidant, and anxious-resistant. [12] These patterns are observable in very young children and communicate the strength and the flavor of the relationship between a child and her primary caregiver.

Secure attachment is the most robust and healthy form. During infancy, you will develop secure attachments to your caregivers if they provide consistent, satisfactory care. You learn that the world is a kind place and that people who care about you will support you and make sure your needs are met. Anxious-resistant attachment, often called ambivalent attachment, is potentially a result of a caregiver who is overly unavailable. A young child needs the love and support of her caregiver, but experiences a caregiver who is not adequately present in the relationship. Anxious-avoidant attachment describes the relationship between a child and a caregiver who may have interjected abuse or neglect into the relationship. It is as if the need for attachment is present, but the futility of seeking engagement keeps the child from initiating it. Lastly, disorganized attachment manifests as confusion for a child in terms of her response to the presence, departure, or absence of her caregiver. This may arise from a child's inconsistent experiences with her caregiver, which lead to a confused, disorganized response.

In terms of friendships, if you extrapolate some of these early scenarios into adult-to-adult connections, you may recognize some of the qualities of those friends you might describe as "toxic." Their behaviors may actually be self-protective behaviors that were modeled in unhealthy early bonds. For instance, an ambivalent child may grow into an ambivalent young adult who desperately longs for warmth and social connections. However, her early failure to receive the positive, supportive presence of her primary caregiver in her early years may have left her unskilled in the mutual give-and-take necessary for friendships. She may be willing to go out of her way to please a friend, err on the side of codependence, and be almost overwhelming in her need for approval and enmeshment. She may also be the friend who encourages your less than best behaviors (e.g., addictions, promiscuity, and so on) so that she can be the one you depend on or the one who enables you. [13]

The avoidant child may grow into the friend who stays on the periphery of your social friendscape. Having been hurt by social relationships early in life, she may be hesitant to seek out close relationships as an adult. The expression "once burned, twice shy" is an apt description of the friendship-avoidant adult. She may long deeply to feel belongingness within a group, have a close, intimate best friend, and be present and available for others; however, she just might not know how. She can be that "on and off" friend whose dependability and sense of empathy may be a bit spotty. The disorganized-attachment style results in a friend who seems to be always on her guard, afraid to fully trust, and ready to spring into action if threatened. It has even been suggested that a person who learns this style of attachment may seek to add chaos and dysfunction into her adult relationships, as this is what is familiar to her. [14] In summation, the potential for bringing "toxicity" into a current friendship may be predicated by our past experiences in our earliest one-on-one relationships.

Self-Awareness and Self-Appraisal Are Essential to Healthy Relationships

Throughout this book, a variety of friendship stories and behaviors will be described. Some of this material may leave you feeling a bit uncomfortable or uneasy if you recognize some of your own behaviors in the examples of toxic friendship exchanges. If this is the case, use this new self-awareness to begin making changes in how you choose to engage with your friends. While people are often quick to blame the other person when a relationships fails, it is critical to accept that regardless of where you place the blame, the only person whose behavior you can change is your own. Therefore, if you are currently ending a toxic friendship and perceive yourself as having been in the right, you may need to reflect on and revise any behaviors that might have contributed to the friendship's derailment. Alternately, if you are coming out of a friendship breakdown and recognize that you may have been a large part of its demise, use the information in the book to enhance your friendship skills so that you can build healthier relationships. Bear in mind that our past relationship experiences may play a significant role, for better or worse, in our current and future relationships. Recognizing the areas in which you may need to further refine your friendship skills can be the first step in transforming yourself into the type of friend everyone longs to have in their lives.

Whereas counselors never want clients to feel that it is okay to lay all of the blame on their parents for what is going wrong in their lives today, our early experiences can shape how we approach friendships or other intimate relationships. More than one client has jokingly asked me if her therapy goal could be "a happy childhood." There is also a T-shirt that promises "It's Never Too Late to Have a Happy Childhood!" While we cannot alter the past, we can learn how to minimize any negative vestiges of control it holds over our current relationships. However, some friends seem to be hanging on to past relationship patterns for dear life, and their inflexibility can lead to sabotaged friendships and frustrated friends.

CONFLICT AVOIDANCE AND CONFLICT MANAGEMENT

Some of us might remember when we were younger and could spend huge chunks of time with our friends—spending the night at each other's home, spending long weekend days or summer days playing together and sharing meals at each other's family table. Do you also remember what often happened after too much time together? Squabbling, arguing, sharp voices, and maybe a liberal dose of whining and complaining about who was always getting whose way? While most of us relished the time we spent with our friends, eventually we would grow a little tired of their company and conflict would erupt. At this point, parents might have been quick to intervene and call for separation and some downtime before fists flew or recriminations got too loud. Even the best of friends can experience conflict in their relationship. Learning when and how to let go of conflict or address it head-on is a skill that is gained over time, and the metaphorical battle lines are different for every friendship dyad.

When we asked women to share their most significant instances of friend-to-friend conflict or to describe toxic friendship behaviors, the responses were as varied as the women who shared them. Friendship breakers included such critical incidents as stealing romantic partners or potential partners, public criticism, borrowing money that had never been repaid, revealing confidential conversations to others, going too long between communications, calling animal control for a barking dog, and refusing to pick up a friend's sick child at school when the child's mother could not get off from work. Women give their hearts and souls to their relationships, but when conflict rises up, some women are quick to cut their losses and move on, while others are willing to give a friend chance after chance. Learning to know when it is best to let go can be harder for some of us than for others.

Sometimes, choosing to end a relationship is the healthiest choice. Other times, opening a dialogue to address and resolve the incident is the best path. If you are currently in the throes of a friendship conflict, there are several important factors to consider before making the decision to let go or hold on to the relationship. We encourage you to consider the upsetting incident in terms of patterns—is this a new blip on the radar or one more betrayal in a long history of letdowns? We encourage you to consider the overall value of your friendship in terms of the past, the present, and the potential future benefits. We also encourage you to consider your own role in the relationship. Your boundaries, tolerance, self-esteem level, and willingness to play into a friend's poor behavior are areas that also warrant self-assessment. As noted in the preface, we provide suggestions and guidelines to help you determine the path that best fits your current circumstances. The appropriate solution may range all the way from letting the incident go to addressing and resolving the conflict, or even to ending the relationship.

TIME TO SEEK NEW FRIENDS?

How do you decide when it's time to seek out new friends? Researchers, and logic, indicate that the threat of social exclusion from your current friendship circle is a significant motivating factor. Due to our undeniable and immutable drive for social connection, fears that we no longer fit in with our group can send us foraging for new friends. The threat of exclusion also motivates us to work harder to get along with others, to see potential new friends as more inviting than we might ordinarily, and to invest more into a new friendship more quickly than we might have in the past.[15] We want to maximize the likelihood of successfully establishing new friendships, and we are willing to make a heavy initial investment. However, behaviors beyond group exclusion might compel women to sever existing friendships and seek out new connections. While each woman's tolerance for another's poor behavior varies due to multiple factors, implicit social contracts and rules are embedded in our culture and in our expectations of our friends.

In this book, we take an in-depth look at ten unspoken rules that are necessary to keep relationships on track. Prior to an examination of the individual rules, the next chapter will provide an overview of the friendship needs and friendship development patterns of girls and women over the life span. We all need assistance from our friends, but what that help looks like shifts dramatically over a lifetime, as described in the following chapter.

2

FRIENDSHIP PATTERNS FROM GIRLHOOD THROUGH OLDER ADULTHOOD

Several decades ago, Irina Dunn coined the phrase "women need men like fish need bicycles" to humorously describe her stance on women's independence.[1] A modified version of that phrase may actually be more accurate in its summation of women's social support needs: *women need friends like fish need water*. Females are ready to build relationships with others just about as soon as they take their first breath.[2] Gazing at their caregivers and attending to and responding to vocalizations are the earliest ways that infant girls work to forge relationships. And as girls grow into women, most gain traction and more sophisticated skills during each successive year.

While the need for social support makes its presence known from earliest infancy, the value of friendships and our friendship behaviors shift over the course of our lives. Social identities also may change dramatically across the life span depending on our unique maturational paths. Girls can go from "zero to homecoming queen" in a heartbeat if the social environment and their social confidence support this type of zeitgeist change. However, many women have shared that they tend to stay relatively consistent in their preferences for social group size, composition, and function. With the advent and proliferation of social media platforms, staying in touch and maintaining friendships have never been easier. Friends are able to touch base, make plans, share news, and offer support in what almost feels like "real time" even when miles and miles apart.

While there is really no single right way to "do friendships," there are some relational behavior similarities across age groups. A stage-by-stage overview of what researchers currently know about the role and function of friendships over a woman's life span is presented in the following sections, but bear in mind that your own experiences may differ based on a variety of individual factors.

YOUNG GIRLS AND ALMOST TEENS

Early in life, girls are generally quick to seek out friends in their neighborhoods, their preschools, or their day-care centers. In fact, between the ages of three and five, most kids have already identified a "best friend" in their social circle.[3] By the time children are in elementary school, most can name three to five *best* friends.[4] These early friends may very well be a part of our support system for a significant amount of time.[5] For some young girls, the role of "best friend" is filled by different players depending on the day of the week or hour of the day. Others may show unflagging fidelity to a single best friend, and their relationship may endure throughout their lives.

Although a child's earliest friends are most likely children of their parents' friends or nearby neighbors, as children's worlds expand they begin to intentionally seek out friends with whom it is easy to get along and who are temperamentally similar to themselves.[6] Even very young girls already know what kind of friends they prefer and understand "in-group" and "out-group" dynamics. Moreover, young girls begin building metaphorical boundaries around their friendship groups, or cliques, by the early elementary school years.[7]

The value of belonging is keenly appreciated by girls, and they learn early that there is power in groups. They also learn that the exclusivity of a group requires gatekeeping in order to maintain its selectivity. Unfortunately, whether due to media exposure, changes in child-rearing practices, or changes in the environment, even the youngest girls are showing tendencies toward "meanness" at earlier ages than in the past. Research findings suggest that kindergartners and preschoolers already take action and satisfaction in intentionally excluding other children.[8] This can be accomplished through a variety of means ranging from social isolation of other girls to verbal taunting, all the way to physical aggression, if a girl feels it is necessary. Although toddlers throw tantrums, preschoolers are learning how to use relational aggression to get the responses they want from peers. Mean girls may start out as "sugar and spice" but show a tendency toward "spit and vinegar" early on. While these types of hurtful behaviors are not the norm for the majority of young girls, the need for females to fit in continues to intensify as they mature.

Almost Teens

By around age eight, young girls have grown into the "tweenage" category, which is a contemporary label for girls between eight and twelve. This period is the extended rite of passage into teenagerdom during which parents witness significant changes in their daughters. A transformation occurs as childhood trappings give way to early adolescent passions and identity development efforts. By the time girls reach those tween years, many are usually finely skilled in their ability to navigate and influence their social environments. Young adolescent girls strongly rely on their friends to help them cope with the day-to-day challenges they face, and it is clear that friends are especially helpful in handling social challenges presented by other peers.[9] Unfortunately, the tween years are also the period in which verbal, social, and cyberbullying behaviors are ramping up even though physical bullying behaviors are thankfully dwindling.[10] Researchers and practitioners are working hard to find effective and innovative ways to eradicate bullying behaviors. For example, one school has even explored the practice of teaching self-defense to middle school students as a way to combat bullying.[11] Regrettably, there does not seem to be an easy cure for the harm caused by some girls' misguided efforts to meet their social goals, which can range from social domination for some to simply social acceptance for others.

TEENS AND NEW ADULTS

This period is perhaps the most intensely friendship-oriented of a woman's life, and these relationships are essential for healthy social development during this period.[12] True, women value social capital from the cradle to the grave and the playroom to the boardroom, but teenagers "feel" their friendships in an ardently intimate and primal manner that is seldom matched again. Not only does being a part of a friendship group provide social support and belonging, it also gives teenage girls the "mirror" they need to see their own identities more clearly.

Whether adolescent friends are experiencing conflict or mutual support at any given moment, aspects of the identity development process are being affected by their interactions.[13] In fact, friendships in adolescence play an integral role in the shaping of a young woman's individual identity. Peer groups provide the reference points by which teenage girls seek to establish their individuality by faithfully embodying the norms of their friends as well as their fashion, hairstyles, expressions, speech, and other characteristics. Adolescence is often a period of unforgiving self-evaluation during which girls obsess about their skin, their hair, their bodies, their clothing, among other things. Although only pockets of change are visible, the media are starting to reflect a rejection of airbrushed perfection. One example of the changing and more realistic beauty representations is found in the innovative Dove advertising campaign that encourages female adolescents' self-acceptance. Ads such as these represent the front edge of an effort to change our current culture of self-judgment and the internalization of false standards of beauty. Unfortunately, adolescents still have a difficult time being patient with their own DNA-dictated physical development. Thus, having a group of supportive and accepting friends can greatly ease the transition from girl to woman.

Not only do friends provide acceptance and companionship, they are also potential pathways to popularity for some teens. Depending on a teen's goals, her choice of potential friends may be based solely on their social status rather than any special, more intrinsic qualities. Popularity, however, isn't always based on strong social skills. In fact, it can often be the teenage girls who are the least socially responsible and rule oriented that earn the highest level of popularity.[14]

Over the long haul, teenage friendships that are established only to serve as "status friendships," meaning relationships that are designed to send a message about the members' relative social standing in the larger group, are unlikely to endure for long. Further, girls who choose friends based on what they can get from the alliance in terms of status or tangible resources seldom maintain lasting popularity as a friend among their peers. A young woman who establishes relationships built based on mutual affinity and the shared goal of intrinsic satisfaction is likely to have greater success as a friend over the long term.[15] Strong friendships provide social support, acceptance, and belonging; they may even provide some insurance against involvement in harmful romantic relationships. [16] Ideally, friends are able to help ground their teenage peers during this tumultuous period of development. As older adolescents move into the next phase of life, friendships will more clearly reflect exactly who a young woman is on the inside, not just the persona she wants people to see on the outside.

THE TWENTIES AND THIRTIES

Due to recent intriguing studies of the human brain's developmental course, it is now believed that the adolescent period actually stretches into the early to mid-twenties. To describe the next phase of life, the years between adolescence and around age forty, we are using the term *twenties and thirties* as the descriptor. During these years, women are starting their careers, entering significant long-term romantic relationships, and taking on responsibilities beyond what they carried in their earliest twenties. In this book, the adult developmental path is described as being segmented into three distinct phases: *twenties and thirties*, *midlife*, and *older adulthood*. While there are not hard-and-fast age boundaries for these stages, the developmental focus and the experiences of each stage are clear.

Women in their mid-twenties and thirties are immersed in a multiplicity of milieus as they focus on the development of their relational, community, and professional roles. Two syndicated television shows, *Sex and the City* and *Friends*, provided rich examples of how this period of life may unfold. Women in this period tend to rely on friends for support as they tackle new jobs, romantic relationships, relocations to new neighborhoods, and so on. While the value of "heart and soul" friends never dims, friends of convenience also have great value. For instance, building friendships with other women at work can be beneficial to your career success and job satisfaction. Neighborhood block parties or dinner clubs can be a welcome element of social connection in new communities. Establishing friendships, not just trading hellos over the fence, can deepen the pleasure you experience in your community.

During this life stage, women are expected to show up and perform in a wide variety of social contexts. The energy available to meet these new commitments is often balanced against the energy required to establish and maintain a significant romantic relationship, another typical focus of this period. During these intensely busy years, it is really not any surprise that research found that the majority of women between the ages of twenty-five and forty found it challenging to keep friendships strong and vibrant.[17] These years can be filled with opportunities to move up the ladder, across the country, and into new clubs and organizations. Being able to create connections with people at the places where you are headed, when you arrive, and where you want to go next is often a more valued skill than hanging on to relationships from your past.

Although the number of women who opt to have children was on a steady decline during the last several years,[18] and the United States ranks near the top of the list for child-free women,[19] the median age for a woman's first pregnancy is still right around twenty-four.[20] And millennials appear to value motherhood more strongly than marriage as a goal.[21] Regardless of age, any woman who is headed toward motherhood as the next step on her path will find that having friends right where you are can be integral to successfully navigating this portion of your journey.

MOM-TO-MOM NETWORKS

Having company in the form of supportive friends along for the ride on the "mommy track" is not only pleasant, it is essential. Upward mobility is frequently related to career paths that require geographical transience for women and men. Given the current economic climate, it is likely that you may need to relocate just to get that first job. As children arrive in families far from extended family members, developing a social support network of other mothers is often the key to successful child rearing and sanity maintenance. Regardless of whether she is employed outside the home, mothering is a 24-hours-a-day, 365-days-a-year job for a woman. Without a group of understanding friends, a mother's mental health and emotional health both take a huge hit. In fact, without a good support system in place, new mothers are five times more likely to suffer postpartum depression.[22] As babies grow into preschoolers, the need for social support continues as mothers face what seems like a myriad of new challenges, new anxieties, and new questions as children develop. Connecting with other mothers whose children are the same age or a little older than our own is extremely helpful,[23] as it can sometimes seem as if no one but another mother would ever understand what we are experiencing.

In addition to building and solidifying friendships with other mothers who can provide empathy and support, mothers frequently rely on friends for a variety of instrumental support needs. These can include carpooling kids to and from school and extracurricular activities, sharing "room parent" duties or taking your place at the school event if you are unable to show up, picking up your child at school in an emergency if something prevents you from getting there, babysitting on a moment's notice, and the list goes on. One mother shared that one of the benefits she valued most in friendships with some of the other mothers she knew was their willingness to have her child over for an afternoon as a companion to their own—even if a mother did not particularly like *her* all that much. No matter how you consider it, motherhood can be intense, and the shared understanding of exactly what good mothering requires allows mothers to be supportive and friend-like, even if a true friendship does not develop.

There are as many different types of mothers as there are types of children. Mothers, like everyone else, typically find it easier to build strong friendships with women who share their interests. They also find it easier to befriend those who have parenting styles somewhat similar to their own. However, a finding regarding the relationship between parenting styles and children's friendships might be surprising. The parents who were more laissez-faire in their parenting, rather than being either rigid or flexible, actually raised children who developed better friendships.[24] Rather than a suggested method for helping your kids build healthy friendships, however, this may be more of a reflection on whether a child's friends provided more relationship structure and predictability than her parents. The arrival of children into a family is almost always accompanied by some measure of unpredictability, but with friends around to provide support, it is easier for mothers (or fathers or comothers) to keep the family rolling steadily along.

As children turn into teenagers and gain more independence, you may realize that some earlier established friendships with mothers of your children's friends no longer offer the value that they once did. However, new friendships may develop as your children get involved in new activities. There are "booster clubs" for parents of high school athletes, band members, and cheerleaders. Traveling athletic teams invite a great deal of parental investment of time. School-based drama groups often send out calls to parents for assistance with sets and costumes. These are just a few of the possibilities for mothers to connect with other moms who might be potential new friends. Before long, though, the high school child will become a young adult and emotionally (if not yet physically and financially) leave the family nest. This transition heralds a change for mothers on many different fronts, and this typically happens just as women begin taking the initial steps of the passage into the middle third of their lives.

MIDLIFE CONNECTIONS

The term *midlife* has grown increasingly fluid and somewhat nebulous as we hear it used to describe varying bands of ages. For our purposes in this book, we will be using *midlife connections* as the descriptor for women from about the time they are ready to celebrate their fortieth birthday throughout the next couple of decades after this milestone. We are looking at this period of life truly as a "connection" between early adulthood and older adulthood. C. G. Jung, the founder of analytic psychology, described the middle years as a time in which we explore and integrate aspects of the psyche that had been obscured from awareness during our earlier years.[25] It is a time when we do a fair amount of self-reflecting and taking stock as well. During these years, many women are able to reclaim more personal time. The previously required heavy investments in raising a family or solidifying a career are ebbing, and women are able to shift their priorities to fit their changing needs. Of course, there will always be exceptions, such as women who are beginning new careers or who had their children later in life, or who are grandparents now caring for their grandchildren. While external circumstances differ, the inner development typical of this period will be ongoing.

With this shift of focus, there are often significant transitions in social relationships. Friendships that were built on the shared needs of instrumental assistance and emotional support during the taxing "child-rearing years" may have run their course. Taking up new pastimes, letting go of old responsibilities, and having more freedom to spend your time as you see fit all provide opportunities to edit your social relationships as you desire.[26] Existing friendships may deepen during this time, as authenticity is easier to offer others and self-judgment often decreases with age.

Women who can accept their own shortcomings and faults may also more easily accept their friends' imperfections when they are irrelevant to the relationship. On the opposite end of the spectrum, women may distance themselves from friends who have little to offer in terms of honesty, acceptance, or fulfillment of their share in the bargain of friendship.

One survey respondent, Cheri, believes staying in touch is the key to maintaining an authentic friendship, especially during the midlife years: "That's the bottom line: don't drift apart. Marriages, children, grandchildren, jobs, [and] time constraints all put severe pressure on friendships as you grow older. You have to really make the friendship a priority and give it time and space to exist!" The need for social support is present throughout our lives, but the types of individuals that we feel comfortable "letting in" to our lives shift with maturity. Some of us may open our arms widely as we seek ways to give back to our communities. Others may draw in their friendscapes[27] a little tighter as they reach the point where personal priorities overshadow others' demands for the first time in decades. The friendscapes we cultivate during the middle third of our lives may greatly influence the well-being we experience as we enter the final phase of our lives.

OLDER ADULTS

Entering the final third of your life can be accompanied by significant upheavals in virtually every sector of your life—social, professional, geographical, personal, and even familial. The loss of loved ones is typically an inescapable facet of growing older. It's no wonder that having a social support network in place is extremely important to your emotional and physical well-being in older adulthood. Whether you are facing high-stress or low-stress events, good friends will help you cope with the ups and downs of life.[28]

As we grow older, life events often affect the size of our friendship circles, and they tend to grow a little smaller as we age. As a matter of fact, our friendscapes undergo the greatest amount of transition during this final third of our life.[29] Luckily, however, this is a case in which size *doesn't* matter. Whether a woman has just one good friend or one hundred friends, positive relationships will positively influence her health and welfare. And if one of those friends is considered a *best friend*, then a woman enjoys a little added natural protection against emotional depression and compromised well-being. [30] Women in this life stage are becoming more reliant on social media sites and electronic communication. In fact, a recent report from the Pew Research Center noted that over 45 percent of individuals sixty-five years and older use social media sites. [31] Just knowing that you are a part of a social support network enhances your self-esteem. [32] A sense of belonging, at any age, is key to feeling that you matter to others and that your life has value.

The value of friendship, companionship, and support in older adulthood cannot be overemphasized. Some women depend on their best friends, some on their new friends, some on their old friends, and some on their family members to help them meet their support needs; however, there are basically three types of social-support-system friendscapers. [33] Some women are *independent* friends who do not need deeply intimate relationships but enjoy having friends available for specific activities. Others are *discerning* friends who enjoy a small number of deeply connected relationships. The last type is the *acquisitive* friend who takes joy in her ever-growing collection of friends. Regardless of how we craft our support networks, it is clear that being a friend to others is possibly the most valued role of all as we age. [34]

THE RULES OF THE GAME

As we move through our lives, our interactions with others educate us on the unspoken rules of friendship. Researchers have been exploring these rules for many years, and Argyle and Henderson are some of the earliest researchers to empirically investigate the roles and functions of friendships. In fact, in their culturally diverse studies, they uncovered the presence of over forty friendship rules in place. [35] These rules fall into four categories: exchange rules (trading favors and services); intimacy rules (mutual trust and confidence keeping); third-party rules (accepting that friends engage in additional relationships); and coordination rules (friends should stand up for one another). [36]

In preparation for this book, we invited women to share their experiences with "toxic friendships." We asked them to share exactly what happened, how they responded, and what they learned from these relationships. We used their responses as guidelines in determining which rules are most prevalently breached today. The next section of this book includes ten chapters that each focus on a separate rule, or flashpoint, in friendships. The rules that address the most frequently mentioned conflict zones are as follows:

1. Trust and confide in your friends and be trustworthy in return.
2. Show your friends empathy and positive regard.
3. Understand that your friend has other friends and be accepting of these friends.
4. Show your friends emotional support.
5. Volunteer assistance when a friend is in need.
6. Repay favors without being asked.
7. Stand up for your friends and their interests when they are not present.
8. Do not "bring down" or intentionally annoy your friends.
9. Do not criticize a friend in front of others.
10. Do not criticize or be jealous of a friend's other relationships.

The rules listed above fell into three basic categories: *Being*, *Doing*, and *Refraining*. The first three rules suggest "ways of being" with your friends that are essential to a healthy relationship. Rules 4–7 describe actions that should be taken to ensure that the friendship is strengthened and maintained. Rules 8–10 are behaviors to avoid, as they create rifts that cannot necessarily be repaired.

While many of these rules may sound a bit simplistic and appear to be clearly common sense, some girls and women do not appreciate or respect the importance of honoring these unspoken rules within their relationships. Within each chapter addressing a rule, we provide a brief overview of the rule and examples of how breaking the rule might play out for girls and women in each life stage. We also share suggestions for appropriate responses and factors that you might want to consider before taking action when a rule has been broken. While there may be times when ending the relationship seems the only option, we provide questions and insights to help you consider whether a friendship crossroads spells the end of the journey. We will start with what might be the most foundational relational rule of all: *Be trustworthy and trusting of your friends.*

Part II

The Rules of Friendship and Their Role in Relationships

3

IT'S A MATTER OF TRUST

RULE #1: TRUST AND CONFIDE IN YOUR FRIENDS AND BE TRUSTWORTHY IN RETURN

Following this first rule is truly the bedrock of a healthy relationship, and while this rule should "go without saying," too often, friends may say too much. The secrets shared and confidences revealed may be made all too public. As a counselor, one of the authors routinely provides her clients with a space where they can truly let go of their burdens and reveal their secrets, their troubles, their fears, or their aspirations. In fact, one of the most valued aspects of counseling is the level of confidentiality that exists between counselor and client. Virtually everything a client shares with a counselor is kept confidential unless the client has expressed knowledge of or intent to harm herself or others. In the case of friendship, this commitment to a friend's right to confidentiality should also be upheld to that very same point. In fact, trust is one of those key building blocks of friendship that lie at the core of this social relationship.[1] However, when it comes to toxic relationship incidents, betrayal of trust is probably the most frequently cited friendship rule violation. For many women, due to past experiences of emotional or other abuse, broken trust, or a significant breach of confidentiality, placing trust in another may be the hardest task they face in establishing close relationships.

Sometimes we have experiences, thoughts, and dreams that we feel driven to share with a friend. Sometimes nothing feels better than "telling all" to your friends, whether you seek confession and forgiveness or need to share a burden too heavy to carry alone. Perhaps you are recounting the most amazing first date ever or describing what a fool you made of yourself at the bar or revealing something you discovered that maybe you should not have found out. We also use our friends as sounding boards for the big decisions and the small decisions we make in life. We trust our friends with our secrets, because we know that friends won't "tell a soul." In fact, there are likely few females who at one time or another have not started a conversation with those very words, "Don't tell a soul, but . . ." Although trust should be sacred between friends, there were interviewees from every life stage who shared that they were repaid with betrayal for having placed their trust in a friend.

Young Girls and Almost Teens

Little girls enjoy telling "secrets," creating funny stories, enthusiastically exaggerating wildly, and sometimes saying outlandish things or repeating words or stories they know that they should not just for the joy they get in the "shock value" their tales produce. However, young children may also inadvertently reveal "secrets" to which they should not have been privy in the first place. Seeing unexpected things or hearing unexpected words at a friend's house may prompt a child to share her discoveries with other children or her parents. One young woman revealed that she curtailed her daughter's visits to the home of one of her friends when her daughter described explicit magazines that she and her friend found on the coffee table in the family's TV room. This mother used her daughter's secret as a teaching moment regarding the types of "secrets" that are okay to keep and those that should be shared with others. Mothers are in an excellent position to educate their daughters on being a trustworthy friend and keeping their friends' secrets safe when they're safe for keeping. Researchers have found that a mother's modeling of healthy socialization during a girl's childhood will have a lasting effect across the years.[2]

During the years heading toward adolescence, young girls begin genuinely to appreciate the value of loyalty in a friend, the support inherently found in friendships, and the freedom to open up and share their inner thoughts and feelings with their friends.[3] Whether a preadolescent is sharing the identity of her secret crush or revealing fears about her parents' relationship, she is learning to be careful in whom she chooses as her confidante.

Teens and New Adults

Research shows that revealing personal secrets is traditionally one of the most intimate forms of social exchange between friends,[4] and an adolescent girl's world is potentially a landmine of secrets. In fact, self-disclosures are a significant part of the friendship satisfaction equation. We use self-disclosure almost like a glue to bond our relationships more tightly.[5] For better or worse, teenagers share with their friends information not only about their likes and dislikes but also about the big moments in their lives such as their first kiss, their first taste of alcohol, and other important "firsts."

This sharing by adolescents is evidenced by a story shared by Janie, a woman now in her late twenties. Janie noted that she can still recall the odd mixture of pride and shame she felt when she was in high school and confessed to her best friend that she had a one-night stand with one of the football players at her school. Describing herself as "ugly duckling," she had not been popular in high school and spent her junior year, regrettably, just like her sophomore and freshman years, without a boyfriend or even a first date. As junior year was ending, both she and the football "Romeo" were hired for the same summer job of lifeguarding at the beach. A group training/cookout early in the season led to something she'd never expected to happen. That night, Janie and the boy "hooked up" on the beach. Janie recalled that she could not wait to tell her best friend about it. Unfortunately, after the incident was shared, Janie's best friend could not wait to tell another friend what had happened. This "other friend" happened to be the sister of the young man, and, of course, the secret was soon common knowledge. As Janie went on to reveal, the fallout for her got even worse when she found out that "Romeo" had laughed about what had happened with his friends.

Janie went on to say that she had been thankful that it happened in early summer, after school was out, and that the "news flash" had lost some of its shock value by the time the new school year began. Recalling the event today, however, still has the power to stir up the anger and humiliation Janie experienced when her friend broke her promise of secrecy all those years ago. When Janie asked her friend why she had shared her secret, the friend's motives were far from malicious. Her friend told Janie that she had assumed that Janie and the football player were going to be a couple, and she was happy for Janie and simply excited to share the news with the boy's sister, another friend. Thus, even the innocent sharing of a friend's news or experiences can lead to inadvertent betrayal. It is always best to ask for explicit permission from a friend before passing along significant news related to romance, professional issues, academic concerns, and similar topics.

In adolescence, knowledge is power, and sharing personal information—about a friend or oneself—seems to be increasingly accepted behavior. In a world where your identity and your life are chronicled in a public forum, whether through instant messaging, texting, Facebook, Instagram, or Snapchat, "secrets" just don't seem to be kept as tightly as they once might have been. A "good reputation" also seems to be less valued than a generation ago, as the cultural mores regarding sex, drugs, and other once-taboo activities have loosened. In fact, a recent study indicated that over 50 percent of one university's freshman class had texted sexually explicit messages (termed *sexting*) before they turned eighteen and over a quarter of these students had sent sexually explicit photographs of themselves via text messaging even though there are legal ramifications related to this form of communication.[6] Keeping sexting private between you and a romantic interest relies on your romantic partner's trustworthiness. Unfortunately, the sharing of such sensitive messaging can happen much too easily with today's "reply all," "forward," and "post to wall" technologies. However, it appears that adolescents who recognize that sexting has legal consequences are less likely to sext than those who are unaware of its illegal nature.[7] In addition to the legal deterrents, adolescents who have been victimized by the sharing of their private messages are likely to curtail their sexting, based on some of the stories shared by our interviewees.

The Twenties and Thirties

Life can be full of challenges, transitions, and new opportunities during these decades. Sometimes new beginnings also herald the passing away of something that no longer serves a purpose in one's life. Trust can be violated in many ways, and when a friend can no longer be trusted, it may be time to assess her value in your life. One young woman described her own experiences with broken trust very broadly: "When a friend takes too much from the relationship and doesn't reciprocate. Also, when a friend constantly crosses your boundaries or tries to change you into someone you aren't. Additionally, a friend who judges others too harshly, which causes you not to trust being yourself with them. These are all toxic because intimacy cannot be achieved with someone you can't trust." The interviewee's last sentence sums up a basic truth about friendships or any other close relationships: intimacy requires honest vulnerability. Yet when there is fear of negative ramifications from honest and open self-disclosure, authenticity of the relationship is compromised, and it cannot grow deeper.

Women in this stage of life are heading off in so many different directions seemingly simultaneously that they definitely appreciate it when friends can be consistent, if not constant, in maintaining a sense of mutuality in the relationship. Unfortunately, when the only consistent behavior is letting go of promises, sharing information that should remain confidential, betraying you by lying, flirting with your significant other, or letting you down, then it is time to take away the friend's power to do these things within the relationship by exiting the friendship. Taking a wait-and-see approach is one option, but cutting your losses by drawing the line may be the best option you can select. Other times, your friendship might just need a "cooling-off period," and then it can be gotten back on track.

Mom-to-Mom Networks

Most mothers spend a fair amount of time making creative solutions during the course of their daily lives. Some of the on-the-fly solutions may stretch the limits of believability and sensibilities, but desperate times can call for desperate measures. Desperation can also lead to some retrospectively humorous circumstances that mothers feel are worthy of sharing for the comic factor alone. The old expression "thick as thieves" can describe the bonds of moms and their friends. A couple of sociologists have suggested that the self-disclosure of misdeeds between "thieves," or those who push the legal boundaries, places each one at risk of being blackmailed by the other. Thus, with this shared liability between "thieves," a shared trust is established.[8] Mother-to-mother friendships, like the much-needed bonds of trust between "thieves," are deep and rich.

Sometimes mothers themselves push the envelope when they have run out of diapers, wipes, clean baby clothes, or patience. Sharing your parenting mistakes with other mothers can be freeing. Confessing always seems to make us feel a little better. In fact, this is one of the reasons that "talk therapy" can be so effective. Trusting your friends with a tale of how you left your child in a dirty diaper longer than you would have liked because you were waiting for your partner to get home later that afternoon with a package of the diapers that you had forgotten to buy that morning can lead to your mom-friends sharing similar stories of "oops moments." Moms know what it is like to be overwhelmed at times or to yell at their kids sometimes because their nerves are shot, then apologize to them later as guilt creeps in. They, like you, perhaps, understand how stay-at-home mothers can dread "the witching hour" (a term coined by Dr. Spock to describe those predinner hours from 5-ish to 7-ish, when your patience with your children may be out the door and you are eagerly awaiting the arrival of a supportive partner).[9]

Anne, a mother of two preschool daughters, shared a relevant anecdote. She had confided to a couple of friends that sometimes when a dinner recipe calls for wine, she likes to enjoy a glass as she prepares the meal. She stated that with the kids settled down in front of *Sesame Street* or Nickelodeon, the single glass of wine helps her relax while cooking as she waits for her partner to return from work. After sharing what she thought was a "no big deal" story with her friends, she was shocked when she discovered that one of her "confidantes" was spreading rumors that Anne was halfway to a drinking problem! Anne said that she had never realized that confiding in friends could be so potentially risky or that her friend would be so judgmental. Anne affirmed that she is now a lot more cautious with self-disclosures. Although Anne couldn't get up the courage to confront her friend, another mutual friend did follow up with the gossiper. Anne's protective friend informed the gossiper not only that the story she was spreading was not based on fact but also that spreading rumors about friends was not a behavior that the larger circle of friends would tolerate.

Some mothers shared similar tales regarding cooperative babysitting agreements that fell apart. Several described times when a friend would offer to watch her kids at a later date if she would look after hers for that afternoon. However, when the babysitting mom tried to collect on the offer, the reciprocation offer was put off, canceled, or forgotten. Agreements for carpool duty or school pickups that had been made, but "forgotten," had left more than one child stranded at home or at school or practice. This story suggests that when it comes to mothering, trusting other mothers is essential, especially in regard to sharing assistance for getting kids' needs covered. When a mother bails on her friends, she may find herself in desperate straits herself if her lack of trustworthiness leads friends to decide against extending any more friendship "credit" in terms of instrumental assistance. Mothers need to stick together, and if you are a mother and have a friend who is not dependable, you may want to let her know the risks of exclusion from the "village" that is needed to help raise a child. This may be the wake-up call that keeps her from getting voted off your and other mothers' friend-oriented "island."

Midlife Connections

Midlife is often a time when women are finally able to state what they will and will not accept in relationships. By this time, many women have realized that they no longer have to embody the "sugar and spice and all things nice" identity. Being assertive, making and keeping boundaries, and tolerating the shortcomings of true friends becomes easier; tolerating the misbehavior of superficial acquaintances grows more difficult and less likely. Ridding yourself of friendships that compromise your integrity or lead to hurt feelings or wasted time will bolster your self-confidence and self-esteem and allow you more space to experience the joy of honest and open relationships.

As one woman in this life stage shared, the behaviors that she believed were "friendship breakers" included "constantly being let down . . . for instance, arranging a meet-up, then while waiting, getting a text (when you're already at the restaurant) saying she can't make it or that she might get there, but it will be very late. Lying to you, sometimes for no particular reason and sometimes to manipulate situations [is another deal breaker]." She added that when she had to "constantly wait around for a 'friend' who was always approximately a half an hour late, or a complete no-show, time after time," she eventually "blew up at her and she stormed off . . . and we never met up again!" As the respondent noted, dependability is a key virtue for many women. When a friend continues to let another friend down, her unreliability can eventually short-circuit the connection. In midlife, especially, women are at a point at which they feel more comfortable setting limits and owning and defending boundaries.

Dependability and willingness to consistently be there as promised are clear measures of the value of friends at this stage of life.

Older Adults

It seems that as the years go by, the number of secrets some women keep grows and grows. Interestingly, researchers have found that older women are less likely to reveal as much personal information or share as many secrets as younger women do. This may due to more modesty relative to new cohorts of women who use social media to announce everything from grades and diagnoses to breakups. Older women also may fear judgment by their friends and shy away from revealing too much personal information.[10] However, when a friend betrays the confidence of any woman—even in older adulthood—the friendship can become a source of distress and tear away at a woman's overall well-being.[11]

Regardless of age, confidentiality and trustworthiness are requisites for satisfying relationships. Further, making promises and keeping one's word are of great value between friends of any age. When the years are winding down and much of one's autonomy and independence is slowly—or quickly, in some unfortunate cases—being reined in, a person's word is one of the most long-retained abilities. When you let down a friend through willed choice, not unexpected circumstances, you step across a line that may be difficult to retract. Keeping promises and honoring confidences is a way to show your word is good and your support and appreciation for your friend are steadfast, no matter what your age or your circumstances.

FINDING THE SOLUTION THAT WORKS

When it comes to friendship, loyalty and trust are essential aspects of the most basic definition of this relationship. When a friend betrays you through sharing what you had expected to be private communications or not fulfilling a promise that had been made, it can be grounds for ending the relationship. Trust, once broken, is often difficult to rebuild. Here are some thoughts and perspectives to consider as you decide how you would handle a friend who has let you down or spoken too freely.

Information as Currency

Let us return to the anecdotal story shared earlier in this chapter regarding Janie, the young woman who was betrayed by her best friend. In response to the story, some may wonder how it all went so wrong for Janie. She trusted her secret to a friend who simply didn't perceive the potential consequences of her actions. Why would anyone reveal a good friend's secrets? And how would she not recognize the potential damage that may result? This is a question with as many different answers as there are people who answer it. Some people may truly be clueless, as in the case described above. For others, insider information is like currency—having something to share, that should not be shared, is like having money in their pockets. Some people may trade this information, your secrets, with someone else for some other type of valuable commodity, such as the social status that comes with being a "person in the know," or to receive another person's bit of "privy information" in trade. Gossipers somehow "forget" that they promised to keep the information you shared confidential. These friends may also assume that once you've shared with them, you are going to be sharing with others.

"Hey, Did You Hear About . . . ?"

In the case of another friend, revealing a secret may not even be something she intended to do, but she allowed herself to get carried away in conversations. These "friends" do not intend to breach the request for confidentiality; they may believe that they are adding to a conversation or keeping someone in the loop. They may casually open up a conversation with a "Hey, did you know . . . ?" as they spill the beans. Some people truly have no filters and just share whatever comes into their heads without a second thought. Whatever the reason, the result is still the same. Therefore, the actual secret holder must really manage the revelation of her confidences. Simply put, if you cannot trust a friend to maintain your confidences, then you need to avoid sharing confidential information or personal secrets with her.

This friendship rule is about ethically inspired relationship agreements. Without keeping your friends' secrets safe or living up to your promises, you may find the number of trusting friends you have quickly diminishing. When we enter into relationships, we have to realize that no matter how close we might be to another person, we still cannot control anyone's behavior but our own. Trust, then, is a liability, and we take risks when we trust our secrets to others.

Once Shared, You Lose Control of the Content

Controlling the "controllables" in a friendship means controlling your own communication, your own behaviors, and your own expectations of that relationship. Remember, even the innocent sharing of another's news can create fallout from which recovery is difficult—for both friends and for the relationship. Trust is earned, and you must provide the trust your friend needs as well as the respect your friend deserves. And if you find out that a friend is broadcasting your secrets to others or failing to live up to her promises, you can take control of where your role in the friendship goes. Edit what you share. Edit the time you spend together. Edit your expectations. Let your friend know that what she's doing is not okay. Let her know how you want the friendship to play out. Learning to trust again can be a challenge, but a solid friendship is rarely built without a few obstacles to be surmounted along the way.

CONCLUSION

When relationships are tested, they can either grow stronger or wither and die. Weigh the cost of the loss of the relationship against the benefits of maintaining it. Decide what the best path for you might be and, please, take the high road! Don't let yourself follow your friend's poor example of "tell all communications" even if you drop her from your "friends and family" circle. Practicing the behaviors we expect from others is the surest way to receive them in return and for others to see you as someone to trust.

4

JUST THE WAY YOU ARE

RULE #2: SHOW YOUR FRIENDS EMPATHY AND POSITIVE REGARD

Empathy and positive regard are two of the basic *core conditions* of counseling.[1] These two conditions contribute to the facilitative relationship between counselor and client, and they also must be present to establish and maintain the relationship between two friends. Empathy allows us to understand our friends, and positive regard is necessary for us to actually *like* our friends.

Colloquially, empathy is described as the ability to walk in another's shoes or see the world through another's eyes. Essentially, empathy is the ability to understand your friend's world and experiences as if you *were* your friend. Empathy leaves us in tears as we watch movies in which someone loses out at love, experiences a painful loss, or experiences triumphant, unparalleled joy at the most unexpected, moving moment. We don't just cry because we are "sad" that someone's heart has broken; we cry because we have stepped into the world of the movie character and we are feeling what she feels *as* she feels it. Empathy is a powerful skill that enables us to immerse ourselves and to care deeply in the experiences of another.

Empathy is said to exist almost from birth in some children, as evidenced by their "sympathy crying" when they hear other babies in distress. Empathy develops over the next decade or two, and girls typically develop the quality more quickly than do boys.[2] As a girl reaches adolescence, it appears that her mother's own level and modeling of empathy affect how well she will develop this skill.[3] Thus, we generally see a range of empathetic responses among our friends.

Positive regard is the appreciation and fondness we feel for a friend. We may assume that our friends must *surely* like us, but when we have feelings of insecurity about ourselves in the relationship, we begin to believe that our friends are just "pretending" that they hold us in positive regard.[4] In fact, once a person begins to doubt the authenticity of a friend's commitment to the friendship and to her, the relationship will likely begin to weaken and crumble. Authentic positive regard is what we need from our friends, and when we doubt that it is present, we turn what we fear, an unstable and insecure relationship, into a newly constructed current reality—a fraying friendship. Thus, mutual, palpable positive regard is essential to a strong and enduring friendship. In the following sections, we share stories illustrating how a lack of empathy or acceptance can create friction in friendships, potentially leading to the end of the relationship. Also provided are points to consider in making the decision of whether to repair or terminate the relationship.

Young Girls and Almost Teens

For young girls, friendships are frequently based on moment-by-moment allegiances. For example, children who sit at the same assigned table in class may develop friendships that are related to proximity and the situation. Other friendships may be born out of shared interests, as exhibited during recess or free center time in school. However, even elementary school girls already know the power of the words "I don't like you anymore." These words can cut a girl or woman deeply, regardless of her age.

Reciprocal relationships during these years grow more intense over time, and the need to belong to a social clique ramps up as girls move toward middle school. Positive regard is often communicated through the choices a girl makes when she picks a partner for school activities, sends invitations to her slumber parties, and decides whom to sit beside at lunch. Yet for the young girl who is sitting alone or never invited to other children's parties, the feeling of being disliked can have a lasting effect on her self-esteem and adjustment.[5]

Exclusion from friendship groups, name-calling, bullying, ostracism, and baiting are just some of the unacceptable behaviors that girls use to torment each other. Friendships may even be formed to trick an unsuspecting girl into trusting another girl. The girl who is duped may then be made fun of cruelly or teased for fabricated reasons or for any weaknesses she may have revealed to the false friend. Less popular girls may also be victims of cyberbullying (see chapter 9 for more information on cyberbullying). This form of bullying has a heartbreaking public side and involves emotional cruelty that playground name-calling does not.[6] The proliferation of news stories about emotional and social damage done via social media among youth from late elementary school on up underscores just how integral the role of social acceptance is to healthy development. Educating young women about the potential damage that social rejection or exclusion can have on acquaintances may help them extend their natural empathy to include those they might not typically befriend.

Teens and New Adults

The need for social approval continues to grow in significance throughout this next developmental period. The desire to find a group in which you feel accepted and have a sense of belonging is intense. The gym class, the long morning break, and the cafeteria are just a few of the hot spots where teens desperately need one or two *companions*, at least, and *friends*, at best. Many of us can recall the stress we felt in high school when finding out our class schedules and assigned lunch periods. Quick communication via phone or text often followed so we could find out our friends' schedules. When a girl ends up in the "wrong" lunch period, the one that none of her friends were assigned, she may feel anxious as she scouts out the potential lunch buddies those first few days. Finding just one person who is a candidate for this situational friendship can make a huge difference for her. Feeling that just *one* person in the room likes you can ease anxieties in high school cafeterias, and years later at events such as large, impersonal cocktail parties or wedding receptions. Most of us know what it can be like to walk into a large group, similar to the ones listed above, and check out each knot of people to look first for familiar faces. If none are seen, we seek out people who look like they have the potential to be "conversational companions" for at least the first few precious minutes needed to get acclimated to the room.

While finding someone we think will like us is more of a challenge for some than others, adolescents can be extremely fickle as they sort out their places in the social pecking order. It can be painful when a friend you have known for years suddenly transforms her self-identity and moves from one social clique to a new one, leaving you behind. There are certain periods during adolescence when young women seem driven to reinvent themselves or let go of false identities that no longer serve them. The periods between middle school and high school, junior and senior year, and high school commencement and college or work are all prime times for reinvention. When a teen re-creates herself prior to entering the new setting, she may also make changes in her appearance, behaviors, and attitudes to reflect those of the new group with whom she wants to fit in. The need to be liked and accepted shapes the identities of many teenage girls. However, in seeking to be accepted, liked, and understood by a new clique, she may be letting go of ties to her former friendship group. This can leave behind bad feelings among those young women.

One young woman, Manda, described the pain she felt when a lifelong friend, Kami, transformed herself over the summer between high school and college. The close friends were both heading to the same university but had decided against being roommates after having been warned that the best way to lose a friend was to room together. Unfortunately, Manda learned that there were other ways that college could break up a friend-ship. Manda was studious but fun-loving, and she had chosen the pre-dental track. Kami was equally academically minded but was more inter-ested in the social sciences. When they met up on their first evening on campus, Manda said Kami already "looked" different than she had a week ago back in their hometown. The changes in her friend's hairstyle, makeup, clothing, and the way she carried herself made her seem like a stranger.

Manda related that she was not surprised when Kami shared that she was going to be rushing sororities that first semester and wanted to look like she fit in from the beginning, in case some of the women she met on campus or in classes turned out to be members of the sororities that she was hoping to be asked to join. As Manda described it, "It was like she was a stranger to me that night, I didn't understand the new Kami and it was like she didn't like the same old me. Twelve years of friendship had evaporated. Just like that. And when a friend turns into someone that wouldn't like you now if they were first meeting you, then it is like those years of friendship were all a lie. The only time we really spoke after that was when we happened to be sharing a ride back to our hometown."

Research shows that as young women move through late adolescence, they are less likely to identify as strongly with particular cliques or groups.[7] As they mature, they begin to place much higher value on each individual relationship and each friend rather than having as much concern over the group to which a friend belongs. When friendships hit crossroads in this period, it may be easier to let go of an unsatisfying relationship to conserve energy for establishing new and more rewarding friendships.

The Twenties and Thirties

As we begin to forge our new identities—in either the work world, the family milieu, or college or graduate school—we seek out friends who really "get us" and understand the experiences and lives in which we are immersed. Some women shared that when they chose to return to graduate school, they felt irreparably separated from many of their friends who were devoted to climbing the corporate ladder or building families at that time. For some women in this age group, networking may be more important than building deep friendships. Grad students connect with law students, executive trainees connect with other executive trainees or those just a level above them, newly partnered or married women enjoy connecting with other coupled-up women. Women who are enjoying life without romantic entanglements may prefer adventuring through life with other single women. Friendships with those you don't initially *like* can develop based on shared experiences that allow each of you to empathize and understand one another's life.

While these friends serve a useful purpose in your life, you may also need friends whose company you enjoy and with whom you have a mutual affection. One woman shared that she had been let down in friendships in which her perspectives and experiences were discounted and/or disregarded. She shared with us the steps she now took to avoid suffering similar letdowns in relationships: "My current friends are chosen more carefully. I listen more with a balanced attitude. I'm not holding back my voice or editing so closely to not 'offend' the other person. I take a lot of care to see how they are in their lives and ask questions but not too invasive. I try not to offer unsolicited advice. And I'm accepting things as they are. I always mean what I say and communicate clearly and seek to understand."

Another woman shared an experience in which she felt that one of her friends liked her only for what the friend thought she saw in her, not her authentic self. As she described it:

> Tina often referred to me as her best friend. I don't know where she got this idea. We had a few things in common, but I never felt comfortable opening up to her, and I certainly didn't consider her my best friend. She was popular and seemed well liked, so I was flattered by her attention. I ridiculously tried to be what she wanted. And predictably it was a disaster. She became overbearing and pushy and I took it for as long as I could and then finally stood up to her. That she could not tolerate. She dropped me and now ignores me and while it hurts to be treated like that, it is a relief to be out from under her control.

When a friend tries to make you into something you are not, an authentic relationship is simply not possible. Many of us can be flattered by the interest and attention of a potential new friend who seems to embody the qualities or status that we long to have for ourselves. However, if that person seeks to change you or seems attracted to aspects of your behavior that are not a true reflection of your core self, it is doubtful the new friendship will endure.

Another woman in this group shared how challenging it can be to understand another's perspective and to maintain a sense of positive regard when a friend is behaving in ways that challenge your core beliefs. Describing a toxic friendship experience, our respondent recounted, "I had to support my girlfriend through multiple affairs that she was having on her husband—a really great guy. That was really hard, to not be angry with her and say what I really thought, but to be supportive and understanding of her feelings and listen to why she was doing what she was. Especially since I have my own very strong feelings about the sinfulness of affairs, but we had to keep our discussions about her and her experiences." This friend went beyond the limits of what many might do to provide support and empathy for a friend. When a friendship requires that you temporarily let go of values that you hold dear, it may lead you to question your own behaviors and choices. Unless there is an equal return and commitment, friends who expect unflagging loyalty and support of their questionable behaviors may not be the ideal friends to possess.

Mom-to-Mom Networks

Motherhood, as we touched on in earlier chapters, can create a wedge in some women's friendships. Child rearing entails new responsibilities that can sometimes keep moms from participating in activities that they enjoyed prior to the arrival of their children. Sometimes it seems that only mothers can fully empathize with other mothers, and some friendships do not survive the transition to motherhood. Some mothers shared that it can be difficult for some child-free friends to understand that choices such as partying until the wee hours of the morning, smoking when socializing, meeting up at restaurants where children are unwelcome, or gathering at homes that lack adequate childproofing no longer work for them. And on the flip side, a child-free woman shared that she felt her friendships suffered because "most of my friends work and have children. I work, but no kids, so finding time to get together is hard."

Mothers are often in a unique position in which they navigate their social commitments and relationships guided by their children's social activities and friendships. They may hang out with the parents of their children's friends at playdates or birthday parties, even if the desired positive regard is replaced with benign indifference. Motherhood has been called the hardest job in the world, and that metaphor arguably can be taken a little further. If it is true that you do not have to like the people with whom you work, it may be true that you do not necessarily have to like the other mothers on whom you rely for shared child care, outings, and so on, as long as everyone can get along and do their fair share. When a mom in your group shows disinterest in you but is still a great mom to know and the mother of your own child's good friend, sometimes you have to accept that not everyone will be your friend and that not everyone will appreciate your perspectives. Mothers of young kids often walk a tightrope trying to balance a family's social priorities. Recognizing that not everyone in the village can be best friends may help you handle those acquaintances who play a valuable role through instrumental assistance but offer little in terms of warmth and friendship.

Midlife Connections

By the time women reach this stage of life, most are relatively confident in who they are, what they need, and what they will no longer tolerate in life. Energy for seeking new friendships or turning superficial acquaintanceships into deeper friendships may begin to wane. Midlife is a period in which women assess their lives and relationships at levels of scrutiny that they may not have used since adolescence. If a friendship is found lacking, there is less fear of what will be lost by letting it fall away. A woman in her forties shared her perspective on friendships that turn toxic: "A toxic friend is a friend asking you to help her reach her own goals, but gives you nothing in return but an empty glass. You just have this gut feeling that she is cold and empty, that she no longer cares about [you] or anyone or anything but herself. These kinds of toxic friends have their own agenda and they will use you and make you think that they really care about you, but they really don't."

By midlife, if friends lack positive regard or seem unable to understand you and your experiences, you are likely ready to let these friendships end, unless there is some significant instrumental or historical justification for maintaining them. Another woman in this age group shared her suggestions for how some of her less rewarding friendships could be made better: "[Women need to] realize that friendship is not just take. They need to appreciate what they truly have in life, rather than their 'poor me' attitudes. They need to show more understanding and consider others' perspectives once in a while. Friendships need effort from both sides." When there is little interest in your own well-being and a lack of understanding of the road you have traveled, there is little incentive for maintaining the friendship.

Midlife brings you to a place in which you may see the worth of friendships in ways you previously have not. If relationships are no longer reciprocal, they can be ended more easily now. However, if you are committed to rebuilding the friendship, be honest about the perspectives and perceptions you have of a friend's poor treatment of you. Some women are blind to the power their words or actions wield even when unintentionally causing you harm. Letting friends hear your side of the story may be helpful, but remember that some women are incapable of providing the warmth and kindness you desire. This does not mean that you should automatically terminate the relationship. You will just need to bear in mind the limits some friends have in providing the qualities that you prefer.

Older Adults

Not surprisingly, older women are typically wiser in their social-relationship decision making than younger women. Eloise, a woman in this stage of life, shared that "as I have grown older, I have streamlined my inner circle. I am [choosier] about whom I trust." Circumstances often limit the amount of energy and time available to expend in maintaining relationships, so they let go of those that serve no purpose and work quickly and effectively to solve their relational issues. As we age, we also value more strongly those friends who are similar to us in terms of beliefs, morals, and spiritual practices. We prefer to be in the company of those who share similar histories, and this preference leads to choosing and maintaining empathetic and understanding friends. As a woman in her sixties affirmed about her own choices, "I am less inclined to have friends just for friendship's sake as you do when you are young. [I] definitely [value] quality over quantity."

When asked what the breaking point for her might be in a friendship, another woman shared that "not being accepted for who I am" spelled the end of friendships for her. However, when a friendship bridges differing lifestyles, caring deeply and holding strong regard for a friend can allow the relationship to endure. This same woman went on to describe the lessons she learned about developing empathy for friends whose lives were following a path different from her own. She suggested that it was helpful to "keep a respectful distance. Remain silent, but have the kettle ready for a cup of tea. Let things go when offended and wait for the friend to return to my world, rather than me saying I am offended." She had seen a friendship end through her own unwillingness to accept diverse differences in the past but now realized that when you care for someone, you need to be kind and accept that *understanding* another is not always possible. She also shared that when a friendship has been unalterably broken, sometimes the best path is "simply walking away and not looking back when you know in your heart it ain't gonna work."

FINDING THE SOLUTION THAT WORKS

In terms of offering friends positive regard, it really is as essential a condition as the presence of trust between friends. Truly, if you do not feel a sense of affection or fondness for a person, an acquaintanceship is unlikely to become a friendship. Therapists offer clients unconditional positive regard, which translates into acceptance of a client with no personal judgment entering the relationship. With friends, a healthy dose of positive regard is also essential, but it may be tempered with an "I like everything about her, but . . ." and you can still call her a good friend. If the assessment of your fondness for her deteriorates into something more along the lines of "Everything she does drives me crazy, but at least she . . ." the friendship's depth and authenticity may be fraying a little more than might be easily repaired.

As studies show, empathy varies among individuals. Some people develop empathy early in life and can "walk a mile in a friend's moccasins" almost as early as they can walk. Others may have had poor parental role models, so their own levels of empathy may always be a bit on the lower side of average. However, everyone's level of need for empathy from others varies. Some women do not feel the need to display their vulnerable emotional side with friends and may not even notice that they have befriended someone with less empathy than another. However, some of us may have highly developed levels of empathy and tenderness and desperately need our friends to meet us where we are in terms of empathetic understanding. In the following sections, we will address the potential mismatched "empathy quotients" between friends.

Do You Need This Person in Your Life?

At times, situational friends, or perhaps *situational companions* is the more appropriate term, are every bit as valuable as closer, more authentic friends are in other circumstances. For instance, if a high school girl needs someone to sit beside her during an assembly, a class where she has no other closer friends, or at lunch, sitting with someone who is even halfway kind can be better than sitting alone. Some women are willing to hang out with moms of their children's friends even if they don't particularly like them all that much, just so that they can facilitate the development of their children's friendships. Sometimes what is most needed is an impersonal, nonobjectionable companion, even if a friend is the company that we would prefer. In situations such as these, perhaps it is best to be satisfied with less than a friend and more than a stranger. Just like little girls who need someone to be their "swim buddy" at camp, sometimes merely having someone along for the swim (or ride) beats hanging out alone on the sidelines.

Are You Better Off with Her or without Her in Your Life?

There is a difference, of course, when the impersonal companion sitting with you now is someone who was once a close friend. People can outgrow or phase out of relationships. This can happen for many different reasons, some of them related to personal or developmental changes and others attributable to external circumstances.

Some of us have friends we have known for years and through a million different incarnations of identities. You may have the type of friend who chose to "run with the wolves" one year and the next she was "running with the wolves" of Wall Street. Even if you just can't fully empathize with what drives her or fully understand where she is coming from, if there is a deep, authentic, mutual connection, you may be pals with her no matter where she is in her head or her life. If the positive regard remains, a friendship can prevail.

On the other hand, you may have a friend who went from being your hard-driving, business-savvy, motivated colleague and strongest competitor at the law firm to a barefoot, craftsy, stay-at-home mom or vice versa. You may have tried to maintain the friendship but realized that you no longer are on the same page or even in the same book, and that trying to find a way to reconnect is waylaid by attitudinal, situational, and chronological challenges that are too pervasive to surmount. Or a friend may believe that you no longer fit in her life, her affection for you has waned, or you are just too far from the same wavelength to understand her new identity now.

Positive Regard

When there is nothing resembling mutual admiration or affection between a pair of former friends, there is little motivation to continue to invest energy into the relationship. As the stories shared in this chapter demonstrated, when you are consistently left feeling as if you hold no value for one another, it is doubtful that the relationship is worth pursuing any further. When a friend only seems to "like you" when she is in need, red flags should go up and you should step back to see the relationship more objectively. You may need to ask yourself if the occasional feelings of care and warmth she offers are worth the periods in which you feel ignored or disregarded. One woman shared her own perspective on reciprocity in personal interest and regard:

> The breaking point for me is usually when friends only talk about their own problems, issues, wants, needs, and desires, and will not tolerate listening to anyone else and their problems. I have found that sometimes people start out as great and involved friends but will start to migrate over to complete self-involvement over time. I used to think the switch might be temporary, but it never is. I have a clock near my phone, and when I think a friend is starting to self-obsess too much, I start timing how long the friend talks about herself, and how much time I get to spend talking about what is going on in my own life. When I notice a large time imbalance, I cut the cord.

Although some may find this a little cold or too severe, or if you are not ready to give up yet on your own relationship, you should initiate a discussion with your friend regarding your unhappiness with the relationship and her level of regard and lack of empathy for you. Unfortunately, however, the friend who has the greatest need to continue the relationship generally has the least amount of influence to change the relationship. As one twenty-something interviewee summed it up, "The hardest thing I've had to do in a friendship is be the one who cares more. It leaves you being more vulnerable than the other." Almost all interpersonal relationships reflect this dynamic, but if you know you care too much and you have a friend who you feel "cares enough," you may be able to work out the current conflict if you feel that your expectations can be shifted to meet with the relational reality.

CONCLUSION

For healthy friendships, the ability to empathize with a person and a feeling of mutual affection are essential building blocks. While not every acquaintance is going to be transformed into a close friend, if you feel that the energy required in maintaining even an acquaintanceship with another is draining, then perhaps it is better to let the relationship draw to a close. When a friend no longer provides you with the feeling of being understood or no longer seems to take pleasure in your company, these are signals that the relationship has likely run its course. Opening yourself to new potential friendships may be more productive than trying to resuscitate the dying relationship. When you reach this type of crossroads, you can give your friendship one more nudge to determine if you need to follow a different path or pick up where the challenging relationship broke down.

5

ANY FRIEND OF HERS
IS A FRIEND OF MINE

RULE #3: UNDERSTAND THAT YOUR FRIEND HAS OTHER FRIENDS AND BE ACCEPTING OF THESE FRIENDS

The focus of this friendship rule is the importance of embracing, not excluding, the other people in your friend's life. This means a couple of things in terms of healthy relationships. First, this rule emphasizes the need to avoid behaviors that would suggest that you view the other friends of a friend as rivals or competition for attention from your friend. Second, it provides encouragement for you to envision your friend's other pals as *potential* friends of your own.

THE FRIENDSHIP PARADOX

Cultivating friendships with the friends of a friend can be a straightforward method of strengthening your own social support network. Some of the early work of identifying potential friends has already been completed, since these potential friends are already in the friendship pool of your friend. In fact, research on the relative sizes of friendship groups revealed something mathematically interesting and a little mind-boggling. According to Feld's theory of *friendship paradox*,[1] the pool of potential new friends (who are already the friends of a current friend) may be quite large.

Statistically speaking, your friends, on average, have more friends than you do. This truth is derived from a complex mathematical formula that has to do with weighted averages. Of course, it also suggests that among your own friends, you may actually be the most popular and befriended member of someone else's friendship group. However, researchers have recently extrapolated this finding to suggest that your friends also may be more interesting than you are.[2] Therefore, being open to befriending your friends' friends may definitely have value for a variety of reasons, as you can add to your friendship network as well as increase the diversity of your friendscape. Moreover, if you are that friend who is most interesting or has more friends, it would only make sense that you would enjoy the opportunity to add variety to your social support system.

Have you ever shown up at a good friend's party, met another of your friend's friends, and spent the whole evening building a new friendship? It feels good to connect with someone new and with whom you already have something in common—your mutual friend—and then realize that you are building your own social network through the newly established friendship. We choose our friends based on shared interests, activities, or life stages. Thus, when it comes to a current friend, it may seem natural to believe that "any friend of hers is a friend of mine."

Researchers have found that the *perceived* similarities between people determine how quickly an acquaintanceship intensifies between two potential friends.[3] Moreover, if a mutual friend believes two people have strong similarities, this also fans the flame of friendship.[4] When a friend says, "You and my other friend are going to really hit it off—you've got so much in common," you and the not-yet-met other friend are already building a friendship, even if you do not consciously realize it. Unfortunately, researchers have found that people tend to make overly optimistic estimations of the similarity between themselves and their friends.[5] Thus, when true feelings about controversial issues arise, unexpected conflicts can occur between friends if they hold opposing views. While we are predisposed to like the friends of our friends, these potential new relationships can go awry in many ways. In addition to the obstacles created by conflicting personalities or conflicting beliefs, potential new relationships can be obstructed if jealousy or insecurity enters the relational triangle.

Young Girls and Almost Teens

As young girls mature, their play also develops. Solo play of earliest childhood gives way to parallel play, then group play, and finally to cooperative play during the early elementary years. However, most young girls have a strong preference for even-numbered, not odd-numbered, cooperative play groups. Whenever three or five girls are together, one girl always seems to be left out of the group. This sense of isolation, even if temporary, can be painful, and attempting to break into the play of friends can be difficult. It can be distressing when a young girl views her good friend's "other friends" as merely rivals for her friend's attention.

Parents and caregivers who oversee playdates or who handle "chaperone duty" at the playground have likely witnessed the drama that can erupt when one child is intentionally, or unintentionally, excluded from a group. Encouraging your own child to play with other children in the classroom, on the playground, or in the neighborhood can be the best defense when she is being squeezed out of another dyad or group. Modeling for her by developing friendships with friends of your own friends can be a valuable long-term investment in helping her to be open to potential new friends. As a young girl moves toward teenhood, however, there can be times when acceptance of her friends' friends as new friends raises concerns for families. Adolescence is a time of rebellion and for pushing past approved limits.[6] Teens are driven to explore beyond the safe boundaries that had been in place for over a decade. Sometimes the friends a teen daughter brings home are ones parents wish would have stayed beyond their daughter's reach.

Teens and New Adults

During adolescence, social groups are often the "smallest unit of measurement" for females. For most teens, the more friends two youths have in common, the more likely the pair is to be friends, themselves.[7] In addition, high schools are a breeding ground for group labels in which membership describes where you stand in the pecking order of popularity or acceptance. Identification with the "jocks," the "cheerleaders," the "hipsters," or the "grinds" can tattoo a label on a young woman that has the power to define her entire high school experience. Breaking out of a stereotype can require that a young woman break out of her social group, regardless of how comfortable its familiarity may be.

Social networking makes it much easier to forge new acquaintance-ships with friends of friends by making a single click for a "friend request." Depending on individual privacy settings, you can learn a great deal about a friend of a friend well before you initiate an online connection. Just checking out the potential acquaintance's "likes" or "comments" on your current friend's wall can provide a wealth of data. This can make it easier to find common ground and isolate a shared interest on which to build a new friendship. One young college woman, Beth, however, realized the dangers of opening up too much of her profile, posts, and friend information to even "friended friends." Beth went to a concert with friends; afterward, the group went out and ran into other friends of her friends. They all had fun playing darts and talking, so Beth had no qualms about "friending" the new friends that night. Unfortunately, one new friend appeared to be a "friend stalker," as Beth described her, and began adding comments to Beth's recent and older posts. She then began sending friend requests to Beth's other Facebook friends. Beth blocked this person on Facebook when she found out about the "creepy" behavior of this new acquaintance. Encouraging young women to be careful online cannot be overemphasized. With the easy access to strangers who pose as potential friends, online social networking needs to be handled with care.

During this stage of life, social networks can grow exponentially if you are open to befriending the friends of your current friends. However, social media and open access pose problems that may be more difficult to resolve than simply "unfriending" a person. On the other hand, refusing to stretch your social network and refusing invitations to events that include new people from beyond your current clique can be unfortunate. When you encourage a friend to put other relationships aside to focus only on your friendship, you may be steering your friendship toward its dissolution. Behaviors to avoid, according to our interviewees, include insulting a friend's other friends, refusing to hang out with a friend if other friends are present, or expressly demanding that she drop other friends. Few friends want such an exclusive relationship, and if you refuse to "join the party," you may end up hanging solo a lot longer than you would like.

The Twenties and Thirties

During these years of building and fine-tuning your adult identity, it is extremely beneficial to expand your social and professional networks. You never know who might be in the right place at the right time to help you take that next personal or professional leap. However, this is also a time in which your choices may define how others see you. Making decisions that make sense for where you are headed, not just where you are, can be an important consideration in your networking/friendscaping pursuits. Thus, willingness to opt in when invited to get together beyond the office, the gym, or the yoga class may help you make connections that help you clarify your identity and where you fit in.

Unfortunately, some friends' aversion to sharing friends with others can make it hard for new connections and friendships to develop. One woman, Allie, shared the following anecdote describing a "friend of a friend" situation that turned toxic:

> A friend of mine, Gail, was very demanding of my time and she had a hard time understanding why I would want "time off" from hanging out with her to spend time with other friends. So I was surprised when Gail invited one of her work friends, Jennifer, to join us one night when we were meeting up for dinner. Well, it turned out that Jennifer and I really clicked and realized that we had a lot in common and shared a love for running. As she and I began spending more and more time together either on the trails or just hanging out, the friend who had introduced us became extremely jealous. When I tried to organize get-togethers for all of us, Gail would show up, but behave like we did not want her there. After a while, I got tired of Gail acting like a spoiled child and stopped trying to include her. Although Jennifer and I are still great friends and training for the Chicago Marathon together, the friendship with Gail has pretty much petered out for me.

We choose friends who like the same things we do, but it is not always as easy to accept that our current friends might like our new friends better than they like us. Furthermore, it can be disappointing when our friend's friends are not the kind of friends we would choose for ourselves. Learning to skillfully and intentionally design your social landscape is especially important as you settle into your professional, social, or familial identity. These decades are typically spent in active pursuits, and having a network of supporters can make the journey a lot more pleasant. Being open to growing your network through meet-ups with friends who bring along other friends, getting to know business friends outside of work and meeting their other friends, and going alone to the party hosted by the one friend you have in spin class are all ways to create a stronger and more flexible friendscape. By limiting your willingness to be "the new kid" in a group, you may be limiting your future opportunities for fun and adventure.

Mom-to-Mom Networks

Friendships with other moms are essential during this period of life. Many of us like to check in with other mothers on every aspect of infant development as well as every button pushed by adolescents who are turning us gray well before the seven-passenger SUV is paid for or traded for the two-seater sports car. Connecting with friends of friends can happen frequently during these years. For example, if your child wants to play lacrosse, you likely ask your friends if they know anyone else whose child has tried the sport. Or if your child needs serious orthodontic work, you may ask friends if they know anyone who goes to Dr. Brecklewhite. These are just two examples of a multitude of resources that our friends and *their* friends might provide. This informal "mother-to-mother resource connection" provides a service very similar to Angie's List but doesn't cost a dime.

There are times, though, when "friends of friends" relationships may not take off in a positive direction. Values conflicts, child-rearing practice differences, and simply divergent personalities can present barriers to friendship development. Since not everyone is going to be your best friend anyway, this should not be a big deal for most women. There can be times, however, when "her friend" might become more like "your enemy." One such instance was described by Sue, the mother of two daughters, eleven and five years old. Sue shared that her daughters were excited by an invitation to a holiday cookie exchange tea party being held by a relatively new friend of Sue's who had a couple of daughters close in age to Sue's own.

Eager for the event and the opportunity to get to know more people in the town to which Sue and her family had recently moved, the trio thoughtfully chose their cookie contribution recipe, baked the treats, and shopped for dresses. The girls had a great time at the party and had no trouble meeting and befriending other guests. Sue, however, realized that the friends of the hostess were unlikely to be on her own holiday party guest list. The other mothers arrived in jeans and T-shirts, brought in boxed wines and six-packs of beer, and hung out in the kitchen, going from "tipsy to sloppy" while the little girls, all in their holiday best, watched videos, ate cookies, and played computer games. When it comes to motherhood and friends of friends, values carry great significance in predicting the development of new friendships.

Midlife Connections

By midlife, we are usually much more confident about who we do and do not want to let into our lives. New friendships are generally more intentionally crafted, and we are more careful in how we invest our energy. As friendship circles shift, though, older friends may begin to feel uprooted by new relationships that better fit our changing needs. A woman in her forties shared the following story about this type of situation:

> I allowed my old friend Lisa to live with me and my husband for a week while she was in between living situations. My friend was being really needy during this time, so I decided to plan a kind of "date night" with her. When we got to the restaurant, the whole conversation centered on her dislike for one of my newer friends. She tried to convince me not to be friends with her.
>
> I tried to be cool and tell her, "Look, how you feel about her has nothing to do with me and I'm sorry you feel that way." However, she kept on insulting my friend and trying to convince me of how bad of a friend she is to me. . . . I finally got a bit mad and told her to stop trying to manipulate me. She got so defensive and angry. She showed me a really ugly side to her and I took a good mental note: this woman has some deep-rooted problems and I am not sure this is the kind of friend I need in my life right now. . . . [Over time], I started to think about her and all the red flags that had gone off in my head, plus how I felt that she was being ungrateful since I let her into my house. I then decided that I did not want to have anything to do with this person again and that it was the end of the friendship.

When you have reached this stage of your life, it is time to begin carving out boundaries that protect you from negative forces and friends who detract from your life. Moreover, if you notice red flags in a relationship, you should listen to your intuition and your gut instinct.

Older Adults

As older women's friendscapes begin to decrease in size, there tends to be less interest in building new relationships. As one woman shared, she has *streamlined* her friendship circle for greater ease in maintenance. Yet, with the risk of friendships fading away due to a friend's infirmity or death, it is essential to stay connected to others and to be open, at least, to considering befriending the friends of your friends—or even friends of your children.

Maggie, a widow, shared that she was heartbroken when she first had to let go of her own home and move into the home of her son and his wife in a nearby town. She felt that her existence was growing smaller and smaller, as she felt isolated from her former neighbors and her church family. Maggie recalled how worried her daughter-in-law became about her well-being as she saw Maggie becoming increasingly reclusive. Eventually, the daughter-in-law successfully cajoled Maggie into substituting at one of her monthly Bunco games when another friend had to miss the game. Maggie laughed in sharing that she had not had that much fun in ages, and she realized that the good time enjoyed by her daughter-in-law's friends and herself was well worth the effort it took to bridge the generation gap.

No matter what life stage you are in, being mindful of your social support network is important. As your network shrinks, it is important that the friends who remain are those on whom you can count for uplifting, satisfying support. When your own friendscape has thinned out too sparsely, it is greatly beneficial to respond positively to invitations to connect with friends of friends or friends of family. If someone who cares about you should happen to try and "force friend" you, be open to the opportunity of enriching your support system. Good friends and a sense of belonging make life especially enjoyable, especially during this stage of life.[8]

FINDING THE SOLUTION THAT WORKS

When we throw a party, we may smile and assert "the more the merrier" as our invited guests show up at the door with their own friends in tow. We may be thrilled by a dinner invitation from a good friend whom we haven't seen in a while but cringe when we drive up and see three "strange" cars already in the driveway and realize that the evening is probably not going to provide the chance for the relaxed heart-to-heart chat you had been hoping to enjoy. Perhaps you have been the person who has shown up at an invitation-only function thrown by a friend and simply expected the host to rejoice at your arrival and embrace the other three friends you brought along? Sometimes we assume that any friend of ours will be equally loved by any of our other friends. However, sometimes a friendship is "big enough" between just a pair of friends.

Humans definitely enjoy belonging to social groups, but sometimes we all want to be the "best friend" or "closest friend" or "special friend" of someone whose friendship we cherish. At times, though, we must handle being part of the "three" that make a crowd when we'd rather be part of the "two" that means company. The following questions will help you decide how to handle your place in line.

Is Your Good Friend Making Poor Choices?

Have you ever had that eye-opening experience when you accepted an invitation to an event from a new friend—whether it's a dinner invitation, a birthday party celebration, or a weekend at their lake house—and arrived at the scene only to be surprised by some of the other guests who were there? If you feel uncomfortable with some of the unexpected, although not uninvited, guests, etiquette suggests that you make the best of a bad situation. Staying long enough to be "seen" and having a believable justification for needing to scoot out early are essential if you do not want to risk your relationship with the hostess.

If you are truly concerned about your friend's choices, you may want to open up a conversation about this topic at a later date. This would only be appropriate if you feel that is in your friend's best interest and you feel comfortable and confident that it can be done in a manner of curious concern, not judgment or condemnation. To conduct this discussion effectively, you need to be able to provide objective facts about the situation, examples of specific behaviors that you observed, and clear descriptions of how the other person's behavior has negatively affected this friend. These conversations can turn out very poorly if the speaker is not prepared and comes across as making accusations rather than sharing objective information with caring and concern.

Is Your Ego Obscuring Your Vision?

We all want to be liked, most of us enjoy being liked "best," and some of us may get a little miffed when a person we consider one of our "best friends" has loads of others she considers just as close. If this happens to you, perhaps it indicates not only how popular your friend is, but also how awesome you yourself must be to have built a friendship with someone so popular. We choose friends who are similar to us, so assume that your friend is opening the door to potential new friendships with new people as wonderful as you both are. When friends encourage us to connect with their "other" friends, you may be pleasantly surprised to see your own friendship circle grow. Besides, being the center of another's friendship circle can be draining. Replace any possessiveness you feel for your friend with gratitude for her having other good friends in her life, and this attitude shift may increase your friendship's longevity.

Would You Like the "Other Friends" under Other Circumstances?

This is an essential question to ask yourself, and its answer really should help you decide whether to pursue the formation of a new friendship with your friends' friends. Within any environment in which you are active—for example, professional, neighborhood, group, or club—there exists a diverse array of personality types and potential friends. Imagine these friends of your friend as members of one of these other settings. Would you naturally gravitate toward them or away from them? Sometimes even an adult is capable of "cutting off her nose to spite her face." If you would enjoy getting to know someone under different circumstances, opening up your friendship circle to these friends of your friend may be the right thing to do. However, if you feel strongly that there is no setting in which you would strike up a conversation, much less a friendship, with these individuals, then just handle any group gatherings with grace. You do not have to "fake friendship" with every friend of a friend, but if you value the original relationship, it can be important to be kind, if noncommittal.

CONCLUSION

In this chapter, we have explored the rule that you should be open to befriending the friends of your friends. Being too open and accepting of persons about whom you know little can be risky, but unwillingness to take time to potentially expand your network can also have negative consequences. It is clear that this chapter's rule touches on the need to refrain from possessiveness of your friend's time and attention. Exclusive relationships may be expected in romance but have no place in healthy friendships. Having a BFF (best friend forever) can create a special and gratifying relationship, but trying to co-opt every bit of her leisure time or her attention seldom leads to a positive outcome.

6

BEING THERE WITH EMOTIONAL SUPPORT

RULE #4: SHOW YOUR FRIENDS EMOTIONAL SUPPORT

As a counselor, I've learned that there are many situations in life in which little can be done to make things *better* for someone beyond offering your warmth, caring, and authentic presence. While clients frequently come to counselors to be "fixed," a large number come to be heard, understood, and experienced in their authenticity without judgment. These are valuable gifts of self that even untrained professionals also should offer their friends as a matter of course. Unfortunately, as therapists know all too well, not every woman can find a group of supportive, nonjudgmental friends. And those who do not often end up asking themselves (and their therapists) what is wrong with *them*, not what is wrong with *their friends*.

Sometimes we may be to blame for wrecked relationships and frayed friendships if we do not offer the qualities necessary for relationships to thrive. Other times we may invite relationship difficulties if we befriend individuals who do not possess the traits necessary for maintaining healthy friendships. Some people do not yet exhibit the emotional stability or maturity necessary to create or maintain healthy relationships. Learning how far short some people fall of our expectations can be a painful experience as described in the following sections.

Young Girls and Almost Teens

In early girlhood, learning to care about one another is supported by our cultural tendency to outfit every young girl with at least one or two play dolls that need care and tending. Little girls will "ooh" and "aaah" and "poor baby" their dolls as they begin practicing caregiving skills early. As little girls grow and enter school, their innate and nurtured support-giving skills may face challenges, especially when their social worlds grow more complicated and less simple.

One woman, Jenny, recalled an early experience of riding the bus to school for the first time after her school year had already been in session for a few weeks. Jenny's parents had driven her to school prior to her inaugural bus ride that year. While this arrangement made family mornings a little less hectic, it also set Jenny up for a much more distressing experience later on. Because she had not ridden the bus initially, she had missed the time when everyone found their favored seat and seatmates. She recalled that the first day she got on the bus, she stood there by the driver and looked with terror at the seats, which all had been filled with at least one rider. Nervously glancing at the sea of faces, she finally saw a friend from her class sitting beside a girl Jenny did not know. Jenny and her friend's eyes met and locked for a moment before the seated girl broke eye contact, shook her head "no," and went back to chatting with her seatmate. This one moment of interaction was powerful enough to inspire Jenny to vow that she would never leave a friend unsupported as she had been. Being there for friends at this age may mean saving a seat in the cafeteria or on the bus, walking home with a friend when she gets a detention, or comforting a friend when her pet dies or her parents separate. Most young girls are well attuned to distress signals in other people for many different reasons. These range from being genetically prepped for empathy responses to being immersed in cultural socialization to be caregivers. When a friend leaves a friend hanging and hurt, she probably has some idea of the pain she causes.

Moving from childhood into the almost-teenage years can bring another layer and phase of emotional and personal development for girls that requires the renegotiation of social support networks. Middle school often brings together students from several different elementary schools and, as new networks form, the rungs on the social ladder may shift. Physical development rates are also highly variable, and as young girls mature, slower-to-develop girls may negatively compare themselves to their friends and experience the feeling of being misfits or "ugly ducklings." Emotional support from friends can provide the necessary sense of belonging that is especially valued as girls reevaluate friendships and self-concepts during these years.

Teens and New Adults

Adolescence is fraught with a million opportunities to be emotionally hurt by others, including peers. The path through high school and into adulthood can seem like a series of landmines in which maturity, independence, conformity, and belonging are tested. Young women check in with friends for emotional support for an expansive variety of decisions, including the outfit they choose to wear the first day of high school, entering sexual relationships with their boyfriends, or what to do after graduation from high school or college. It is also the time when women are probably most likely to withhold support intentionally to punish or exert power over peers. Regardless of where a young woman fits into the social strata in her community, a feeling of social belonging is essential to high school survival. Our friends reflect our projected self-identities, and we turn to them for support and understanding.

Some adolescents may actually be doing themselves a disservice with their tendencies to engage in group rants or to *co-ruminate* with their friends.[1] Co-rumination is basically the tendency to discuss your problems to an excessive degree with others. Adolescents typically find a significant amount of satisfaction in this activity, as it can elicit a great deal of voiced emotional support from their friends. However, co-rumination can have negative consequences for young women, as the intense focus on problematic situations can lead to a negative emotional state that is associated with adolescent depression.[2] Brainstorming solutions and sharing feelings can definitely work to bond friends; however, an obsessive rehashing of negative events and reactions can be detrimental to mental health.[3]

Although virtually all teenagers are going to experience and need to process negative events in their lives, one adolescent, Kriss, shared a story about having a friend who refused to look for solutions or change her perspectives. Kriss affirmed that her friend's consistent focus was on how badly she was treated by her parents, how teachers had it in for her, and how her sometimes-boyfriend was too unpredictable and often unavailable. When Kriss realized that spending time helping her mother do housework was more appealing than spending an afternoon with her negative friend and that Kriss could do nothing to support her friend "enough," she decided it was time to let the friendship fade away. Adolescence is tough enough, but having friends who are bottomless pits for sympathy and support can be more than most teens can handle.

As teens head further toward adulthood, the situations in which they may need their friends' emotional support can vary widely. Some young women may deal with eating disorders and need friends who do not "bail" on them when they are actively in a binge/purge cycle and who do not encourage these behaviors either. In cases where friends are making risky choices that have health-related consequences, it is essential that you support their efforts to get help—even if this brings up your own issues around the disorder or behavior. When it comes to substance use, if a friend is expecting you to cover for her or enable her to use and abuse illegal substances, you may need to withhold this type of support for her risky behaviors. Quality support of your friend may also require that you step up and encourage her to seek treatment. Good friends support their friends' efforts at sobriety and clean living and remain loyal even when their friends struggle with use/abuse triggers and slip-ups. Coping with and overcoming substance use problems is seldom simple, but good friends who stick around even when things get rough can make a significant difference in the long run.

In speaking with college women, stories about support addressed issues about social and romantic relationship conflicts. One interviewee, Rochelle, shared that her worst social experience in her college career to date was when she and a good friend went to their first fraternity party during their freshman year. She said everything was fine for the first hour or so, but then her friend disappeared into the kitchen and never returned. This friend had left Rochelle by herself with a group of inebriated people she did not know. Rochelle later found out that her friend had left the party with a boy from one of her classes without considering how this decision would affect Rochelle. Rochelle said that she "pretended" that it was all okay the next day when her friend called, but that was the last time Rochelle counted on friendship or support from this person. Good friends should never leave one another stranded at a party or event when the original arrangement was to arrive and depart together.

The young-adult period of life is filled with uncertainty and possibilities for disappointment. When a friend finds it too difficult to get outside of her own perspective and recognize a friend's need for support, the friendship may be on its way to a well-warranted ending. Finding a balance between independence and interdependence during these years can be challenging, but young women definitely should be able to count on their friends for emotional support.

The Twenties and Thirties

As one twenty-something women stated, the most significant reasons she could name for ending a friendship included lack of support and compassion from a friend. Support may be needed to help us cope with losing out on a job opportunity or professional advancement, to commiserate with us when a romantic relationship fizzles or explodes, or to help us deal with weight gain, heartache, or bad hair days. Compassion and support should be givens when it comes to authentic friendships. Asking for help, of course, may be a lesson that many women need to learn. Although women today are taught early to be bold and fearless as they follow their professional and personal dreams, calling on others for backup or guidance might still present a challenge. Knowing how to respond to a friend's failure to provide needed support is explored at the end of this chapter.

By the time three-quarters of the women in this country reach age thirty, they have already entered into their first cohabitation with a partner.[4] Furthermore, experience shows that new romantic relationships can affect friendships much more strongly than new friendships affect romantic relationships. At the opposite end of the romantic spectrum, thirty to thirty-one years of age is the median age for first divorce for women.[5] During this type of life event, our friendships are likely to rise in their level of importance as we rely on friends to help us manage the emotional roller-coaster that breakups may bring. Women who have failed to be present for their friends as they've placed all of their energy into their romantic relationships may painfully regret this choice if a romance fades and they are now trying to mend friendships that they had allowed to wither. When asked about past toxic friendships and what had led to past friendship breakups, a woman in her mid-thirties revealed, "For me, it was her consistent dropping off the face of the earth as soon as she was in a romantic relationship. She would call me and ask for dating advice, but never make any effort to actually connect." She felt abandoned by her former friend and, without reciprocity of support, she had no reason to continue investing in the friendship.

Mom-to-Mom Networks

Entering into motherhood can be a brave decision as a woman embarks on a totally new way of being and living; instrumental support and emotional support are often essential ingredients in a successful journey. One young woman shared an example of just how early the need for support might be felt as a woman begins her journey to delivery, as well as how hurtful a careless and thoughtless friend can be. As the new mother related, "After having struggled to get pregnant, my husband and I were elated to discover that we had finally conceived. Two months later my friend announced she too was pregnant and followed with 'and it didn't take me as long as you.'" The callousness of this friend was heart wrenching, and the young woman added that she let the relationship fade into more of an acquaintanceship. She is now careful to surround herself with friends who are more secure in themselves and more able to offer emotional support and empathy. We heard of another woman who was quick to build new boundaries when a toxic friend not only withheld much-needed support after a traumatic loss but also went on to tell her that her "full-term stillbirth was an act of punishment by God." This woman quickly ended the friendship and is now less likely to open up to friends as easily as in the past.

Learning to be a good mother can be challenging. When a child is ill, there is an even greater need for the emotional support of friends. One woman shared that when her child was placed on dialysis, she had two good friends with whom she quickly shared the news. Unfortunately, she said that neither of them "bothered to phone or be a shoulder to cry on. . . . I was always there for them, but when my time came, they just walked away. It was hard for me then and still is today."

Although the incidents shared in the previous paragraphs may be uncommon examples, new mothers need emotional support for extreme circumstances as well as the ho-hum, everyday challenges that mothers face. When children do poorly in school, have trouble making friends, are cut from the athletic team, or fail to meet expected developmental milestones, it is important to have friends who offer emotional support coupled with a nonjudgmental attitude. Most mothers try hard to do the right thing when raising their children; emotional support from friends when new mothers do something right or wrong can mean so much to their future sense of competence.

Midlife Connections

Once we reach our forties, most of us have lost patience for mind games and pettiness in friendships. We are ready to "call it as we see it" and move on, if need be. Emotional support is perhaps the most essential ingredient of our friendships at this point. Typically, midlife women know who they are, and while there may still be some uncertainty about their next adventure on the journey of life, they are sure about the type of friends they want along for the ride. When a friend has been in our lives for decades, it can be especially disappointing if she fails to provide emotional support when it is most needed. One woman, Yvonne, shared a story that illustrates not only the absence of emotional support but also the complications that arise when friends "choose sides" in the breakup of romantic relationship:

> My only real heart-to-heart friend informed me she would be attending the wedding, across the country, of my ex-husband and the woman he had been sexually and romantically intimate with during our marriage. He was still my friend's neighbor and she stated she wanted to be respectful and attend. We went through a month of back and forth in regards to her decision. She knew it hurt me but stated she wanted to go and she was giving me fair warning to get over it. Through e-mails, calls, and in-person meetings we both explained how we felt. It became clear to me that my feelings weren't important enough. She had watched me go through the affair start to finish and I just couldn't understand her position to celebrate their union. I told her I could no longer continue our friendship. She stated that I would come around. It's been two years since I've spoken to her.

When it comes to solving dilemmas such as this, there is seldom an easy solution. Whether you believe Yvonne was being too rigid or her friend was being too insensitive, what matters most in this situation, as it does in any friendship conflict, is the value of open communication.

Although the current situation was deemed too toxic for Yvonne to continue the relationship, her willingness to actively open the initial lines of communication regarding her friend's choice is an important attribute in a friend. Unfortunately, her friend's inability to provide the level of emotional support that Yvonne needed suggested that the friendship was more one-sided than Yvonne had assumed. Regrettably, research has shown that people who have more trouble establishing and enjoying close relationships are less likely to be able to offer emotional support.[6]

Another woman shared that she had to end a friendship with a friend who simply could "not be there during hard times. She just wanted to be there when times were fun." She went on to add that this friend could not be present for her or console her after the death of someone for whom she cared deeply. Another woman shared that her friend of over two decades not only was unsympathetic and unsupportive when she shared that her partner was losing his job but also began persistently cajoling her with encouragement to "not worry about the future and just have fun today." She felt that her friend could not appreciate the severe financial stress the couple was feeling because of the loss of income.

Most women appreciate and long for a friend's emotional support as they face unexpected emotional stressors, such as a divorce, or expected losses, such as losing an elderly parent, or facing normal but disruptive life events, such as transitioning to a newly empty nest. This period of life can be one in which relationships deepen as women gain greater self-knowledge. In many cases, your supportive presence can make a significant and positive difference when a friend is moving through physical, emotional, and relational transitions. Giving too much of your own emotional energy is not encouraged; being steadfast and available while also clear about your own limits to be there is essential.

Older Adults

As mentioned in chapter 2, our interactions with friends change as we age. For most of us, however, the need for someone's warm presence and understanding never fades, no matter how old we are. Life transitions might now be more emotionally trying as increased longevity means we have even more decades to turn habits into immutable patterns. Losses, too, sadly become a routine part of living—and run the gamut from losing independence to losing a lifelong partner. Friends can be a balm for the suffering that is experienced during these years. Friends who do not show up or support women during these transitions may be missing out on one of the last opportunities to exhibit their concern, loyalty, and care for their friends.

Good times in life can also arise out of transitions. The ascent into grandmotherhood can bring significant joy and potential stress to a woman's life. One woman shared a story of a friend who voiced resentment of her spending what the friend considered "excessive" amounts of time with her grandson. Her friend was also unable to support her willingness to allow her grandson and his mother, her daughter, to move back into her house when her daughter returned from military service abroad. This lack of support and the selfishness shown by her friend were sufficient cause for the relationship to end. As the circle of friends gets smaller as your days grow shorter, emotional support may be the most valued gift a friend can offer another, and it should be the resource most easily and abundantly available to provide.

FINDING THE SOLUTION THAT WORKS

Emotional support is a key component of friendship—having a group of people to whom we matter is what social connection is all about. Friends, though, also have lives of their own, and sometimes we must make allowances for their priorities at the expense of our own. At times, however, a line must be drawn regarding acceptable and unacceptable supportive behavior. Following are some questions to consider in determining your next steps in the relationship.

Does the Lack of Emotional Support Reflect the Climate or the Weather?

When working with clients who are experiencing any type of mood disorder—depression, anxiety, severe stress, or just a blue funk—counselors need to know the duration and intensity of the concern. The climate refers to the long-term, overarching state of affairs. Some of us might always be a little unhappy, pessimistic, or cynical. Other people might exist in a climate of joy, hope, and optimism. Typically, you will have friends who represent a wide variety of different climates or temperaments, which is totally fine. The weather is the temporary state we're in—and generally reflects the current circumstances of our lives. A normally unhappy person might feel a brief surge of joy when something extraordinary happens in her life. A normally joyful person may drop into despair when something unfortunate befalls her. These are normal reactions to abnormal circumstances.

When a normally supportive friend fails to provide support, you may need to determine whether the incident reflects a temporary behavior choice (the weather) or a more permanent and less changeable personality trait[7] or change in their commitment to the friendship (the climate). Even our most cantankerous or cynical friends should be willing to offer some form of emotional support when we are in need. When a normally supportive friend has failed to be there at a critical moment, you may want to explore the circumstances a little more thoroughly.

If a friend who is normally supportive just cannot be there for you because of something that has unexpectedly shown up in her own life, cut her some slack. We cannot necessarily control our responses to unexpected or unpleasant events that show up in our lives. There are also times when intersecting needs for support occur between friends. Storms can appear out of nowhere and disappear just as quickly, but regardless of how prepared we believe ourselves to be, emotional storms can take an unexpected toll. If the weather is rough, hang on and wait for things to clear. However, if you feel that the relationship is suffering more than a normal dip in its give-and-take, this may indicate a more significant shift in its strength or stability. Some of us can tolerate "arid, desolate conditions" better than some, while others of us can more easily handle the "rainy seasons and monsoons." Only you know when you need a climate change.

Have You Been There for Her When She Needed You?

Sometimes our own immediate desire for attention, support, or an audience will skew our perceptions of our own behaviors in a relationship. For instance, you might remember that night when your friend called at 2:00 a.m., needing to talk to you about the ugly argument she had with her partner. You listened, comforted, and chatted with her on the phone until you fell asleep at dawn. Unfortunately, that night was almost a dozen years ago, and you have screened her calls since then and picked up only on the rare occasion when you were bored or feeling lonely yourself. When the give-and-take of emotional support becomes undeniably unbalanced, you may need to reflect on whether your own "giving" warrants the amount of "taking" that you want to receive. Looking honestly at your shared history may open your eyes to the disparity in what each of you has invested and the dividends each of you has received.

Do You Make It Easy for Others to Support You?

Some women can be their own worst enemy when it comes to receiving support. They might minimize the efforts made by their friends and judge them as inadequate. They might trivialize their own difficulties, which can obscure any clear message regarding the need for support. The need for some women to appear "together" even when life is raining down problems and suffering can keep friends from recognizing just how grateful these women would be for expressed support. For women who are aloof and distant, friends may have a hard time reaching out for fear of being rebuffed. Researchers found that women dealing with serious illness and strongly in need of emotional support were potentially limiting the support they received through their own behaviors.[8] It was found that the more frequently they used curse words or swore, the less emotional support they were offered by others. Before recrimination of your friends for failing to be there for you, it may be useful to engage in some objective and honest self-reflection.

Vaguebooking

Facebook is a powerful social tool, and when assistance is needed, many women resort to putting out an "all hands on deck" call on their Facebook page. The ability to communicate with a large number of people at one time can be intoxicating, but some needy friends may also use Facebook to "vaguebook" their friends. This is the practice of posting status updates that are designed to prompt friends to post back for more information or support, but provide little in the way of actual content. Examples might be "I cannot believe that a friend would treat someone like this!" or "Okay, officially frustrated." This is not a healthy or effective method of seeking support from others. If you are a vaguebooker who feels friends are not providing adequate support, it may be helpful to be more open and clear in expressing genuine needs. If you have friends who vaguebook and then complain that their friends do not offer the support they expect, you might want to have a one-on-one, direct but supportive conversation with them regarding the message sent by their ambiguous communications.

Are Your Expectations Realistic?

Sometimes we may want a friend to be more than a friend; we may want a friend to be our mother, our therapist, and our psychic all rolled up into one. While it may be normal to occasionally want that kind of support, it is not normal to receive it from a single person. For young adolescents, friends are practically full-time companions—through face-to-face contact, phone calls, or texts. When they need a friend, they can find one as quickly as they can text 911 on their cell phones. As we grow older, however, our friendships begin to take a less central role in our lives as we begin to focus more on the less purely social aspects of our lives. As noted in the earliest chapters in the book, romantic relationships can eclipse friendships just as professional responsibilities or motherhood might. The amount of emotional support a friend can provide may be strongly affected by the balance of the other priorities in her life.

Have you ever noticed that after you have experienced a trauma or crisis in life, you feel the need to tell and retell the story of the event to others? For instance, an older adult may know exactly where she was and what she was doing the afternoon she learned that President Kennedy was assassinated. For the current adult generation, the tragedy of 9/11 may be the mass trauma that is still so fresh in our psyches that we can provide a detailed narrative of where we were and what we were doing the moment we first heard about and saw the news that the Twin Towers had been struck. We feel the need to tell our story over and over, as if we are using familiarity and repetition to integrate the experience into our mental framework. This is a normal process for abnormal events. However, if you also feel the need to tell and retell your stories about frustrations at work; disappointment with your significant other; anger at your parents, children, or the cop who gave you the speeding ticket; the rude person who cut into line in front of you at the bakery; and so on, you may be expecting more support and attention from friends than they should be expected to provide.

Friends cannot provide an unending supply of praise, patience, encouragement, comfort, or reassurance. Just like you, they can hit the "emotional empty" mark. When the support you ask of a friend is enough to cause "emotional bankruptcy," you need to honor the limits of this friend. If you know that you are especially "high maintenance" or "needy," you may need to cut your friends some slack. If your friends seem to have less tolerance for your complaints or lamentations, you might benefit by asking them if you come across as too needy or demanding. If you realize that the problem friend is really yourself for needing too much, not your friend for giving too little, take steps to scale back the need for an audience of supporters. You can research some self-help practices for self-soothing and self-care. Meditation, yoga, journaling, and exercise are all excellent ways to gain self-awareness and self-control, in terms of understanding and making sense of the events in your life. Truly, being a good friend to yourself is one of the most enduring and positive developments you can manifest.

Are You Better Off with Her or without Her in Your Life?

Counselors often ask this question of their clients who are trying to decide whether to stay in an iffy romantic relationship. The same question applies to friendships—if a friend brings other resources to the relationship that outshine her ability to be sufficiently supportive when needed, then you may decide to bend the support rule. Emotional vampires, those friends who suck your energy and demand your support but give little or nothing in return, are the kinds of friends we can all do without. Negative relationships actually compromise a person's health and well-being. You have to decide if this woman's presence is worth the cost of her friendship. If you choose to maintain the relationship, it is important to acknowledge that you are intentionally making this choice so that you can focus on the positive aspects of the relationship and allow the negative aspects to remain in the periphery of your emotional lens.

CONCLUSION

It is pretty much a given that friends are expected to provide emotional support to one another during the good and not-so-good times. Unfortunately, each woman's need for emotional support and capacity to give emotional support can vary based on life stage, priorities, commitments, as well as many other variables. When a friend cannot meet your needs, there are several choices for resolving the situation. One option is to open a dialogue with your friend to explore the imbalance you perceive in the relationship and make adjustments in expectations or behaviors. Alternately, you can choose to step back from the friendship if you believe the friend is incapable of offering what you need from this relationship. You also could choose to end the friendship if you feel that investing any additional energy into the relationship would only drain you further with no likelihood of replenishing your emotional resources. We rely on friends for support, but when a friend does not offer it as adequately or as freely as we would like, careful evaluation of multiple aspects of the relationship is suggested.

7

A FRIEND IN NEED

RULE #5: VOLUNTEER ASSISTANCE WHEN A FRIEND IS IN NEED

Being able to rely on friends to be there to offer emotional *and* instrumental support when things get rough is an essential ingredient in the maintenance of healthy friendships. The value of concrete support is evident between the youngest of friends as well as the oldest of friends. As one young interviewee shared, "If someone is never there for you, despite you being there for them in their times of need, then it is worth ending the friendship."

Most of us tend to take pride in independently meeting our own needs. Probably a lot of us might feel a little guilty or hesitant in asking others for help. Many might hope or assume that our friends can sense and respond to our needs without us having to make a direct request. Despite possible reluctance, take a moment and reflect on exactly which friends you would be willing to call on for assistance if the need arose. Who would you have an easier time asking—new friends or old friends? Friends or family? Most of us would probably have to answer, "It depends." Situations and circumstances call for different "SOS signals," and different friends are able to rally or assist in some cases better than others. There is probably nothing you would not do for the friends you count among your closest if they sent out a call for support.

According to many women we've interviewed, the true test of a friendship can be the measure of *comfort* a woman feels in asking someone for assistance when needed. If a friend seems hesitant to ask *you* for assistance or turns down offers of assistance you willingly provide, it is unlikely that you would feel comfortable asking *her* for assistance. Expectations surround reciprocity between friends; however, one woman respondent shared that friendship should be about generosity, not simply reciprocity. But when offers of assistance are rejected, there may be something deeper going on for your friend or within the relationship.

Expectations about support are usually implicit or unspoken, and this may be a part of the significant pain that we feel when assistance is not provided when needed. Asking for help can take courage. Refusing to provide it when needed can totally derail a friendship wherever we are in life.

Young Girls and Almost Teens

For little girls, a friend in need can be a very important asset indeed. Entering the new world of preschool or elementary school can be challenging for many young children as they leave the comfort of their own backyards or day-care centers to enter unfamiliar environments where the unspoken social rules and the major players may differ dramatically from their home turf. The need to find one's place can be felt as acutely by little girls as it can be by high school students. Unfortunately, the playing field for little girls is just as fraught with drama and friendship vagaries as any other time in life. In fact, as noted earlier in the book, mean girls are breaking in their bad behaviors before they ever reach elementary school. [1]

We interviewed a woman who still recalls a day, twenty years in the past, when her "best friend" stood silently by as other girls on the playground grabbed her new glasses and ran off across the playground with them. The friend's only response to the situation was a suggestion that Barbara had better run after those girls quickly to get her glasses back! That day ended a friendship, and, sadly, it left Barbara with a lack of trust in others that still exists today. The look on her face and the tone of her voice as she shared this experience emphasized what a powerful mark this social lesson had left on her.

By the time we reach middle school, most of us have already learned our place in the social pecking order in our schools and neighborhoods. Depending on our place in the social strata, we may be surrounded by friends who are eager to step in and help us meet our needs. However, we may also be at a lower stratum where social pressure keeps others from lending a hand. According to Wiseman's[2] description in the book *Queen Bees and Wannabees*, a person who sees our need but stands by while we are alternately tormented or ignored may be wrestling with her own dilemma. She may feel totally bound by allegiance to the social leader even though she is morally torn by a desire to respond to our need for help.

The years between ages five and twelve have been described by Erik Erikson[3] as the stage in which we focus on the issues related to the developmental crisis of "industry vs. inferiority." During this period, we focus on playing by the rules and keeping an eye on the level of fairness in life. Allowing ourselves to ignore the need of another to maintain our own sense of competency is a challenge that can be overwhelming to tweens. Often, the "nice girls" are the ones whose needs are most frequently ignored if their niceness does not equate with popularity. It can feel better to be on the "winning team" than to risk exclusion by helping someone with less social clout.

Teens and New Adults

As tweens grow headlong into adolescence, this may create even more deeply embedded patterns of conforming behavior for some. Other teens, however, embrace a stronger sense of individuality and exhibit more autonomy in their identity development. These teens have less need to seek the approval of peers. These teens often are the friends who can be *authentic* friends. They are the ones who can see beyond the superficial image that adolescents portray and judge a peer's worth based on values deeper than superficialities such as fashion sense and hair. Unfortunately, even less superficial teens can get wrapped up in their own expectations and nonconforming identities and make bad decisions regarding friendship behaviors.

When asking women about the types of behaviors that might end a friendship, lack of support almost always comes up. For adolescents, support can take on many different guises. For one girl, it might be friends who cover for her with her parents when she is engaged in behaviors or with people with whom she shouldn't be engaged. Support might be a friend getting another friend safely home when she's intoxicated or giving her a ride to school when she does not have a car.

Teens may have to make a lot of judgment calls on what type of support is okay to offer and what type of support is really "enabling." These are tough calls that most adolescents are still trying to figure out, as they are not yet able to make mature, rational decisions.[4] Thus, adolescents' decisions about relational reciprocity, fairness, and depth may all be based on skewed views that arise within their own unfinished, still-developing brains. Some teens may decide that it is better not to support a friend's misbehavior, but the fallout of "doing the right thing" can be outright hostility, resentment, or a broken friendship. Adolescents' decisions can have powerful impact on their social status.

The Twenties and Thirties

These emerging and young adult years include many transitions, often including and beyond romantic commitments. We've heard from many women that they value the support their friends offer during this period of their lives as they move from student to professional and as they become active members of their greater communities. Instrumental support may include everything from carpooling to work together to accompanying a friend to a party so that she does not have to go alone. Support can also be shown by friends who are willing to loan one another a few dollars or pick up the tab for drinks when the month is lasting a little longer than their available cash. Unfortunately, not everyone can count on their friends as much as they might need and/or wish.

One young woman shared a story of having gone out with friends to a club that was twenty miles from their neighborhood. She became separated from her friends during the evening, and they left her behind when they departed. She related that when she realized they were no longer at the club, she had phoned one of her friends and asked her to come back and get her. The friend offered to do so, but for a hefty price. After that experience, the friend who had been left behind says she is cautious and highly discerning in whom she befriends now. Friends should be willing to offer a helping hand when they can, and she firmly believes that friendships end when friends expect unreasonable "compensation" for their assistance. Learning your limits is healthy, but the circumstances that sometimes surround the lesson can be harsh.

The Mom-to-Mom Network

Regardless of the overwhelming and continually growing number of books addressing motherhood from virtually every angle, including planning for natural childbirth, knowing what to expect during pregnancy, soothing colicky babies, speaking the right language of love with spouses and children, parenting difficult kids, and so on, we doubt that a mother exists who has not needed to call for face-to-face support in a moment of sheer desperation at an untimely moment.

Mothers are typically extremely adept at and willing to help out other mothers, as children bring in a million different new needs for assistance from friends, and reciprocity is a vital part of these friendships. In little time, a mom quickly may realize who she can count among her friends and who is out of the circle. In fact, one mother shared that the final straw for one of her long-term friendships occurred on what was one of her all-time worst days of motherhood. This woman described being already overwhelmed with caring for her spouse and two of her three kids, all suffering from the stomach flu; a dog that had fled the fenced-in backyard and was running through the streets of the neighborhood; a plumbing emergency that constituted more of an emergency than it probably should have been; her in-laws' flight arriving that particular afternoon; and the expectation that she was to be at the airport to pick them up later that day. The woman was desperate for someone to run by ball practice at the school to pick up her third child so that she could drive the two hours to the airport to collect her in-laws. The friend she called was the one for whom she'd done the same type of favor in the past with no hesitation. However, her friend astounded her with a totally unexpected refusal to help out, instead sharing what she assumed was a clear and logical rationale for withholding support. The friend had just had her car detailed for an upcoming airport pickup of a business contact for her new company, and she didn't want to risk having the child come down with the stomach bug the rest of the family had while in her car.

There are some moments in which a friend's temporary lack of support can be forgiven and even expected. At other times, a lightbulb goes off and a woman recognizes a pattern or a signatory event in which she realizes that a relationship might be beyond repair. When a relationship presents a "deciding moment" such as this, you might need to step back and ask yourself the questions listed at the end of this chapter as you consider the steps you need to take.

Midlife Connections

As noted previously, midlife is a time in which women face a slew of personally transformative opportunities and challenges in their lives. Children may be launched into adulthood and out of the nest, professional landscapes may shift, caregiving responsibilities for older relatives may be assumed, and romantic relationships may also take on new focus as long-standing relationships might end and new "second-chance romances" are begun. Friends can be needed to offer all types of instrumental support during the midlife years.

Unfortunately, not every friend is as willing to be present in our lives in the way that we feel we deserve. When asked to describe the "breaking point" in a friendship, a woman in midlife described a friend who began "ignoring everything in [my] life . . . even life-threatening events." Another interviewee shared that her friendship ended because of a friend's lack of concern or compassion for how she was doing even as she was facing significant, newly diagnosed health concerns. As we move into a period of life when health and well-being take on greater significance and the need for instrumental support might increase, we may value having friends around us offering support more than earlier in our lives.

In fact, social support is an essential component in our ability to cope successfully with major illness and disease.[5] Support can be provided in a variety of ways during these years—a friend may be needed to provide transportation for medical treatments, to walk your dog or water the garden if you are out of commission, or to volunteer as your "walking buddy" to help you keep diabetes under control. However, the presence of toxic friends can only exacerbate precarious physical health problems as well as worsen or generate emotional health problems.[6] Cleaning up your friendships at midlife can be an important step as you move into the next phase of your life.

Older Adults

Support can also be especially valuable to friends headed toward older adulthood, according to Charles Lauer.[7] In fact, he used the word *tragic* to describe the inequity of failing to stay in touch with those friends who have been present in our lives to provide support. These friends have reached a stage in life when they desperately need support.

Mary, an amazingly capable ninety-four-year-old lady, recognizes that she is beginning to face undeniable limitations in what she can physically accomplish nowadays. She relies on assistance from neighbors, she shared, much more than she would like. However, living as she does in the snow belt of the Midwest, the weather adds significant challenges to her basic household chores, such as getting out the door and down her front steps for her daily walk or getting her trash cans to the street. Mary admits that she can be ornery, but she surprised herself with the unexpected anger she felt toward a neighborhood friend who neglected to throw her paper up on her porch on a particularly blizzardy morning. Her anger, she knew, was out of scale to the issue, and she realized that it wasn't the friend at whom she was truly angry. Mary elaborated that she was angry at her own frailty and inability to support herself in an undeniably increasing number of ways. Her perspective illustrates the wisdom of her years, but she went on to note that when it came to truly "toxic behaviors," she saw them in family more so than friends. This makes sense, as younger family members are expected to step up and assist their maturing relatives both instrumentally and emotionally, but not everyone who is needed is willing to provide this type of support.

FINDING THE SOLUTION THAT WORKS

The fifth unspoken rule of friendship addresses a foundational aspect of rewarding relationships, which is that friends offer support when needed. Period. There can be times, though, when we do not get what we most want or need from our friends, as the stories above illustrated. How do you know when it's time to sever the relationship? Following are some questions that you need to ask yourself as you consider your response to a situation like this.

Was Your Need for Support Clearly Expressed?

If we do not indicate or if circumstances do not clearly show that we need support, we have to recognize that our friends are not mind readers.

Actively communicating your need is the surest way to increase the chances that your needs will be met. This can be important to remember when you find yourself blaming a friend for not "knowing" you needed her to show up even though you didn't send out a call for help.

Is This a Friend to Whom You Would Give What You Want to Receive?

It would be wonderful if a friend could drop everything to rescue you from a bad date, a visit from in-laws, or lunch at the least favorable cafeteria table, whenever necessary. Unfortunately, you have to remember that your friends have lives of their own, and circumstances do not always allow for immediate gratification of your needs. Would you leave work in the middle of an important meeting to come to her aid? Or would you wait until the meeting ended and you could gracefully head out the door to assist? Would you kick your kids out of their beds in the middle of the night to give her a place to sleep if she just walked out on her partner, or would you offer the couch? Situations and circumstances dictate what "reasonable expectations" should be. Consider how far you would go for this person before you make a decision on the future of the friendship.

Do You Spend More Time "Calling in the Troops" Than You Do as a Part of the Cavalry for Your Friend?

Sometimes we have to take an honest look in the mirror and determine if we are perhaps a tad more "needy" than other friends might be. Are you perpetually in need of instrumental support? Do you tend to "owe more favors" than other friends do? These are tough questions, but if the investment we ask our friends to make in our friendship is consistently higher than the investment we are making, we may begin to see the return on our investments shrinking. This shrinking occurs as friends seem less willing to provide support. You may need to proactively show a little more independence and learn a few new skills—whether it's time management, basic carpentry, or some other area where you find yourself withdrawing others' energies from the friendship bank. Figuring out the area where your expertise is a little weak is an important first step in growing your competency and relying less on others.

Is This the First Time She's Failed You or Just Another Step toward the "Friendship Cliff"?

In relationships, some of us may be optimists about the outcome and others of us may be realists. Those of us who tend to be optimists always assume that "next time, my friend will be there for me." You assume that your friends are capable of giving you what you need and you always hope that the balance of the relationship will even itself out. However, if you have been let down repeatedly, it is probably time to reevaluate the relationship. If you cannot recall the last time your friend was an active member of the relationship—and she's let you down once again—it might be time to save yourself from future disappointments and ease out of the friendship. Hopeless optimists have a hard time ending relationships. However, if this is you, when you are consistently looking around for the friend who never shows, you may grow a bit weary of singing solo when what you really long for is a chorus. In healthy relationships, friends are willing to provide backup support when a task is too heavy for one person alone.

Realists, however, accept that people seldom change without a sizable motivating force. They are more easily able to assess and accept the limited future of a friendship when the friend has been heading steadily toward that "friendship cliff" over lack of support. If it's a "first time for everything" event, give your friend another chance. If you notice that the pattern of a friend vanishing when you need her most is clearly established, the decision to end the relationship might be the best path to take at this point.

Is She "Part of the Group" or "One of a Kind"?

If your "no-show" friend is a part of a larger, tight-knit group of friends, it can be very difficult to terminate the relationship. When you continue to show up at the same parties, girls' nights out, and weekend barbecues, it can be difficult to hide your negative feelings. Therefore, if you believe ending one friendship might negatively influence multiple friendships, it can be especially valuable to sit down with your friend and talk out your concerns about your relationship. Do not compromise other relationships, however, by talking to mutual friends behind your friend's back. Be up front and honest with the friend who you feel hasn't been present in the relationship the way you need for her to be. Opening up communication about friendship disappointments can be difficult. However, one woman offered words of encouragement about the best way to handle rule-breaking situations: "Don't delay saying what's on your mind. Speak openly and promptly about your feelings. Be honest and open." If you find that after having this discussion with your friend her behavior still doesn't change, you may need to accept her as she is. Intentionally shift your attention from the disappointing friend to the appreciation of the positive members of the group and the pleasure you find in those relationships. Do not let one disappointing friend spoil the good times you can enjoy with the group.

CONCLUSION

Social support, emotional support, and instrumental support are essential components of healthy friendships. We need people to lean on when times are rough and to rejoice with when life is good. Celebration, commiseration, and assistance are what we look to friends to provide. When these expectations are not met, we need to take a look at our roles in the relationships, the behavior patterns of friends *and* ourselves, and whether we reap compensatory benefits from the relationship. Only then can you make the decision to ignore the breach, repair the relationship, or let go and move on.

8

KEEP THE "FRIENDSHIP FAVORS" BALANCE IN CHECK

RULE #6: REPAY FAVORS WITHOUT BEING ASKED

Most of us probably have a good friend or two, or perhaps even more, for whom we would spare our last dollar or give the proverbial shirts off our backs. It makes us feel good to do a good deed for others.[1] Although we might not consciously acknowledge it, favors we do for our friends are investments in the friendship that we hope will pay off when we need a favor from a friend. Here in the United States, we especially tend to value friendship exchange systems in which reciprocity over time is enjoyed.[2] One method of describing this expectation is with the concept of the *equality matching*[3] framework. This concept is built on the assumption that both friends possess a shared understanding of the value of the resources that each one will be investing into the relationship and that both agree to honor this unspoken bargain.

Friendship resources include a vast variety of things, both tangible and intangible. For instance, you might pick up the check for your friend's meal when she is short on cash. Then her next payday will mean a payback for you. Your friend's child is going to be a sunflower, a raindrop, or a face in the crowd in the elementary school play, and your friend really wants you to accompany her on opening night. You agree to attend, and a couple of months later, when you need someone to go with you to the opening reception for the modern art exhibit you have been eagerly anticipating, your modern art–loathing friend will go with you because she knows she owes you—and she likes you, too.

Although long-term friendships don't require a "ping-pong payback" right away, newly developing and newly established friendships typically do. Trust within a new friendship is built by taking risks, whether these involve self-disclosure, favor providing, or other tasks. New friends are expected to respond with similar leaps of faith and similar relationship investments of personal, social, or material resources. Once a pair of friends has built up a history of trust and equitable sharing, favors do not need to be returned quite so quickly. However, when the length of time between favor done and favor returned grows too long for comfort, it may leave someone wondering if the old saying is always true that *no good deed goes unpunished.*

Young Girls and Almost Teens

Learning to share is a big lesson that children master at their own pace as they develop. Sharing toys, sharing the right to decide the activity, sharing cookies, or sharing choices about what video to watch are all paths to learning how to keep a friendship balance in check. Sharing is probably the most appreciated early friendship skill children acquire, as a matter of fact.[4] Despite the need to share, some children have a harder time taking turns or sharing their toys than others. If the poor sharer is in your home, you know that the volume of "child's play" can ratchet up shockingly swiftly. If you've had young girls in your home for any extended period, you are probably too familiar with the piercing screams of "give it back!" or "it's my turn now!" Even older girls can end up fighting over screen time, control of the remote, or any of a million limited resources. Allowing a friend to go first can be a painful decision for some young women, whether it's choosing the best slice of pizza, the best seat at the cafeteria table, which video to watch first, or which friend gets to crush on which boy band member.

Favors become more complex with time, and one woman, Tonya, recalled middle school as a time of torment by her "best" friend. Tonya was a math and science geek, and her best friend would take advantage of her academic prowess. The friend successfully coerced Tonya into sharing her homework for copying for a number of years. No matter how Tonya tried to get out of doing her friend this favor, her friend could cajole, wheedle, and shame her into giving in to her demands. To this day, Tonya regrets how easily she caved in to others' demands when she was younger. The middle school years are difficult enough under the best of circumstances, but a friend who is manipulating a young woman's good nature adds to the drama unnecessarily.

Teens and New Adults

While many teens may have lost some of that competitive "me first!" attitude when it comes to friendships, some are developing extremely sophisticated skills of manipulation and persuasion. Young women also learn the value of what they can bring to a friendship. Their innate drives to build friendships and find romantic success provide opportunities for them to hone their *bargaining skills* in relationships. Favors given can include rides to school, seats saved in the cafeteria and at the stadium, clothing loaned, and communication services provided between friends and potential romantic partners. Girls band together, and their belonging-ness to a clique is cemented by the resources they bring to the group. The resources they deliver and receive will vary for the girl with the car, the girl with the coolest clothes, the girl who can ace calculus and helps others prep for tests, the girl who is dating the high school hero, and so on. The roles each young woman plays provide social capital, and their friendships deepen as investments escalate. Of course, there is much room for girls to be hurt when they provide resources but don't receive the expected payback—whether they expect loyalty, an invitation, inclusion, or approval from their friends.

One woman, Terry, recalled her experiences with a former friend whom she considered her best friend as a teen. In high school, both Terry and Lisa were known for their good grades, involvement in the drama club and the school newspaper, and being pretty much "good girls." Both were thrilled to be accepted into the flagship state university and decided they would room together when they headed to college. While Lisa's popularity rating shone a shade or two brighter than Terry's in high school, Terry often provided instrumental assistance to Lisa, including lending clothes and providing rides to events. Terry enjoyed basking in the reflected glow of Lisa's high school social success, and she often felt this was payback enough for all of the favors Lisa asked of her. Once at college, Terry was not surprised or disturbed when Lisa began the next round of "Hey, would you do me a big favor? Can I borrow your . . . ?" Over half a semester passed, and Terry had been asked to lend everything from her own personally monogrammed sweaters to clean forks, stadium cups, and notebook paper. Unfortunately, Lisa did not volunteer to return any favors, and there were no "limelight" benefits for Terry as there had been in high school.

The favor balance was far from balanced for those early months, but the friendship went bust on a Friday morning when Terry returned from class to find a note that read, "Terry, borrowed your black boots and gray sweater—spending the weekend with Angie and her family in Raleigh." Terry shared that the note was signed with a heart over the "i" in Lisa's name, of course. As she summed up, "Okay, I had tolerated Lisa borrowing my socks, then putting them back in my drawer unwashed. She explained to me that she 'didn't sweat,' so the socks were not really dirty. I tolerated her grouchiness in the mornings when I was trying to get ready for my early classes and I tolerated the lights and the music playing until 1:00 or 2:00 a.m., while she stayed up late to finish her homework. But the day she took my favorite boots and sweater and left town, I realized that I had done that girl all the favors I was ever going to do." Unfortunately, Terry did not outright address her anger with Lisa. Instead, she just became distant and backed off from the friendship. The following semester was a very difficult one for both girls. They were stuck together as roommates for those final few months, but neither was willing to address the gulf between them, and they both found different roommates for their sophomore year.

The Twenties and Thirties

"I had a toxic friend who always took more than she gave," complained a woman in her twenties. When women are still trying to make their way and settle into adulthood, which includes the building of relationships and careers, they seldom have surplus energy available for squandering in poor friendship choices. Roommates, however, may be a fact of life even now, when jobs pay little and rents stay high. Learning to navigate sharing living space with another twenty- or thirty-something can be especially difficult if roommates see the relationship balance from very different perspectives.

Gina was a new schoolteacher and her roommate, Cassie, was a pediatric nurse—they both had a passion for helping others, especially children, although their career paths had taken them in different directions. They had become good friends over the course of the year before they decided to share an apartment, and both believed the rent-sharing plan was going to benefit them financially and socially.

Unfortunately, according to Gina, the rosy future she had envisioned turned gray shortly after the second month they'd moved in together. Although Gina loved cats, Cassie's two felines were given more freedom and less attention by their owner than Gina would have liked. Gina found out shortly after they moved in together that Cassie seldom took care of the litterbox, and so Gina began taking care of this duty. Cassie also frequently visited her boyfriend back in her hometown on weekends. Due to Cassie's absence, Gina was cat sitting a couple of weekends a month as well. In addition to getting "dumped on" for cat duty, Gina resented splitting the utilities down the middle, even though Cassie washed clothes every night after work and Gina waited for full loads to save money.

As the lease's renewal was growing near at the end of the first year, Gina knew that she could not take another year with Cassie. She dreaded the moment that Cassie asked her to sign a new lease, as she really liked Cassie as a friend but felt that another year of investing in their relationship would lead to what Gina's finance professor called a *sunk loss*. No return could be expected. Gina was frustrated that Cassie would never understand that she had broken a bargain on which the two roommates had tacitly agreed when they first moved into the apartment together.

Feeling compelled to keep score with a friend is not conducive to an optimal relationship. Most of us would like to believe that our friends will be available to assist us without feeling that they "owe" us. Unfortunately, some good-hearted women end up shorthanded regardless of the kindnesses they offer to friends.

Mom-to-Mom Networks

These years are full of the giving and receiving of favors between friends and neighbors. For instance, working women may need friends available to let in the repairman when they cannot leave work, or homemakers may need friends who can give them a ride to pick up the car when it is ready at the shop. Of course, these are just examples at the "40,000-foot view" of what favors between friends might look like. However, when it comes to real life, the favors a woman might need or provide may involve a great deal more than just a gallon of gas or a spare key. When asked about the most difficult thing she had ever had to do for a friend, one woman, in her thirties, described the kind of favor that takes a deep commitment to the relationship. It is also one we would hope, for our friends' sakes, that we would never have to repay in kind:

> A friend rang me once at 4:00 a.m. as she was having what later turned out to be a miscarriage. Her husband was away working and she knew I'd be there for her. I rode with her to hospital in the ambulance and stayed with her until her husband arrived. I made all the necessary phone calls. She remained in hospital for a week, during which time I cared for her two children.

This friend is the kind whom most women would love to have in their lives, but not everyone can be as present and helpful as this woman had been. When describing relationship killers, one-sided friendships are universally distressing. One woman shared her frustration with the lack of mutuality: "I listened to her constant moaning quite well [and for too long], but in the future I wouldn't wait as long to recognize that the friendship was extremely one-sided and I was getting nothing from it. In fact, I often gave up things to keep her happy . . . [including] missing my son's football game!" Most of us feel good when we do a friend or stranger a good turn, but when our kindness leaves our stomach churning, it is a warning sign that a change is needed.

Midlife Connections

By the time we reach the end of our thirties, we are hopefully able to assess relationships and social exchanges more objectively. Women don't need piles of friends the way they might have when they were younger and are comfortable being more selective of those they let into their lives or *keep* in their lives. As women mature, the relationship balance may also be measured differently than when they were younger. Financially successful women may happily pick up the tab for their less economically stable friends—at lunch, for drinks, and even for vacations.

One woman, Keeya, with whom we spoke described an experience of what she first thought was surprisingly good fortune but resulted in the fraying of a formerly strong friendship. Keeya was a licensed counselor, as well as a fiber artist, and she wore her heart on her sleeve and felt the need to take care of every struggling soul with whom she came into contact. She gave her energy to charitable causes, lost causes, and all of her family and friends, as she was able. A single mother of two teenage children, she worked in private practice and was never as financially secure as she would have preferred. She was good friends with a couple who were planning a dream vacation to an exotic location that coincided with one spouse's annual professional conference. Since this meant that the other spouse would have plenty of free time to sightsee, they invited Keeya to accompany them on the trip. They offered to use their credit card points to pay for the third airline ticket, and they had already booked a two-bedroom condo; thus, Keeya's lodging was covered as well.

The trip was as wonderful as Keeya had hoped. It was only after the return that the balance of the travelers' friendship seemed to shift. Once they were all back home, Keeya's friend began asking for favors that ranged from expected tasks like giving a ride when needed to unexpected requests for gratis original artwork by Keeya for gifts for other friends. When Keeya tried to protest and explain that her art was a big part of her livelihood, she was reminded that "the trip should be investment enough to justify providing the favor." Keeya relinquished one small work of art but refused to budge on the matter again. Keeya laughed with irony as she noted that the friendship had fizzled before her tan lines had faded.

Older Adults

As we age, our instrumental needs increase as we are less able to do for ourselves. This can lead some women to be more dependent on others than they would like, and some might feel that they are either giving too much to their friends or not being given enough. A woman in her sixties described the impetus for ending a friendship: "When you realize that you give more than the other person and you get very little back. You only hear from your friend when she wants something. When she dumps everything on you but doesn't give you the opportunity of actually talking or sharing, dismissing everything you say, interrupting you, taking the conversation back to herself, and never once asking if everything is going okay with you."

What may also be interesting about the need for balance between friends during this stage of life is that women prefer not to be "overbenefited" by a friendship.[5] As one interviewee complained, "I have one young friend who wants to do too much for me . . . she makes me feel like an old lady. I try to get her to stop, but she complains that I'll have a heart attack cleaning out my gutters. I'm eighty-three, have lived alone for almost twenty years, and know what I can and can't do by now." Women in friendships that were equitable or in which they felt "underbenefited" were actually more content with the relationship.[6] When friends try to do too much, it can create a sense of obligation for some women or a sense of guilt for others. No matter what age you might be, keeping relationships balanced is clearly important to your own sense of self-efficacy and self-respect.

FINDING THE SOLUTION THAT WORKS

This rule is a reflection of our expectations that we be treated fairly by our friends and that the investments we make in our relationship are equaled by our friends. When a friend does a good turn by us, we should be on the lookout for opportunities to do a good turn for our friend. Yet there are times, as described above, when one friend seems to be doing all of the giving and another seems to be doing all of the receiving. What are the factors that should be considered when you feel that your friend has "overdrawn" her credit in the relationship or when you feel that you are getting a higher dividend for a smaller initial investment?

Do Circumstances Justify the Unbalance?

How do you measure your friendships? Is there a universal gauge that can be applied to each different type of social relationship? Or do your expectations of return on your friendship investments vary based on the parties involved? Most likely, your expectations differ depending on the length, proximity, and emotional closeness of the relationship.

From time to time, we recognize that our relationships may be unbalanced due to unexpected or unpredictable circumstances beyond either member's control. If we experience a crisis, we would like to believe that our friends, if necessary, will assist us beyond what we may have previously invested in our relationship. If a friend needs you more today due to bad luck yesterday, and you value the friendship, you will jump in to help. As one woman shared in a discussion of equity in relationships, sometimes a mother might love one child more than another during a moment of special need by that child. So long as the other child is the one you love best when he needs it, temporary inequity can be just a normal part of a long-term relationship.

What Is Your Expected Payback?

What do you expect from your friendships? Are you a "high roller" who risks a lot if you are feeling lucky or have a feel for the odds? Or do you parcel out your risk taking and play the penny slots? In high school, some girls befriend the popular and powerful girls in their class as an investment in their own hope for "popularity by association." Some girls are excellent *followers* and knowingly sacrifice their own interests in the hopes that the "high school top dog" will reward them with glory and shared attention. The payback expected is high, and the willingness of a girl to subjugate her own needs and wishes can make sense when you consider what the payoff might be for her in the high school cultural setting.

If you feel that you are constantly being the hero, picking up the pieces, and giving it all you've got but the return on the investment has been less than what you feel is due, then it is time for a review of the relationship. A discussion and clarification of the expectations of both you and your friend are essential to mapping out the future of your relationship. As one woman shared, "Friendships are give and take, and not one-sided, where one person is always doing all of the taking, while the other is doing all the giving. When I see that a relationship is heading in that direction, I quickly get out of it. Because it's probably only going to get worse." When the payout is less than expected and your investment is draining you dry, it may be time to cut your losses and walk away.

What Is Your Economic Philosophy?

This may seem like an irrelevant question at first; however, research shows that romantic couples argue more about money than any other concern. In fact, disagreements about money can be heated.[7] A close second for hot topics between couples is the equitable balance of shared housework responsibilities.[8] If you are the kind of person who believes strongly that "a penny saved is a penny earned," then you might have a harder time giving more than a friend in the early stages of a relationship. However, if you are not willing to offer a new friend at least a 1:1 matching program, the relationship is less likely to endure. If you cannot imagine ever "buying a round for the gang" or picking up the tab for the person in the line behind you in the Starbucks drive-through, it may also be difficult for you to invest tangible resources in a friendship.

No one should allow herself to be the one who is always giving, but there will be times when a friend's needs might outweigh her investment. That leaves it up to you to decide whether it is worth your time, energy, and investment to keep the social exchange in place. If you are always saving for a rainy day, you may miss the opportunity to take a last-minute cruise with a friend, or splurge on a girls' day out at the spa, or go crazy at the Coach or Prada outlet. If you are flat-out broke, in debt, or living from paycheck to paycheck, and you love your friend, withhold judgment of her financial decisions and find ways to enjoy her companionship that don't put your opposing economic circumstances or philosophies in the spotlight. For example, she may be able to afford to treat you to a massage, and then you may repay the favor by offering to train with her as she prepares for the upcoming half marathon if she asks!

CONCLUSION

While earlier rules remind us to offer both emotional and instrumental support to our friends, this rule encourages us to recognize that an exchange system is at work here, too. Some of us might use the term *karma* to describe the benefits of keeping the friendship balance in check, while others might connect this to the earth religion–based Law of Threefold. This is the belief that whatever you send out into the universe comes back to you multiplied by three. Others might rely on the wisdom of the Golden Rule, which is pretty much endorsed by every faith group around the globe. Even if our friends don't keep a scorecard, literally or metaphorically, it is important to show your appreciation for their good deeds to you by doing them a good turn every chance you get.

9

DEFENDING YOUR HONOR

RULE #7: STAND UP FOR YOUR FRIENDS AND THEIR INTERESTS WHEN THEY ARE NOT PRESENT

Showing loyalty to your friends through your actions is the focus of this friendship rule. This includes refraining from gossiping about your friends as well as not tolerating the gossip of others about your friends. There is an expression that "silence gives consent," and when you fail to speak up when your friend is criticized, she may consider you as much at fault as those who verbally attacked her. Audre Lorde once stated that "your silence will not protect you." When you fail to show loyalty to a friendship, you put yourself at risk of losing a friend.

This rule speaks to the necessary practice of exhibiting loyalty to your friends. When you silently allow others to speak ill of your friends, you are likely perceived as being in agreement with the expressed opinions of your friend. Friendship allegiance requires that you support and defend your friend's good name. If you feel that you are in a situation where that is not possible, your friend might have reason to be concerned about the depth and authenticity of the relationship. When a situation occurs in which a friend fails to show loyalty, a relationship can quickly reach a crossroads. In the following sections, we share examples of how this can happen and provide several suggestions and starting points for how to respond.

Young Girls and Almost Teens

As girls move from childhood toward adolescence, their level of authenticity in relationships proves to be a harbinger of strong friendships and psychological well-being over the long term.[1] Conversely, the damage done by "friends" at this age can have a lasting influence on young women, as recounted by a young woman in her early twenties: "When I was nine years old, I overheard a girl, who was supposed to be my friend, telling a group of kids that she was not really my friend, but had to be nice to me because her mother told her she had to, because 'it was the Christian thing to do.' So now I tend to make sure people are sincere before I commit to cultivating a friendship with them."

Some girls may have more trouble than others distinguishing between truth and fiction. One study indicated that a quarter of the children in the study, between ages five and twelve, had imaginary friends.[2] Thus, some young girls may have a difficult time distinguishing between truth and falsehoods about a friend. Unless she knows for a fact that a story about a friend is untrue, she may innocently assume that it is true. On the other hand, she may be a quick and pure defender of a friend's character when others are trying to tear her down.

As young girls head toward adolescence, the social strata begin to solidify more firmly, and some girls may be placed in a position of sacrificing their friends in order to cement their position in the next higher stratum. Gossiping is one method of bonding with others.[3] Shared information about someone who is not present can create a sense of deeper connection through mutual knowledge of intimate information about another. While young children grow out of their tendency to merge fact and fiction, the older young girls become, the more likely they seem to be to accept gossip as truth.[4] Thus, when a friend is being talked about in unflattering terms when she is not present, some girls will be drawn into believing that the words are based on fact. Speaking out against group opinion, too, can be very difficult for those with lower self-confidence or those who have lower positions in the social hierarchy.

Cyberbullying

The damage done by cyberbullying could fill multiple volumes, as it has lasting effects on victims. We have space only to touch briefly on this topic, but it is worthy of attention due to its prevalence and potential lethality. The power of cyberbullying to do harm and wield destruction is greater than many adults may have expected when they opted to bring the Internet into the home or place smartphones in their daughters' hands. The stories of the trauma suffered by young women who have been mercilessly bullied via online communications and social network sites are heartbreaking.

Research has shown that cyberbullying is more detrimental and induces greater fear than covert or face-to-face bullying.[5] Much of its power is found in the unpredictability of strikes and the Internet's omnipresence in most young women's lives. Schoolyard bullying happens only at the school and only when the victim is physically on-site. The victim, afterward, also has a good idea about the identity of her tormentors, as a rule. Cyberbullies are stealthier in that they can torment their victims twenty-four hours a day from virtually anywhere and under total anonymity. Cyberbullies hold a power that can strike fear in people even when they are in their own homes and whether they are alone or with others. It is important that young women recognize the harm that can be done through this activity. When several young women get together and decide to engage in cyberbullying, it can take a very courageous member of the group to withdraw from the activity or a member with a strong level of social influence to call it off. Good friends should not allow another friend to be harmed, but there is a feeling of innocuousness when young women are hanging out in familiar surroundings as anonymous messages are relayed so quickly and efficiently.

Young women need to be encouraged to recognize the danger that can come from this intentional attack. Cyberbullying is *not* a harmless prank and has negative consequences that reach far beyond an individual incident. News stories and personal anecdotes of the dangers of this form of bullying should be teaching tools to help young women understand the destructive power of their behavior. Perhaps most disheartening is that research shows that those individuals who have cyberbullied another tend to be less negative in their evaluation of this type of behavior and seem to minimize its power to harm others.[6] It is essential that information about the harm done by both face-to-face bullying and cyberbullying be clearly communicated to young people and essential that parents do not condone or encourage this behavior.

Teens and New Adults

During early adolescence, young women can reach the zenith—or per-haps *nadir* is the more appropriate word—of their potential for "mean-ness." Social standing and social acceptance drive much of the daily behaviors and responses of this age group. Middle school and early high school cliques are typically pretty clearly defined, and it can be difficult for females to move between different groups. However, as young wom-en move through the later years of high school and past commencement, the process of degrouping is set in motion.[7] As friendship packs lose their intensity, young women are more able to select their friends based on individual identities, not group approval. This is a transition to a more adult form of social network development.

Unfortunately, even as young women begin to exhibit greater inten-tion and independence in making friends, they may still betray others. One young woman, Diana, shared that she had been the target of a toxic friend who vacillated between ignoring her, bullying her, and making snide comments about her in front of their mutual college friends. For her, this was the turning point in their relationship. Diana said that the "friend" was inconsistent and that she had, in return, been too passive for too long and allowed herself to be bullied for too long. When mutual friends described how she was being talked about her behind her back and excluded from social gatherings, she finally ended the relationship with the disloyal "friend." This can be the only choice in situations in which a friend has lost respect for you. Diana shared that her biggest regret, beyond trusting the friend, was that she had to walk away from a long friendship without knowing the real reason behind her friend's be-trayals. As she summed up, "The issues got too big because we were not honest with each other and didn't address things head-on."

Another young woman in her twenties shared this story when asked to describe any experiences with having to end an unhealthy friendship: "I ended a friendship only once, and unfortunately this was the most impor-tant friendship that I have ever had. My friend betrayed me twice in just three years. First, she stole my boyfriend, and I was able to forgive her. Then she stole my job; that was the end of that friendship for good. She had been my friend since we were seven years old." Honesty between friends is essential, and honesty about friends with other friends is an additional expectation. Tearing down a friend by gossiping about her or standing quiet while others do so is a very poor choice of methods to build yourself up or fit in with a group. Outright betrayal is an equally unacceptable behavior that is an example of a friend "not having your back." Traditionally, the late teens and early twenties herald women's movement away from clique-focused friendships. As you move away from former cliques and social groups, new opportunities to broaden your friendscape will arise, and you can establish relationships with greater intentionality.

The Twenties and Thirties

These decades are prime time for building your adult identity, as noted in chapter 2. While our culture has shifted dramatically in the past half century in terms of women's rights and their professional goals, immutable biological differences between the genders still influence our behavior. For instance, evidence indicates that there is a difference between the crisis responses of males and females.[8] When faced with a threat to physical or psychological safety, women will respond with a desire to *tend and befriend* rather than the *fight or flight* reaction that most people believe is the typical de facto fear response.[9] Thus, passively allowing others to defame a friend—or even joining in—might be some women's "go-to response" when they feel stressed or anxious when a good friend's reputation is being attacked. While she may first try to defend her friend, if others are more persistent and they disregard her words of support for her friend, she may silence herself and step back from the discussion. Trying to argue against a group of women who share a single belief can be a significant challenge. Even though adult women are typically less likely to worry as much about fitting in and conforming to others' expectations, many continue to have a hard time speaking out against majority opinion in social situations.

Even more disappointing than a friend who does not speak up in your defense is the friend who actually takes the lead in spreading gossip or outright lies about you. We heard from a woman who learned that one of her friends was saying horrible things about her to others behind her back as well as flirting with her boyfriend. This was especially painful because she had considered this person to be her best friend for many years. She was willing to take some time to consider rebuilding their friendship, as she related: "I tried to just distance myself from her for a while to just get some space, but she was tenacious and wouldn't leave me alone. In the end, I had to send her a text message and tell her that I had heard what she had been saying about me and that I would appreciate her not contacting me again."

While sometimes a little bit of distance from a situation can help you clear your head, without taking the next step of openly addressing the issue between yourself and a friend, the friendship is not likely to heal. Conflict is not as easy for women to handle and address as it typically is for men. Women are seldom taught how best to handle their aggressive tendencies or their anger. Thus, many women err on the extremes of the emotional expression spectrum. Some women swallow their anger and quietly tolerate being treated poorly or silently slip away from the relationship. At the other extreme, women may explode and inappropriately express their anger through harsh words or physical acts. Some may simply dump all of their negative feelings at the feet of the "enemy" and dramatically exit the relationship. Choosing a more levelheaded but assertive path that opens up a dialogue between friends is a much more effective means of handling conflict. Even more valuable is the modeling of authentic, open communication that you are providing your friend. If poor communication practices and disrespectful messaging are at the root of the conflict, inviting an honest conversation about the damage of these behaviors is a very powerful message to send.

Mom-to-Mom Networks

As noted in earlier chapters, having a wide and diverse social network is essential to managing motherhood. Unfortunately, the bond of motherhood does not mean mothers are above sharing gossip or speaking ill of the mother who is not present at the park that day. Gossiping, as a behavior, works to build alliances between those who are present through the sharing of potentially privileged information as well as serves as a method of communicating knowledge between people.[10] When mothers get together, they often seek advice or suggestions on problems with their children, their partners, their extended families, and so on. When a mom shares a story about how another mother dealt with a similar issue, but *wrongly*, she is potentially providing helpful information, but at the cost of the reputation of the absent mom. Unfortunately, some friends are more interested in making a point and educating someone on what not to do or how something can be done wrong, rather than considering how her words may negatively affect you.

One young mother, Heather, shared an upsetting experience that involved her daughter Lindy, her daughter's good friend, and the mother of this friend, who had long been a friend of Heather's. One afternoon, Lindy returned from the friend's house and shared that the other woman had said "mean things" about Heather to the two girls. When Heather called her friend to learn more, she was told that it was true in that when Lindy asked for more soda, the other woman had unkindly reprimanded the girl with a comment along the lines of "Your mother clearly lets you have too much sugar at home!" Heather and the other mother were able to laugh about this incident, but it gave them both a wake-up call about the potential weight of the words they spoke in front of other mothers' children.

Midlife Connections

During this period, as women get to know themselves more authentically, they may now recognize which friends will stay the course with them and which ones might best be left behind. When a professed friend prioritizes loyalty to a woman below her desire to gossip about the friend behind her back, the friendship is likely no longer worth maintaining. One woman in this period of life shared the following story: "I have ended a friendship when the friend was really not a true friend at all, but just pretending to be one. Behind my back to mutual friends, she tried to make me look incompetent and as just a bad person, in general." She said this hurt most because the gossiper was "still hanging out with [her] with a smile on her face." She shared that she ended the "farce of a friendship" when there had been too many coincidences in which mutual friends knew confidential information about her life that she had never shared with them.

Midlife is also a period in which you typically feel free from prior obligations to tolerate the bad behavior of friends just to "fit in," as a rule. Although you may value activities in the community such as women's clubs, church groups, professional associations, and other similar groups, you may also value autonomy and a sense of congruency in your relationships. The recognition that others, even those whom you assumed to be friends, may not have your own best interests at heart may serve as encouragement for you to exemplify the values you hold and the identity you claim. When a friend has failed to support or defend you in a group setting, do not give away the power you can hold in proving them wrong. Living out your values is the best way to encourage the type of relationship you most value.

Older Adults

A couple of the types of older women portrayed in the media include the "nosy neighbor" and the "gossip." As women age, they continue adding to their vast store of knowledge about people, places, and things. They may share their perspectives quite openly and honestly with others. Where once a group of women may have gossiped about the woman whose piecrust was the toughest, they may now be gossiping about whose recent Botox injections make her look more like a Picasso than a Rembrandt. Just like with any friend, when the disparaging remarks or gentle digs are more entertainment than intentional insult, you may be able to let the friend off the hook for being a part of the conversation.

At times, though, a friend's silent agreement with another's negative opinions about you cannot be ignored, and you must carefully reflect on the value of this friend in your life. Although research has shown that older adults tend to be treated much more kindly by friends than younger people might be,[11] sometimes peers can be less thoughtful. While you cannot control the behavior of your friends, you do have the power to control how you respond to their unkindness. In fact, speaking up and expressing your feelings grows easier for many women over time. As you mature, your opportunities for developing new relationships may be more constricted. Thus, it becomes even more important to be cautious in what you share with friends with whom you have less trust and to focus your energy on enjoying the relationships with those with whom you have greater trust.

FINDING THE SOLUTION THAT WORKS

Loyalty is absolutely one of the most crucial elements of healthy friendships. Therefore, it can be very difficult to accept that a friend has allowed others to speak ill of you—either by quietly allowing others to speak against you or by actively joining in the discussion. If you discover that this type of conversation has occurred, it can leave you feeling vulnerable, angry, and hurt. As counselors know, expressing anger is often easier than expressing hurt. Vulnerability can be hard for many people to acknowledge, but when someone you had trusted and embraced as a friend betrays you in this way, it can leave you feeling raw and exposed. Choosing to continue the relationship may hinge on your responses to the questions below.

What Is Your Personal Assessment of the Damage That Was Done?

Sometimes the damage that is done during an incident of this type seems larger and more significant than it actually may be. If someone shares a little too much information about you that is not as glowing as you would want it to be, it can be retroactively embarrassing if the information was accurate, or absolutely infuriating if the information was false. Deciding how you will handle the situation depends on the overall value of your relationship. If you feel that your reputation has been damaged in such a way that your comfort with this friend and other friends is irreparably compromised, you might decide that the friendship has lost its value. If the incident was just a flash in the pan and likely to be less memorable than last year's *Survivor* finale, then you may decide that the relationship is worth maintaining. Regardless of the path you decide to take, offer your friend some honest feedback on how the incident affected you and left you feeling. Without clear communication, boundaries and expectations are not as likely to be honored.

What Was the Intent of the Breach?

Earlier in this chapter, we noted that gossiping about others is relatively common behavior that serves multiple functions; one function is to keep others from making mistakes. If you know that you really did something ridiculously dumb, or if something happened to you that you would not like to see happen to others, then you may be able to accept that your friend really was providing a helpful, reality-based example of what not to do. When you see a "what-not-to-wear" photograph in a magazine, the woman's eyes are generally obstructed to protect her identity. It can be painful when a friend "blows your cover," and the unflattering anecdote or "urban lesson" is directly linked to you by name. If you believe the friend made an honest goof and you can step back and see the bigger picture, the conflict may be just a minor blip on the screen. However, if the intent was more malicious, the outcome might be very different.

When a friend makes a habit of talking about one friend to another to create animosity between groups or to wield power over others, it can be very difficult to see the value or marshal the energy to do the necessary revision on this type of friendship. Some women build alliances by sharing negative perspectives about a mutual friend. Denigrating the targeted and absent friend may create a stronger bond between the women present. Some women will use this strategy with multiple friends to create a collection of "us vs. her" groups with a different "her" in each group. When your reputation is sacrificed as a power play by someone you consider a friend, this may be the catalyst to end the relationship. As many women have shared, if a friend speaks ill of mutual friends to you, it is likely she is also speaking ill of you to mutual friends.

Are You Better Off with Her or without Her in Your Life?

Some friends are timid and lack the self-assurance to stand up and defend you when others are making unflattering or insulting comments about you. Some people have a hard time asserting themselves when they hold the minority opinion on an issue. While you might hope that every friend would be willing to put her loyalty to you above her own hesitance to speak up, it will not always happen that way. Of course, if your friend frequently finds herself in groups where these types of conversations are occurring, it may be worth exploring more fully your mutual friendship and the relationships you have with the other individuals involved.

Discretion is often the best choice when it comes to speaking with a friend about gossip that has been shared about her. Some friends, though, seem to take a perverse pleasure in relaying the content of gossip to its target. If you have a friend like this, there may be more problems in the friendship than her tendency to share information. A discussion of her motivation for spending so much time with those who are speaking ill of you might be helpful, as would a conversation about her motivation for sharing the gossip with you. If she is trying to gain loyalty from you by revealing unkind remarks of others, this relationship may not reflect the healthiest of friendship dynamics.

Some women may just be hard-core gossips who mean no harm but enjoy sharing insider information. They simply do not realize the damage that is done by indiscriminate gossip. If you can handle the likelihood that you may be the topic of this type of friend's conversations, accept that she may listen to, not discourage, others' negative remarks about you. If you still enjoy her company, you may decide that she is worth the risks involved.

Other friends may be simply "do-gooders" who do not recognize that the trade-off for sharing your shortcomings, errors, and misfortune to potentially protect others from similar mistakes may actually be the unintentional sacrifice of your good name. These friends may have "hearts of gold" but miss the larger message that their words convey. If this friend is the type you are facing, opening a frank discussion about your concerns is necessary. She may respond with apologies and honest expressions of regret, but you might still need to be careful in what you choose to share with her in the future. When a friend has a disappointing flaw or two among a wealth of strengths that she brings to your life, learning to work around the flaws may be well worth the extra effort.

Unfortunately, a friend who uses the power of derogatory remarks and insults to build her own position within a group is unlikely to change her behaviors without significant motivation. An honest discussion of the consequences of her behavior on others can be a first step in the process, but it may not be enough to produce lasting change. If you decide that you are going to terminate the friendship, remember that whatever transpires between the two of you as you exit the friendship will probably be discussed in her conversation with others. Thus, it is important to handle the ending of the friendship wisely and to be intentional in your behavior. We heard from numerous women who let friendships fade away rather than directly addressing the conflict or relationship termination. These same women often shared that their biggest mistake in ending a friendship was not having these important, clarifying discussions of how their relationship had gotten to this point. It can take courage to address a divisive issue head-on, but there is strong satisfaction in knowing that you asserted yourself in this way.

CONCLUSION

A friend's loyalty should be actively engaged 24/7, regardless of where she is and who is present. When a friend joins others in assessing your shortcomings, finding fault in your behaviors or life choices, or making fun of you, it is difficult to believe that this friend has your best interest or feelings at heart. While some may view gossip as harmless entertainment, the sharing of valuable information, or warnings about mistakes to avoid, when a friend places you in the middle of the conversation, it can be emotionally painful and socially humiliating. Through self-reflection and open discussion with your friend, you can determine whether to maintain the relationship or let it go.

10

BRING JOY TO YOUR FRIENDS

RULE #8: DO NOT "BRING DOWN" OR INTENTIONALLY ANNOY YOUR FRIENDS

This next rule focuses on doing what you can to add to the happiness of your friends, while also doing what you can to avoid bringing them any grief. Friendships should be the relationships that offer a break from the difficulties we face in life or in other relationships. Life is not always "peaches and cream," and we should be there to offer our friends support when they are feeling low. If a friend is *only* a friend when her path in life is blocked, her luck is out, her love life is a wasteland, or she is between jobs, she may have you confused with a therapist rather than a friend. If you feel that she has worn out your welcome mat or that you yourself have become her doormat, it may be time to speak up and share your concerns with your friend. Some individuals may be unaware of the impact their behaviors have on others, and it may take more than a few slight hints to open up their eyes.

When your own life is filled with hurdles or you feel that you are a target for another's anger, disappointment, or frustration, sometimes the company of a good friend is the most effective antidote to the negative energy that is being sent your way. With friends, you can complain about the world in general as well as the particular inhabitants who are causing the grief and suffering you are experiencing. Ideally, friends will respond with understanding, empathy, sensitivity, and maybe even chocolate! Good friends do what they can to cheer you up and help you reconnect with the joy and pleasure you long to feel again. Unfortunately, not all friends bring an upbeat, positive spirit to the relationship. Some friends seem to revel in cynicism, pessimism, and negativity.

Social support is essential for our overall well-being, whether life is going smoothly or we have just made it through a disaster.[1] As life grows more complicated and demands on our time grow more frequent, having pleasant companions along for the journey grows in importance. All of us need sympathetic listeners, supportive friends, and ardent allies. However, when friends exert their own limited energy in nagging us, annoying us, or trying to bring us down when they are miserable, the shared journey may not be as rewarding as we would prefer.

When a relationship is beginning to feel more difficult to manage than it is worth, or a friend seems to have intentionally brought unhappiness to your door, there is an important question to ask yourself: Did the social exchange or incident leave you feeling hurt or angry?[2] Research shows that when we feel hurt by the actions of a friend, we are actually more likely to consider continuing and working to enhance the friendship. When anger is the pervading emotion, this suggests that we are ready to consider ending the friendship. The following examples illustrate how friendships may present crossroads related to the joy or misery a friend might bring across the life span.

Young Girls and Almost Teens

In the earliest years, girls tend to have many different "best friends" depending on the day and sometimes the hour of the day. While this type of changeable affinity is normal, it can create hurtful situations for the young girl who is left on the sidelines when a new "best friend" is chosen. This can be as painful for a mom as it is for her daughter. However, sometimes neither mom nor daughter can do much to change the situation. While involving other parents in the social struggles of young girls may be possible, sometimes this involvement can lead to negative repercussions for a child.

Probably every mother of a daughter has learned the hard way that "two girls are company, but three girls are an emotional breakdown in the making." When two girls are together, taking turns and playing nice are easy. When three girls are present, one of them is almost always going to be left out. A mother's intervention is never as effective as you might like it to be. However, if the girls are at your home and your daughter is aligning with one girl over the other, you may be able to step in and interject some diplomacy into the situation. If the girl who has been *excluded* is your daughter, this may require a different response. Some mothers might provide a brief lesson on kindness and good citizenship at others' homes. Other mothers may suggest the girls join in a more group-oriented activity such as a Disney video, board game, or snack break to interrupt the current group dynamics in play. Sadly, parents will not always be present to intervene when a daughter's friends fail to bring happiness to her life. Despite the desire to protect one's daughter, even young girls must learn to maneuver life on their own two feet.

Teens and New Adults

Adolescents can create misery for parents, teachers, and their friends with what seems like a total unawareness of the reaction their behavior is producing. Kathleen, a high school student, shared her frustrations with another girl, Heather, with whom she had been friends since childhood. Although they both were considered "good girls" by their parents, Heather was always looking for ways to push the limits and had no reservations about nagging Kathleen to join her on a "walk on the wild side." While Kathleen had no interest in serious drinking or breaking curfews, her friend was constantly begging her to cover for her or join her. The friendship was fast losing its value for Kathleen, but loyalty born from years of friendship kept her from letting the relationship go.

When young women head off to college and leave their close friends and familiar surroundings, they may decide to reinvent themselves and to become the woman they had always imagined themselves to be. For some, the transition goes smoothly and they find acceptance and a sense of belonging among new peers. Others, though, may have a more difficult time being accepted or building new relationships. It can be difficult coping with less than ideal roommates or less than inviting potential friends. A young woman's social confidence can be shaken if she is unable to find a niche in the new environment. However, with communication technologies such as texting, Skyping, messaging, and e-mail, young women now have the ability to stay closely connected to distant friends. Research has shown that close connection with a distant but steadfast, strong support group can minimize the emotional fallout a woman may experience from a lack of quality face-to-face friendships.[3]

The Twenties and Thirties

The range of ways that friends in this stage of life can bring down or annoy one another is greatly diverse. In the preceding years, social life and academics were the predominant areas of interest for young women. Now, women are intensifying their focus on careers, long-term relationships, and community involvement. As the stakes get higher, maturity and a focus on the future encourage women to take a more responsible perspective on social relationships. Expectations that their friends will take a similar view of acceptable friendship behavior may not always be met. For instance, one of the most distressing behaviors noted by women who had dealt with toxic friends involved the betrayal of friendship through any form of attempted or successful seduction of a woman's significant other. Whether the seduction is mild flirting, revealing an attraction to a friend's romantic interest, or outright sexual betrayal, this form of disloyalty is perhaps the surest way to end a friendship. No woman who shared that a friend had let her down this way possessed any tolerance for this behavior, and a friend could do very little to reverse the damage and pain caused in this type of conflict.

Other ways in which friends may drag down a woman during this stage of life include constant complaining, whining, neediness, and demands for assistance or support. Financial issues were also frequently noted for their potential to create troublesome situations between friends. As one young woman affirmed, "If a friend asks to borrow money, make sure you consider it a gift. That way you won't be ticked off when they fail to pay you back." Speaking negatively of mutual friends or putting down your friend's choices in life may be a quick way to sink the positive mood in a relationship. While some friends may struggle with their own emotional issues and need you to be more supportive than you might be with others, when it seems that a friend is intentionally trying to distress you, it may be time to revisit the purpose and value of this friendship.

Mom-to-Mom Networks

During this stage of life, friendships tend to fall into a few different categories. These include the "other mothers" and the "child-free" friends. According to many women, there is a great divide in how these two types of friends are experienced. One mom, Elsa, shared that motherhood led to the revision of several relationships with child-free friends and that the outcomes were less than ideal. Understandably, she had become less free-spirited and less able to accept invitations for adventures on a whim as she had before starting her family. Elsa shared that there were times she would love to trade a late night *in*, filled with crying and formula feedings, for a late night *out*, filled with laughter and wine. However, this trade was not one that she felt comfortable making yet. She described one of her friends as being "noncompliant" with her new priorities, constantly cajoling, pestering, and begging Elsa to join her in a night out "just once." Elsa expressed concern that her friend's refusal to understand the changes in her life was jeopardizing their friendship, especially as the complaining and the badgering were wearing on her already-frayed nerves.

Other ways that friends can bring down women in mom-to-mom networks include mothers who spend too much time complaining about their children's teachers, other parents, or the treatment their child received from a coach, just to name a few. One mother, Laura, shared that her neighbor was convinced every other parent in the neighborhood was doing something that would damage her children's emotional health for life and, if given a chance, the neighbor would drone on for hours about this "mistreatment." Laura shared that she had perfected the art of cutting short this woman's lamentations and accusations through the use of excuses involving repairmen on their way, dishes in the oven, doctors returning phone calls, and dogs needing to go out. This was working so far, but Laura expressed her concern that the negative narratives will only get worse as the neighborhood children get older.

Midlife Connections

According to the psychoanalyst and theorist C. G. Jung, midlife is the time when women may begin to embrace and express sides of their personalities that remained dormant in prior decades.[4] One midlife woman shared that when she feels that someone is clearly affecting her emotional stability in a negative way, such as putting her down or picking fights over nothing, she has less tolerance than she did when she was younger. She now describes how she can let these friends go without the guilt that she would have felt earlier in life:

> When a friend consistently drags you down, you don't have to justify the decision to end the friendship, no one has to be right or wrong. It can simply be that you just don't get along. That helped me be free of the guilt-tripping that some friends pulled on me in the past. If it becomes a matter that you and the other person are just like oil and water, then it is time to part. No one has to be the villain. I'm almost fifty, so certain behaviors are just unacceptable to me at my age; if I were twenty, then I'd be more tolerant. But my peers and I, at our ages, are who we are and are not likely to change. So, you have to say to yourself, life is too short to be guilt-tripped into misery by the whiner, the petty arguer, the person who wants to fight over nothing and put you down.

This woman has a clear sense of how to create and enforce her boundaries, but she also acknowledged that when a person is coming from what she termed a traumatizing place, she could be much more tolerant and forgiving of poor behavior. However, she firmly believes that it is not a friend's role to try and "fight a friend's demons." This suggests that we may have significantly different expectations of friends depending on their levels of emotional well-being.

Perhaps women across the life span might benefit from an exercise shared by a woman who used turning forty as the catalyst for revitalizing her life and her relationships. Her story is as follows:

> When I turned forty, I wrote a list of all my friends' names and then reflected on them to determine whether they were giving back. Four were immediate "yes" responses, two were "no," and three were "not sure." I then phoned the "not sure" friends and invited them to catch up. Two responded, and we did spend time bringing each other up-to-date. Then I left the ball in their court as to whether they contacted me again to gauge their level of interest in maintaining the friendship. One of them did not, but one did call back. The third former friend simply dropped off the radar completely. Unfortunately, the one who did not return the call was the wife of a good male friend, but even though

sometimes relationships "make sense," a friend's mutuality might not
be what it should be for the relationship. So when I see this friend and
his wife, I am always polite and warm but do not bend over backward
to make myself be liked by his wife, as that is probably something that
is impossible in the end, and humiliating to try.

Some of us would probably rather not risk checking in with friends whom
we have "misplaced" or with whom we may have lost touch, but it does
provide an opportunity for you to take proactive steps if you feel a relationship has reached a crossroads. Willingness to make that first "check-
in" call gives evidence of your value as a friend. For those friends who
may be wondering where you stand in the relationship, a check-in and
hearing your voice on the phone may bring them satisfaction and joy.

Older Adults

By this point in life, many women have little patience for those friends
who detract from their happiness. Women may be more forthright with
one another when sharing what they think, but they also expect that their
friends will do the same with them. One older woman shared that she felt
that she had earned the right to say what was on her mind now that she
was seventy-two years old and saw nothing wrong with letting her family
or friends know where she stood on almost any issue. While her desire for
authenticity in her relationships is admirable, she said she realized that
some of her friends probably did not appreciate her honesty as much as
she felt that they should. Calling herself a cantankerous old woman, she
said that she was not concerned about her effect on others and was going
to say what needed to be said.

Another woman, Jeannie, is much gentler in her own approach to life
and complained that life was too short to let anyone make her feel bad.
Jeannie shared how important it was to reach out to others and said she
sent out boxes of birthday cards, anniversary cards, get-well cards, and
sympathy cards over the course of a year. Kindness was in her nature, and
she stated that she has learned to just ignore the friends who wanted to
gossip about church members or other neighbors in the community. She
noted that everyone her age had some physical ailment or bad news in
their lives. However, she mentioned one friend, specifically, who wanted
to spend hours on the phone dwelling on these types of things. Jeannie

did not want to hurt this woman's feelings, but she said that she always felt a little down after a conversation with this woman. For women at any stage, learning how to enforce boundaries to minimize negativity in relationships is a necessity but can also be a challenge.

FINDING THE SOLUTION THAT WORKS

The stories above illustrate just a handful of ways in which friends can tear away at our own happiness or occlude our own sunshine with their own perpetual rainclouds. We know that as a friend we must comfort our friends when they are struggling, but this role is different from spending time with a friend who is trying to drag you down with her. Friends who nag at us to change something about ourselves or who overwhelm us with their litanies of woe can wear us down and sap our energy. We choose friends who seem to be a good fit, but when they want us to change to fit their needs, it may be time to reevaluate the friendship.

Does She Try to Match You Woe for Woe?

Unfortunately, some of us may have collected one of the less-than-joy-inspiring friends along the way. These "friends" are those who seem incapable of spreading joy or bringing happiness to others. There seem to be two unique versions of this friendship rule breaker. The first is the friend who seems driven to top every tale of woe you share with an even "bigger and badder" tale of woe of her own. For example, you say that you had a lousy day at work and will be facing three unfinished projects on your desk in the morning. Your friend says she had an even lousier day at work and she may not even have a job to return to in the morning. You share that your "almost teenage" daughter didn't turn in an assignment at school and ended up in detention. Your friend reveals that her teenage daughter missed her period and may be two months pregnant. These examples represent friends who seem to work from the principle that their larger share of bad luck somehow "undoes" or "disqualifies" your own despair for consideration and commiseration. It's not even that this friend is trying to seek your sympathy for her lot in life. Instead, simply winning the "bad luck battle" is her goal.

Do You Believe the Situation Is beyond Hope?

The second type of friend is the type that seems perpetually incapable of bringing any joy to your life or her own. While the friend described above is trying to match you woe for woe, this second type generously leaves tragedy and pathos on your doorstep—with no investment on your part required. This friend can be overwhelming, as she is the one whose life would be nothing without a daily dose of injustice, misfortune, or pure bad luck. You could spend a lifetime desperately trying to help her see the sunny side of life, find the silver lining, and take the wheat and leave the chaff. However, with this relationship intervention, you would probably be just as effective in trying to spin straw into gold. Neither outcome is likely going to result. This type of friend uses your friendship as a dumping ground for all of the resentment and unhappiness in her life. Sympathy, understanding, a cup of tea or a glass of wine, and a shoulder to cry on—these you can offer, but they are seldom the balm that is sought. There is just no way you can mitigate your friend's constant misery in a meaningful manner.

If you notice that you feel worse every time you get off the phone with a friend who calls you daily to recite her list of "you won't believe it but . . ." miseries, perhaps it is time for you to find a way to miss those calls. Life can be difficult enough for all of us; there is no reason to add another problem issue to our daily tasks while all you may be trying to do is to be a good friend and let others feel good. We all need to "vent," but we also need to celebrate the good times with those about whom we care.

Do the Good Times Outweigh the Bad?

If you are low on friends, and the few friends you have make you feel low, life can be a lonely business. Sometimes friends can be companions but not good company. Other times, just having someone there beside you can be enough. Therefore, you have to weigh your options and consider your own investment in the friendship. If you are trying to beat your "bad luck battle buddy" at her own game, you have the power to shift that relationship—just stop playing! Yes, you want to share your own trials and tribulations with someone, but if your friends need to top them, you need to consider if it is worth the trade-off or back-and-forth rounds. Let her get her bid in for the top low, then you can simply acknowledge the unfairness of life, validate her experiences, and let it go. Head out for dinner, hit "play" on the remote, head for the mall, continue your work-outs, whatever. Just let it go and enjoy having company.

Are You Better Off with Her or without Her in Your Life?

For the friend who *only* brings misery and *refuses* to be soothed, you have a couple of choices in how you respond. The first choice is to be the model of a good friend. Be up front and be honest with her. Tell her that her lamentations are really bringing you down and taking the joy out of the friendship. If your words are ineffective and her complaining contin-ues, you may have to make a tough decision. If you are at the point where being alone is preferable to this friend's company, then you can disen-gage from the friendship. Be busy when she calls, be unavailable for future meet-ups, and when interaction is unavoidable, listen politely as long as circumstances dictate and then make a getaway as diplomatically as possible. You probably don't want to provide any additional material for her next rendition of the "bad life blues" with other friends. Friends tolerate an awful lot from one another, but there are some rules for which consequences must be enforced. For example, do not let a friend suck the joy out of your life just because that's how she adds satisfaction to her own.

CONCLUSION

In closing, we want to remind you that if a friend is constantly sabotaging your joy in life, you may be giving her too much power in your life. We cannot expect our friends to be the comedian, the life coach, the court jester, or the personal cheerleader we may wish we had waiting in the wings to build us up when we feel low. However, the balance of the relationship should have a positive tone and offer more dividends than demand risky investments. You have the power to choose which friends you allow to share your resources; this includes emotional resources as well.

11

CRITICISM IS NOT OKAY

RULE #9: DO NOT CRITICIZE A FRIEND IN FRONT OF OTHERS

This chapter offers a look at behaviors that unacceptably cross the line from private to public. Providing constructive feedback one-on-one can be instructive, but making a friend feel bad in front of others is outright destructive. Unfortunately, there are times when someone you have considered to be a friend might make a negative comment to you about your appearance, attire, attitude, or actions in front of others. Seldom is this behavior really considered "okay" between friends, but each situation requires individual attention as you decide the path the friendship will follow.

Akin to this rule is the corollary that friends should avoid putting you down simply to raise their own status. Whether you feel verbally attacked in public or private, it brings a relationship to a critical juncture. Criticism of others is often more likely a symptom of our own insecurity. People sometimes try to build up their own self-esteem through the tearing down of another's esteem. It is unpleasant to imagine that friends would risk their relationship in such a hurtful manner, but this does happen. As we describe in the sections below, there are several ways to respond when this happens.

Young Girls and Almost Teens

Young girls can be spontaneously and unashamedly honest communica-
tors. They do not always have the filter that tends to develop with social
maturity. Listening to their reactions and verbal responses to others re-
minds us of just how honest and authentic girls can be until they learn to
hide their true feelings to meet social expectations. Many years ago, there
was a television program called *Kids Say the Darndest Things*. The
show's host would prompt the kids with questions designed to provoke
humorous answers. In addition to being spontaneous, little girls are very
literal, and they react to the world from this unique standpoint. Thus, one
girl may hear that a friend has gone to the beauty shop. Seeing her friend
when she returns, a little girl might blurt out something like "You didn't
buy any beauty!" If an outfit a friend is wearing looks different or unlike
what is typically worn, a young girl might tell her friend that the outfit is
"ugly." Young children hold strong expectations about how others should
typically look, and any variations from the norm can be upsetting.

For the most part, the authenticity between young children provides a
wonderfully refreshing take on friendships. However, as young girls begin to mature socially, the potential grows for insults tossed out intentionally and with aim. In playgrounds everywhere, you can hear young girls
undoing friendships with the words "I don't want to play with you," or,
even more clearly, "I'm not going to be your friend anymore." Friendships can be fickle for elementary students as girls' understanding of the
social schema in their schools matures. The need to belong to the in-
crowd in late elementary school can lead friends to criticize and slam
yesterday's friends, just to fit in with today's friends.

Teens and New Adults

Teenagers' efforts toward conformity often encourage the development
of extremely tight relationships in which similarity is prized above individuality. These dynamics can create the potential for public humiliation
if a friend doesn't quite "fit in" or if power is gained by criticizing a
friend. When a group leader chooses a target to belittle, the group itself
may quickly follow suit to avoid being the next target. As Rosemary
Bleiszner[1] noted, adolescents push against parental influence,[2] which
then tightens their alignment with their friends, and the role modeling

done by their friends carries a significant weight in how young adults choose to behave themselves.[3] When friends model "ragging on someone" in front of others, it quickly can become the group norm. With television shows that highlight making a fool of oneself (such as *Jackass*), or making a fool of others (such as *Jerks with Cameras* or even *America's Funniest Home Videos*), the cultural norm seems to be outright, full-on insults and mockery of even those you consider close friends. While these shows may appeal more to males than females, the "put-down" culture is unfortunately pervasive across gender and age.

Some young women's self-esteem levels are more fragile than others, and a friend's insults or criticisms can be especially damaging for them. When a friend makes fun of you or criticizes you in front of a group, her words may be the product of her personal envy and insecurity. Her comments may be an attempt at humor, and she may not realize how hurtful her words are. When a group of young adult male friends get together, they revel in the fun of trading insults back and forth with no malice intended. Most same-age females, however, are much less likely to use insults as a way to bond with friends. Other young women have sophisticated skills in the use of sarcasm and irony as defense mechanisms and as ways to demean others. It can be hurtful when a friend criticizes us in front of others. A hasty "I'm kidding" or "just teasing" or texted "jk" tacked onto the end of a derogatory comment by a friend does not always undo the pain.

The Twenties and Thirties

As your identity shifts from emerging adult to adult, it is typical to grow more focused in your goals and gain clarity in your social networking needs. From late adolescence onward, friendships are increasingly developed with intentionality versus conformity as the relationship motivation. As one woman in her early thirties shared, "My current friends are chosen more carefully, I listen more with a balanced attitude. I'm not holding back my voice or editing so closely to not 'offend' the other person. I pursue friends who I feel let me be 'me' and don't criticize and judge. And being with them feels awesome!"

Unfortunately, some women may experience significant friendship conflicts prior to deciding to be more intentional in their friendship choices and before they can enjoy fully satisfying friendships. Being insulted in front of others, receiving harsh and unfounded criticism, and failing to assert oneself in a relationship can all be potential paths to crossroads in which the decision to continue or terminate a friendship must be made. However, many women have a difficult time directly addressing the shortcomings of friends.

One woman shared that she was frustrated by a friend who openly mocked her within their group of friends for being single for so long. She went on to share that she has had to "demote" her friend. She shared that "technically, I have not 'ended' the friendship, but it's certainly 'ended' in terms of closeness." This type of toxic behavior, such as using words to hurt other people, typically influences the way that we face a friendship crossroads juncture. Sometimes allowing relationships to naturally fade away through ignored phone messages, unanswered texts, or unanswered e-mails can be the least difficult way to let go of the friendship. However, as many women have shared, one of their biggest regrets when choosing to leave a relationship has been not taking the time or finding the courage to discuss the concern with the friend. Furthermore, those who have had the satisfaction of openly conversing about the off-the-mark behaviors generally feel much better to have cleared the air, regardless of how well or how poorly the message is received.

Mom-to-Mom Networks

Some women seem to have no sense of shame when it comes to calling out other women for faults they believe are present. Mothers can be especially sensitive to criticisms of their parenting skills when they first enter this role due to their insecurity.[4] One woman, Adrienne, shared that her feelings had been hurt more than once by a friend when they were engaged in a group discussion of how best to handle a particular child-rearing issue. Adrienne shared that she was surprised at the vehemence expressed by one member of her social group toward friends' opinions about a wide variety of topics, including working mothers versus stay-at-home mothers, child discipline, and video game ratings. Although Adrienne stated that she realized this was just the way this woman communicated, she had learned that she needed to sometimes give herself a pep talk before group get-togethers as well as remind herself, in the moment, that she appreciated this friend and simply had to let the harsh criticisms roll off her back.

Another woman shared a very different story regarding public criticism and diverse perspectives on another aspect of motherhood. A young mother, Liz, described a relationship she had with a friend that had to be ended twice. They had been friends since childhood, but during their teens, Liz shared that the friend had a tendency to go after Liz's past and potential boyfriends. However, in their mid-twenties, Liz gave her friend another chance, as she assumed they were both older and wiser. According to Liz, the friendship "plodded along for several years" before its next and final critical incident occurred. She and this woman were at a get-together with a group of friends and Liz was talking about her struggles to get pregnant. Liz was shocked at what the friend did next: "She condemned me in front of our group for considering egg sharing the next time I had IVF (in vitro fertilization) and said I was genetically unfit to have a child!" Liz shared that her friend was referring to her first child's diagnosis of immunoglobulin A deficiency, an illness that is not hereditary and that her son had outgrown. Liz continued relating the incident: "My friend then told me that if I wanted another child, I should let her have it for me! I should have known from the beginning what she was like when she confessed that upon seeing me for the first time that she hated me and that her first thought was 'she is gorgeous . . . all the guys will want her.'" Liz realized that this relationship was never going to develop into the type of friendship that she needed in her life. Public criticisms and enduring jealousy were two things for which she had no tolerance.

Midlife Connections

As a woman begins to focus more clearly on the essential ingredients for her own happiness and satisfaction in her life, friendships may come under scrutiny. The midlife period comes with an increasing awareness of the finiteness of time. Although the urgency varies among women, there is a common desire to have more control over the ways in which they invest their precious time. A woman may be making choices of significance that could be stretching her previous levels of confidence. Starting a brand-new career, choosing to leave a romantic relationship that no longer meets the needs it once did, and so on present opportunities for midlife women to be assertive in life in ways that are new.

One woman shared a story of her own efforts to make new and positive changes in her life only to be belittled by a friend:

> The breaking point for me is when friends who feel bad about themselves make me feel bad about myself by putting me down. I don't put up with that anymore. I recently had some positive changes in my life and am living in a nice new house now . . . and one of my friends who knows how much I've struggled to get to where I am was invited to my home. After leaving, she said that it felt like a "soulless place," and talked about how her own older, full-of-character house was so much nicer. What she said really cut—I had worked so hard to get where I was now.
>
> When I called her on this and said that it upset me, she said "I was just feeling insecure about having bought an older home." I don't think there's any excuse for putting another person down. I think people should deal with their own insecurities without putting this on other people. I would rather spend time alone than with people who do that to me. I have few friends, but the ones I have are quality people.

Sometimes you are in a position to recognize the reason behind a person's hurtful comments, but depending on the situation, you may still not feel it is justification enough to forgive and forget. We all have our own individual level of sensitivity that guides our responses.

Older Adults

As women get older, they tend to be a bit more forthright in their communication and may be more likely to "call it as they see it" even when a friend's feelings may be hurt. Respecting your friends, especially in group situations, never loses its importance. In fact, longitudinal research shows that hurtful social interactions actually compromise older women's physical health.[5] Negative social interactions have been shown to be associated with an increased risk for high blood pressure. Thus, when a friend shares criticisms and complaints about your behavior when others are present, in addition to hurting your feelings, it may be hurting your health. When the price for social support is compromised well-being, you may need to approach your friend about her behavior.

Women in community living settings or nursing care facilities may have few opportunities to fully "divorce" a friend or seek out new friends.

This can be especially difficult given the fact that the majority of older adult women already face the natural loss of so many members of their social support systems during this period.[6] Therefore, they may tolerate behavior from their friends that they typically would not under other circumstances. Sometimes learning to accept the shortcomings of others is the easier path when compared to attempting to change the behavior of others. There is a saying that *the older you get, the more like yourself you become.*[7] If a lifelong friend has always been one to speak her mind or put others in their places, she is highly unlikely to change her behaviors at this stage of life.

FINDING THE SOLUTION THAT WORKS

This unspoken rule of friendship is about respect and common decency. We may see mothers leveling their children with harsh reminders about manners in public, women complaining about something their partners have done in public, or daughters challenging their mothers in front of others. These are not "nice" behaviors, but people get away with a lot more leeway with family members than they typically do with friends. If you have a friend who "calls you out" or criticizes you in front of others, you may want to ask yourself the following questions before you respond or choose to exit the friendship.

What Is Your Personal Assessment of the Damage That Was Done?

Sometimes we believe things are worse than they really are. If your friend's criticism was more of a helpful critique and was not intended to truly hurt you, you need to consider her intent. Some friends may simply be more upfront in their communication styles and not recognize how their words may come across to others. Sometimes in group counseling sessions, a therapist will "take the temperature of the room." This involves checking in with each person present to find out how they are feeling in the moment. This is often done at the start of a session or after a particularly intense or significant event in the group. This style of check-in might be a good model for you to implement when you experience an unsatisfactory situation with friends. If you can't follow up immediately with the friend or group that was present when the incident occurred, you might do so at a later time. It can be uncomfortable for a lot of women to witness this type of personal exchange. Thus, a group check-in may help your friend recognize how toxic her interpersonal behaviors can be for her target and her audience.

Was the Intent to Do You Harm or Good?

When a friend is really trying to step up and provide information that can be helpful but chooses the wrong time and place to do it, her intent may alter your perception of her behavior. Sometimes the urgency of a situation might lead some friends to provide valid and important feedback but at what could be an inopportune time. Irvin Yalom, one of the gurus in the field of psychotherapy, addresses the value of immediacy and feedback in the counseling relationship.[8] To be effective, feedback must be given at the proper time, which is neither when the circumstances are too "hot" nor when the concern has grown too "cold." Sometimes being reminded about a bad habit or wardrobe malfunction in front of others may actually be as close to the "right moment" as possible. This may be true, for instance, if you are heading out the door for a job interview or first date. Other than these moments of absolute urgency, keeping your constructive feedback for a friend under wraps until a private moment with that friend is advised.

In another vein, the subtleties and niceties of social communication actually may escape some women. With no intent to do any harm, they may simply share information at an inappropriate moment. When this is the case, there may be a variety of reasons for your friend's behavior, including nature or nurture. Poor role modeling in her childhood might be a cause, or a physiological or neurological issue might be behind the behavior. Friends cannot undo these types of causes. So if that is "just the way she is," you will need to choose whether to accept her and move forward or distance yourself from group meet-ups, especially if you are particularly sensitive to criticism. Some of us have thicker skins than others and cannot perceive the harm our words may be doing, so you may want to bring up the issue with your friend to help her appreciate the power of her words.

If your friend comes from a place of negativity and has a pattern of using her words as weapons, you may be at a crossroads in the friendship where a decision has to be made. Assessing the value of her relationship overall is essential, but having a frank discussion with her about the damage she is doing is equally necessary. Before ending a relationship that you feel still has some value, make sure that ending the friendship is a step you are ready to take. When a toxic friend no longer provides any added value to your life, letting go of the relationship may be the best decision. Knowing that words are her weapon, however, you will want to be prepared for any verbal assaults that this woman may present at the friendship's demise or with other mutual friends down the road.

Are You Better Off with Her or without Her in Your Life?

As one woman stated, "If someone makes you feel bad about yourself or drains you, they are not someone you need." When you no longer want to be in her company or you are miserable with worry over what she may be allowing others to say about you, then it is likely that the friendship is too toxic to cure. As another woman revealed, "There is a telltale dread that I feel when a friendship has turned toxic, and if I avoid [acknowledging] that feeling, it grows worse over time." Trust your gut and exit relationships that leave an aftertaste of poison. Some friendships, however, are worth the occasional breach and the drama that can accompany these incidents. When you feel that a friend's presence in your life is definitely valuable, you may benefit from simply forgiving her uncharitable comments and moving forward. Friends who tolerate our own highs and lows and our good and bad behavior are often worth holding on to in spite of an occasional misstep.

CONCLUSION

Good friends provide honest, insightful, and helpful feedback to one another. They can serve as mirrors that are often more accurate than our own self-perceptions. We do need to know when our jeans really do make us look fat—but not once we are already at the club. We need to know that our son really is acting out-of-line at ball practice, but we don't need to be called out in front of the whole booster club. There is a time and place for providing the insights that only close friends can offer. Simply put, that time and place is ideally one-on-one, in private, between friends.

12

JEALOUSY IS NOT OKAY

RULE #10: DO NOT CRITICIZE OR BE JEALOUS OF A FRIEND'S OTHER RELATIONSHIPS

This friendship rule is about keeping yourself from feeling jealous of a friend's other relationships. For women, one of the most valuable resources is social capital in the form of social relationships. If we believe a relationship is threatened, we may respond at a primal level with jealousy over the friend. We don't want anyone to take what we believe is ours. However, it is not acceptable to express jealousy or to criticize a friend's relationships with other friends or family members.

When friends are the "resource," we may see their other friends or relations as rivals. We may approach the friend with poorly veiled expressions of jealousy and a fear of being cast aside in favor of other, more appealing friends. This fear can evolve into clinginess. If a friend gets too clingy, most of us respond with efforts to disengage from the relationship even more decisively. A careful balance must be found in the give-and-take of friendships, but bringing in our own baggage in the form of jealousy and criticism can be a surefire capsize moment.

In addition, good friends are careful to guard against feelings of jealousy of a friend's good fortune. As earlier noted in chapter 6, it is important that we can share the joys and high points in our lives with our friends. If your success generates unchecked jealousy in a friend, it makes it difficult to enjoy her presence in your life when things are going well.

Young Girls and Almost Teens

Friendship jealousy may start early for girls. In fact, research continues to indicate that young girls have fewer friends, on average, than young boys.[1] Due to their higher selectivity in choosing friends, little girls have a smaller pool of potential friends. Thus, there is often competition for the "best" friends, and girls expect exclusivity and loyalty from their closest friends.[2] Girls are seldom too shy to demand loyalty from their friends and also often openly criticize friends for spending time with others. Mothers also find out early that when it comes to playdates for their daughters, "two is company, but three's a crowd." With an uneven number of girls in the house, someone generally feels left out and jealousy can quickly creep in.

The unfiltered communications of young children often mature into intentionally hurtful comments by tweens, as they seek to use the threat of "unfriending" a friend if her behaviors don't meet the expectations of the group. This relational gatekeeping requires a delicate balance. Girls must weigh the risks of terminating relationships that hold value against the possibility of being unable to establish connections with new potential friends.

Teens and New Adults

Teenage girls are intensely connected to and dependent upon their friends. A great deal of insecurity swirls around during adolescence as well. With the innate drive to develop her self-identity, yet an equally strong drive to move through these years in a flock of peers, the inner tension and social pressures combine to create a perfect storm for a young woman. Friendships are valued as markers of identity in a manner that will likely never again be experienced with such passionate commitment. Therefore, it makes sense that this age group would show significant levels of jealousy in their friendships.[3] Not surprisingly, the level of jealousy a teen feels about her best friends' involvement in other relationships is affected by the level of self-worth she possesses. This correlation may be the reason most people tend to seek friends who have the same level of social acceptance that they believe they have themselves. This means that if you and a friend have similar levels of acceptance among your peers, it is probably less likely that the friendship will "break up" over other, outside friendships. If you and a friend have similar options from which to choose in the larger pool of potential friends, there is less of a threat of friendship loss to "rivals" for each other's friendship. The real threat is felt if your friend has greater popularity or social capital in the peer group. If a friend has more appealing "potential friend" options than you have, then you may be especially jealous or anxious over her relationships with others. In adolescence, the need for acceptance and the need for conformity act like accelerators in our quest to find our "tribe." For teens, friends are not just fun to hang with; they actually determine one's social identities. When so much hinges on our relational bonds, it makes sense that jealousy over other friendships and criticism of our relational rivals happens so naturally during this stage.

A great deal of drama potentially surrounds jealousy and criticism of a friend's other relationships. In fact, it can be difficult to rein in emotional displays during these years. Although drama peaks during the high school years, relational jealousy does not end at high school graduation. A college-age woman shared that she had to end a crazy-making three-way friendship due to jealousy expressed by both friends over the time she spent with the other. She related that one of her friends "offered to stop being friends with me if it would make the other woman feel better." She remembered thinking, "Aren't we all adults here?" Unfortunately, friendship needs spring from an essentially primal place deep inside that can lead us to respond with less-than-optimal behaviors from time to time.

The Twenties and Thirties

As women begin to find their groove in their professional and personal lives, some of the energy that was once devoted to intensely experienced friendships is now diffused into these other pursuits. However, jealousy isn't necessarily lying dormant. This feeling may take on a pernicious role in the relationships between some women. A woman at this stage of life shared the following anecdote that illustrates the breadth and depth to which jealousy's roots can spread:

> I once helped a friend get a job in the same school where I worked. I networked, spoke on her behalf, and talked her up. When she did come into the faculty, she ignored me and was "BFFs" with a different teacher she'd known in the past. She also became very close to the

other teacher. . . . It was all very unpleasant. During this period of time she admitted to me that she'd been jealous of me our entire lives (we were high school friends) and that she still felt that jealousy. It was all very distressing and still is, if I think about it. She got married and moved away to another state, and when she visits our hometown, where I live and where her family still lives, she does not call me. I don't miss her.

Jealousy and criticism over other significant relationships also create problems and friendship breakups. One woman noted that a friendship had ended when she heard the friend "saying something bad about [her] family that was unwarranted." It is no longer just other friends who will vie for your best bud's time during this period. Romantic partners begin to play a huge role in young women's social lives now. Most all of us have probably been on both the "canceling out" and the "canceled out" end of the "dates over friends" equation. Too many cancellations may inadvertently cancel out the friendship. Another young woman, we'll call her Josie, said that jealousy over time spent with boyfriends killed a former friendship. She shared with us that "[my friend] badgered me about spending too much time with my then boyfriend and said I should balance my life better"—meaning that Josie should spend more time with her friend. Josie reflected on the situation, agreed that her friend might be on target, and adjusted her priorities. All went well for a while, but "as soon as [my friend] got a new boyfriend, she never had time for me or any other friends, which of course hurt me deeply." This was the end of their friendship.

Mom-to-Mom Networks

Motherhood can separate some friends quite quickly if only one of them is riding along the "mommy track." Children take up a lot of time and energy. Friends who do not have kids may lack appreciation for this fact. One woman shared that as soon as she had her second child, non-mommy friends began to drop off her social calendar. She recounted, "Some friends accused me of spending too much time with my children and kept reminding me that babysitters were not the 'evil' I thought they were." Other friends had the nerve to complain to her about her children's manners and their behavior in public places. For this woman, it was an easy choice to furlough some friends—at least, she said, until her kids were a little older.

Another mother revealed her own tendency to be a little too transparent in her feelings of jealousy of some friends' lives and relationships. She confessed to being jealous of what some friends could afford for their families. This had led her to make a snarky (a.k.a. jealous) comment or two from time to time about a friend's partner's financial success. Mothers may also criticize their friends' partners for not being as helpful with their kids as they feel partners should be. Another mom, Mackenzie, admitted that she'd expressed a little too much envy of a good friend's financial wherewithal regarding her friend's live-in nanny and the purchase of the trendiest baby equipment and fashionista layette. Things became strained between the friends after that, and Mackenzie recognized that she went too far in her remarks that day and fears that the friendship may be beyond repair.

Midlife Connections

The number of friends women have in midlife has usually begun decreasing as women typically are more independent and have less need for approval or a chorus of support than they did in earlier stages. As we have described, there is also less tolerance now for poor behavior from friends. Many midlife women consider their primary romantic partners as their closest friend, so the shared primary mutual relationship precludes a good number of potential opportunities for jealousy and criticism of other friends. Yet this deepening relation can create jealousy among other friends: "My friend always seemed to make fun of my husband or find some way to criticize him. Never to his face, only when she and I were alone. So I decided that maintaining our friendship was not worth losing the God-sent relationship that I have and cherish with my husband by having her undermine it with her constant negative comments." This woman went on to say that after weighing all of the facts, ending the friendship was the only option. However, she acknowledged this was a sad decision, as their friendship had spanned many years.

Although this period of life is considered the reward for all of the hard work invested in professional and personal pursuits up to now, there are still women who envy the relationships that their friends have built that seemingly outshine their own. While some women are more prone to jealousy than others, learning to place the value of a relationship over the short-term satisfaction of expressing feelings you may later regret is an important step. This may protect the relationships that you will be grateful for as you move into the next phase of your life.

Older Adults

It has been said that people get more like themselves the older they get. Also, the older we get, the less likely we are to hold our tongues. This is true for many women who now have little concern about letting friends and family know exactly what they think, as the following anecdote illustrates.

A woman, Elaine, had recently moved from her family home into a new retirement community with her husband. The retirement community had a well-appointed clubhouse, and the community offered a range of activities from yoga and meditation classes to bridge and Bunco games there. Elaine was pleased with their move, and she immersed herself in new activities and established friendships with her new neighbors. One afternoon, Elaine had a get-together at her house for old and new friends. Assuming that everyone had enjoyed themselves, Elaine related that she had been shocked by comments from a lifelong friend who stayed late to help her straighten up after the gathering. This friend criticized Elaine's new friends, claiming they were too "hoity-toity" for the "old Elaine and their crowd." This friend then complained that Elaine had "abandoned her true friends" for these new acquaintances. Elaine recognized the jealousy as her friend's fear about the potential loss of their friendship, and Elaine was able to reassure her friend of her commitment to their relationship.

The freedom to say exactly what you think may be one of the perks of growing older. However, that does not mean that your friends will necessarily accept or even tolerate everything you say if your comments include criticism of the people about whom friends care or the relationships friends have with others. Risking the loss of relationships in the interest of expressing your negative emotions, such as jealousy and envy, is seldom a wise choice. As support networks shrink as a function of time and the pool of potential friends also dwindles, the choice may be long regretted. The following sections offer points to consider as you weigh your reaction to a friend who's gone too far or the payoff of speaking your mind for your own satisfaction.

FINDING THE SOLUTION THAT WORKS

Is there a right or a wrong way to handle friends who seem jealous of your other friendships or familial relationships? If you invite a friend to join you in criticizing one of your relationships, what happens if she goes too far? It seems like everyone enjoys a little mudslinging every now and then, but what happens when the mud you've encouraged a friend to sling clings to a person about whom you also care deeply? These are tough questions that require some reflection before action can be taken.

With Privilege Comes Responsibility

When we have good fortune in our lives, we might respond to these circumstances in a variety of ways. Some of us may not even be consciously aware of how our circumstances differ from those of others. We may be oblivious to all that we have, whether it is made up of material or intangible resources. Others might be aware of the value of our resources and feel gratitude for our good fortune. Still others may be aware, but rather than experience gratitude, they exhibit a sense of entitlement and superiority. Our perceptions of our "lot in life" shape how we respond to friends' expressions of jealousy or criticism of our relationships.

For instance, if you are moving blissfully through life unmindful of the relative success of your primary romantic relationship or how well you have raised your children, it can be quite a surprise to hear a friend make a catty remark or express envy of your relationships. Thus, one way to respond to your friend's emotional state is with a simple "Wow, I hadn't realized just how fortunate I am in my marriage/relationship/family/friendships. Thank you for bringing my attention to this aspect of my life."

If you know in your heart just how fortunate you are, let your friend know: "Yes, I am so lucky to have found such an amazing partner (or been blessed with an awesome mother or raised kids who still keep in touch with me or been able to build connections with so many wonderful people)." If you believe that your good fortune is simply what you deserve, and you value your friendship with this particular friend, you may need to reflect on the message you want your response to send. An entitlement-tinged response can be a sure way to get the friendship-termination process started. A gracious response will be the best choice for you if you hope to continue the relationship. In fact, your friend's jealousy may even be the spark that allows you to move from a sense of entitlement to a sense of gratitude for all that you have.

When You Want What Your Friends Have

Good friends recognize that in a climate of financial disparity and economic storms, there will always be material gulfs between themselves and some of their friends. Genuine and deeply valued relationships, however, should not hinge on economic homogeneity. Wanting what your friends have is not unusual. Enjoying the opportunity to share what they have can be a pleasure booster. However, resentment of their good fortune is simply *not* okay. If you enjoy your friend's company and value the relationship, keep any negative or less cordial feelings under wraps—it is what good friends do.

Many women are tempted to express jealousy or criticism of their friends' other friends or significant relationships. Many of us believe that our perspectives are better than those of our friends because we are outside observers. But do not belittle or insult the "other friends" in your friend's life. Even when she is "dissing" a friend in front of you, be discreet in your responses. Do not say things that could be potentially humiliating if, for instance, there is a likelihood that the three of you will soon end up in each other's company again.

So what can you do when your friend needs to vent about a different friend you know is not worth her time? Just take a cue from professional counselors and empathize, empathize, empathize! You can empathize by simply listening and reflecting what she is sharing. For instance, you might say something like "It must have felt awful when Deb did that!" or "I can tell you were hurt when that happened." Or "Yes, it probably did change the way you looked at everyone!" You can provide a shoulder to cry on and an ear to listen. However, you do not have to agree or intensify the criticism of the other friend to show your support.

Words That Can Come Back to Haunt You

There may also be a moment when a friend has absolutely had it with her significant other, or child or mother or some other bound-by-blood-or-law individual. While you may have already spent years wondering how your friend has tolerated this particular individual, this is still not the time to agree with anything she says. Definitely do not add your own horror stories even if she says she has finally reached a breaking point.

The ties that bind us to family connections are strong, often much stronger than many of us would like. While it is difficult to fully dissolve the relationships formed by these ties, it is easy to do damage that can remain painfully present years into the future. Do not risk sacrificing a friendship by trying to build a wall between a friend and her relations. It is better to keep your sentiments in check, because you never know when your words may come back to haunt you, especially if and when fences get mended and relationships are repaired. (Of course, there is always the caveat that if any aspect of a friend's well-being—physical, emotional, or mental—is potentially at risk, then helping that friend take action may be necessary.)

Resentment of a Friend's Good Fortune Is Never Acceptable

On the other hand, your friend's mother may be the greatest mom you know. Her husband may be an amazing handyman or chef. Or her daughter may know more about decorating than a stack of home-design books can describe. Remember, though, that these people are her people. Being jealous of her access to them—or being manipulative by trying to get them to do for you what they do for your friend—is never okay. You can enjoy their presence in her life and appreciate it when their gifts are shared with you. However, do not sacrifice a friendship by trying to insert yourself into relationships in which you do not rightfully belong. Sure, it would be awesome if your friend included you in a lunch date with her mom the next time she's in town, or if her husband and daughter offered to pitch in on your renovation plans. But it should be *their* choice to share their gifts with you. It is never cool to express jealousy or resentment and risk ruining a friendship just because your friend hit the family jackpot.

Turning the Negative Emotion into Positive Change

Jealousy has the potential to be a complex and extremely painful emotion. It can reflect our own sense of inner insecurity and insufficient self-worth. Jealousy of others' happiness and healthy relationships also can hold us back from fully engaging in relationships with people about whom we care very deeply. When we want what others have, it speaks more about what is missing in our own lives than what is present in a friend's life. Thus, if you feel a prickling of jealousy bubbling up inside of you, perhaps this can be used as a "red flag" to encourage you to do a little self-exploration. Examining that sense of deep longing or acute need that jealousy highlights may bring to light areas in which you may want to change or grow. When you explore those "tender spots" in your responses to others, you can create a blueprint for how you might like to shift your own choices, goals, and path in life.

Many of us grew up whining to our parents that some situation of their orchestration was *just not fair*. Parents' universal response is typically "No one ever said life was fair." Although these words do little to placate a child, there is little point in arguing against this simple truth. When a *pattern* of unfairness always draws your attention, it may be time for self-exploration. Reflect on the reasons that you tend to notice a particular scarcity in your life or, alternately, an abundance in your friend's life. This might reveal something about the areas of life that you feel are ripe for change. Do not sacrifice a friendship because you covet a friend's relationship, partner, mother, child, or social life or because you find fault with others in her life. Use your reactions to reshape your own life to bring you more of what you long for so deeply.

13

A RULE-BY-RULE GUIDE FOR PARENTS

It is challenging to deal with toxic friendships in your own life, but when you see your daughter's life being influenced by toxic friends, it can be even more upsetting. Whether your daughter is being affected by a rule-breaking friend or is the one breaking the rules, we provide suggestions for appropriate parental responses. The following sections provide a rule-by-rule breakdown exploring how circumstances might be for your daughter when the rules are broken.

RULE #1: TRUST AND CONFIDE IN YOUR FRIENDS AND BE TRUSTWORTHY IN RETURN (CHAPTER 3: IT'S A MATTER OF TRUST)

Keeping Secrets?

For many young girls, secrets are not always something that they can keep secret very long. Most are familiar with the experience of buying someone a surprise gift, revealing to your child what is contained in the gift-wrapped box, and then hearing your child communicate the contents of the box with the recipient well before the gift is opened or, in some case, even presented. Just as young children have trouble discerning between fiction and truth, imagination and reality, keeping confidences confidential can be equally difficult. Helping your daughter to understand the difference between "public knowledge" and "private knowledge" is a valuable mission, but it may take some time for the lesson to be learned. Encouraging a daughter to refrain from sharing private information with her friends is about all that a parent can do to keep sensitive information from making its way around the neighborhood or schoolyard.

As your daughter gets older, she will begin to realize the value of confidences, and most young girls enjoy having secrets from others. The power of holding insider information is not lost on young women who view shared confidences as a bond between friends. Unfortunately, if a friendship begins to wane, your daughter's heart-to-heart sharing with her once-close friend may be something that she comes to regret. If your daughter discloses to you that she has shared something she should not have, damage control may involve a mother-to-mother chat with the friend's mom or a mother-to-daughter's friend chat, if that is the best that can be accomplished. Letting your daughter know that you are going to follow up with the friend or her mother is important so that you and she may discuss her concerns about this step. Discussing with your daughter the potential consequences of her former friend sharing private knowledge is also important. Talking through the potential negative fallout, mentally rehearsing what you might need to say to defend yourself, and practicing self-talk can make the actual situation less difficult to handle. Imagining the worst case scenario and mentally walking yourself through it step-by-step can also soften any emotional damage that might occur. If your daughter has trouble with keeping secrets, encourage her to imagine how she would feel if her own secrets were revealed.

Asking young adolescents to avoid revealing confidential information to their friends is not likely to be effective. Friends are the ones to whom young women are most likely to turn when they have secrets that need sharing. Discuss the risks of revealing too much sensitive information with your daughter and remind her that once secrets are shared, she no longer has control over who else might learn her secrets. Also, if your daughter tells you that a friend is in danger of harm from others or herself or is in danger of harming others, take your daughter seriously. Depending on the age of your daughter's friend and the circumstances, you may offer to speak to the young woman or encourage the young woman to seek assistance from professionals, or alert authorities yourself if circumstances warrant this course of action.

Learning to Trust

For most girls, the rule that encourages them to be willing to trust and confide in their friends is not hard to follow. Often young women can be a little too trusting of their friends. Regarding this rule, mothers may be more valuable in helping their daughters learn the limit of how far they should trust their friends before a friend teaches this lesson in a way that creates discord or difficulties in your daughter's life.

Games such as "Truth or Dare" begin relatively harmlessly at sleep-overs for elementary school girls. This may be their first experience with being asked to share more about themselves than they might feel comfortable offering. As they turn into adolescents, these games can become riskier than in earlier years. The PG rating can head straight to R and slide into X with one question unanswered and one dare agreed to. Although the Internet and the movie industry have created a slippery slope of what is and is not acceptable behavior for young women, it is never too late to embrace open communication between you and your daughter.

As your daughter begins spending more time with friends out of your sight and out of your home, make sure that you are spending more time assuring her of your willingness to listen to her and support her as she grows into a young woman. One of the most dangerous relationships develops when a mother fails to give her daughter the safety and support necessary for her to open up about sensitive topics. While parents are seen as the enemy for a decade or so, be willing to offer your daughter a truce and amnesty when she has information that should be shared with a parent, not just trusted to a friend. And if you are concerned that your daughter is less than trustworthy for her friends, dialogue with her about the losses and harm she may cause if she fails to respect the boundaries of confidentiality in her friendships.

RULE #2: SHOW YOUR FRIENDS EMPATHY AND POSITIVE REGARD (CHAPTER 4: JUST THE WAY YOU ARE)

Empathy is exhibited by children at surprisingly young ages, and young girls are typically more empathetic than young boys during the early part of childhood.[1] Your daughter's ability to empathize with other children also has been found to be linked with her prosocial behaviors, and these behaviors support her friendship skills.[2] As we noted earlier in chapter 4, you actually play a role in the development and effectiveness of your daughter's empathy level. Friends who understand us or just "get us" are always a special type—less explaining to do and a greater sense of connection between friends are two of the perks. Sadly, not every friend of your daughter is going to have a parallel level of empathy.

If your daughter is particularly sensitive to the lack of this quality in others, you may need to help her find a way to empathize with those friends who are less able to empathize with others. You might remind her that empathy is a skill that develops over time and with experience and that some of her friends may be unable to see others' perspectives just yet. However, when your daughter has been let down by a friend who has wronged her but cannot understand how her actions harmed your daughter, you may have to discuss with your daughter the need to step back from her own immediate feelings and take the perspective of her less empathetic friend. As young girls mature, their levels of empathy also grow more sophisticated, so it may help your daughter to know that she is just a little ahead of the curve. In terms of an adolescent daughter who is wounded by a friend who lacks empathy, encourage her to stretch her skills of cognitive empathy and take on her friend's perspective, while acknowledging that everyone brings a different perspective and sensitivity to an issue. For highly empathetic mothers, it can be painful to see your daughter emotionally raw and wounded by the actions of a friend. Helping her to take multiple perspectives on the issue may help her tease out whether she wants to forgive the friend and maintain the relationship or admit that the gulf is too wide and begin to seek out other, more similar friends.

In terms of friends who have shown a lack of positive regard and appreciation for your daughter, or even seem to dislike your daughter, it is hard to encourage her to patch up the friendship and let an incident of casual or acute disregard go by the wayside. Friendships are based on mutual affection and pleasure in the relationship. When being with someone is hurtful or when someone whom your daughter considers a friend is intentionally mean or unkind, she may need to be encouraged to let the friendship fade or, depending on her age, engage the friend in a frank discussion about her feelings. Allowing your daughter to continue putting herself in a position of emotional vulnerability is not something any mother wants to condone. Accepting this type of behavior from others suggests that a child might be insecure, suffering from compromised self-esteem, or lacking confidence. Helping her to identify her strengths and positive qualities and helping her to find ways to grow these may place her in a much better place to make healthy, meaningful friendships with individuals who truly appreciate her presence in their lives.

RULE #3: UNDERSTAND THAT YOUR FRIEND HAS OTHER FRIENDS AND BE ACCEPTING OF THESE FRIENDS (CHAPTER 5: ANY FRIEND OF HERS IS A FRIEND OF MINE)

For mothers, it can be heart wrenching to watch the vaguely *political maneuvering* within the friendship groups of young girls. As girls mature, the cliques seem to get more solidified. While turmoil may exist within individual cliques, there is less movement of girls *between* groups. Encouraging your daughter to be open to different opportunities for friendship development may help her from being pigeonholed in a particular group. Today's kids may have a laundry list of friendships groups that grow each year and may have begun with "day-care friends," "neighborhood pals," "church school friends," "Mommy and Me gym club friends," and "soccer team friends," just to name a few. With so many settings in which to cultivate friendships, encourage your daughter to befriend a variety of others. Also encourage her to be accepting of the friends of friends to whom you have already given your approval.

Many of us probably recall having heard that "the more you love, the more love you have available to give." Finding a way to share this with your daughter in a way that she can hear may encourage her in accepting and befriending the friends of her friends. It can be painful for some young women to walk into a party and realize, "Snap! I'm the only girl from the swim team/yearbook/part-time job/theater group who's here yet." Encouraging your daughter to have a high level of self-confidence can help her handle the temporary "outsider" feeling that she might experience when meeting up with a close friend and her close friend's "other" friends. You might want to remind her of specific previous successes in building new friendships. For instance, you might share something along the lines of "Remember when you didn't know anyone when you started your third-grade class but you made a best friend there . . ." to bolster her sense of social competence. Self-confidence and the tendency to have fun in life are qualities that we all appreciate in friends; inspiring your daughter to feel good about herself, recognize her strengths, and enjoy what life has to offer—including new situations—will pay dividends for her for the rest of her life.

And if your daughter chose just one friend from her swim team to come to her school friend–heavy birthday party, remind her to make sure the lone swimmer feels every bit as welcome as the other twenty-five guests and to make sure she knows that setting up conversations and connections between guests who have not met previously is an important hostess skill. While any friend of a friend should be considered as a potential new friend for you, sometimes it helps when the mutual friend bridges the gap and creates a connection between the two of you.

RULE #4: SHOW YOUR FRIENDS EMOTIONAL SUPPORT (CHAPTER 6: BEING THERE WITH EMOTIONAL SUPPORT)

As a mother, you learn early on that there are times when emotional support and unconditional love are all that you can offer your daughter when she is suffering from something as painful as colic, earaches, or sore throats. It can be difficult to witness your daughter suffer emotional stressors related to failure in terms of academics, athletics, or professional ventures. It can be the most difficult to see your daughter wronged by friends who do not stick by her when she needs them.

Once called "fair-weather friends," friends who are no-shows when a daughter is in need of emotional support can break a child's heart, but they might engender anger in her mother. It is painful to see your daughter's good nature and trust disrespected by her friends, especially when it is most needed. While wonderful character education lessons can be taught from an incident such as this, no mother wants to have to lead this lesson. When an elementary-age daughter is wrestling with unpleasant feelings related to having been excluded from a birthday party or group outing, the best thing a parent can do is acknowledge her hurt feelings. Acknowledge that sometimes friends do not realize the consequences of what they are doing to their friends. Show her your support and love.

Sometimes, for parents, being emotionally present with compassion is all you can do for a child, just as it sometimes is with friends.

For older daughters, there seem to be a multitude of possible "failures" in life that can require emotional support and cheering up from friends. These include not getting the grade she wanted on a test, not getting called by the boy who asked for her number, not making the cheerleading squad, or not getting first chair in band. It can be especially painful when her best friend did make the team, did get the lead part, or did get the call-back for the part-time job. If the friends who reached the goal your daughter longed for are not there to tell her that they really thought she deserved it, that it wasn't that big a deal anyway, or other adolescent ways of trying to help a friend feel better while jumping for joy inside, then your daughter may be especially bereft of joy. Distraction may be necessary, in whatever meaningful manner would work for her particular situation. Acknowledging her double loss, not achieving something she attempted and then feeling ignored or hurt by friends who were not there to help her feel better, is also needed.

Regardless of your daughter's age, if you have the sense that her friends are usually really good friends and that their absence in this moment is an aberration, and not a consistent pattern, help your daughter see this as well. If, however, this is just one more example of how uncaring her friends can be, you may want to help her brainstorm potential paths for developing new friendships. One of the basic purposes of friendships is companionship in the good and the not-so-good times; when friends fail to be there at either end of the spectrum, it may be time to look for new candidates for better friendships.

RULE #5: VOLUNTEER ASSISTANCE WHEN A FRIEND IS IN NEED (CHAPTER 7: A FRIEND IN NEED)

With some children, getting them to pitch in around the house with age-appropriate housekeeping tasks can be a challenge. Setting and clearing the table are easy early chores, as are matching socks or folding towels. Ideally, parents educate their children about the value of pitching in to help the family. This can go a long way to preparing our children for helping others and giving back to the community as they grow older. It can be difficult for a mother to see her daughter's sadness when she has been denied help by a friend. Depending on a girl's age, a friend's failure to assist may involve a refusal to share her own school lunch with your daughter when your daughter has left her lunch at home, or it might include a friend's unwillingness to help your daughter finish her chores more quickly so that your daughter could accompany the friend to the movies. When your child has been hurt in this type of situation, offering her empathy and kindness is essential. Letting her know that some girls just seem to have a harder time helping friends than others might is also an option. Help her to understand that just because her friend has let her down does not give her the right to let her friend down in the future. Remind her that she can model giving back and helping others, even if friends are not ready to respond in kind.

When your adolescent daughter has been blown off by friends who had better things to do than help her out when she was in need, support and understanding are important. Making sure that your response does not add insult to injury is essential—even if you know in your own heart that your daughter's friends are unlikely to be there and lend a hand when your daughter is in need. Remind your daughter that even if practicing good friendship behaviors won't help this particular friendship, it is great practice for being the friend you would want to be in any friendship. And as you commiserate with your daughter, don't misstep by implying or declaring that your daughter makes bad choices in friends. If your daughter has trouble finding satisfactory friends, you may need to explore what is going on in her social world. If self-confidence, self-esteem, or self-worth are lacking, help plan activities that will help her build up these qualities. If she is trying to befriend the wrong type of friends, encourage her to get involved in activities in which she will interact with different types of peers: volunteering, community classes, civic groups, faith-based groups, and so on. Help her recognize the qualities that she would like in her friends and help her learn how to look for these qualities and be less willing to settle for less invested or less appropriate friends.

RULE #6: REPAY FAVORS WITHOUT BEING ASKED (CHAPTER 8: KEEP THE "FRIENDSHIP FAVORS" BALANCE IN CHECK)

When children complain that "life isn't fair," most parents reply, "No one ever said life was going to be fair." Yet, when it comes to friendships, we all generally assume that a friend will do for us what we would do for her. The rule of equity is much valued in friendships. However, when your daughter lends a hand at her best friend's lemonade stand, but her best friend whines and declines when your daughter asks her to walk around the neighborhood while she tries to sell wrapping paper for her school, this is a prime example of how this rule can be broken. If your adolescent daughter is always willing to take on extra shifts at her part-time job when coworker friends need a day off, but she cannot find a friend to take her hours when she has a last-minute need for time off, that is another example of how friends fail to repay the favors they have been done.

When a daughter is faced with the reality that friends do not always repay the favors that she has done for them, mothers may respond in a variety of ways. Some mothers might step in and remind the friend of her daughter's willingness to help her and how it would mean so much for her daughter if her friend agreed to repay the favor and jump in and help out. Other mothers might tell their daughters that this is what happens in life, and next time they should not be so eager to accommodate a friend. What needs to be determined, however, is whether your daughter is consistently doing favors for others but allowing others to take advantage of her willingness to help them.

If you see your daughter constantly on the losing end of friendship benefits, it may be helpful to gently share your perceptions with her. Do so in a way that lets her hear your words as loving concern, not critical judgment. Beginning with an empathetic statement such as "I see you were hurt by what your friend did . . ." may be a productive way to avoid any hint of criticism. Encouraging her to figure out which friends give as much as they get from her friendship is a good way to build on the positives. Keeping the focus on her strengths as a friend and her worth as a person may help her begin to see all that she has to offer and to refuse to take less than she is due from her relationships. It is important that she not be made to feel bad for her friends' poor track records. Help her change her expectations if she seems to assume that friends let friends down; as her self-worth grows, she will be in a better place to attract friends who give as well as she does to a friendship. When your daughter seems to be giving others the short end of the stick, remind her that her friends may recognize the poor bargain that they have with her and may one day decide to withdraw from the relationship. Let your daughter know what you have observed and encourage her to step back and look at her past behavior as well as consider the potential future consequences of short-changing her friends. It is hard to see our daughters hurt by others, but it can be harder still to see them let down their friends.

RULE #7: STAND UP FOR YOUR FRIENDS AND THEIR INTERESTS WHEN THEY ARE NOT PRESENT (CHAPTER 9: DEFENDING YOUR HONOR)

There are times when a young girl might end up in a group of other young girls in which an absent friend of hers is being judged, criticized, or made fun of. When the other girls in the group hold more social power or prestige than your daughter, she may be easily tempted to laugh and joke at her absent friend's expense. This can be a poignant crossroads that is difficult to maneuver for many young girls who worry that their failure to join in may make them the focus of the put-downs right then and there. Older girls and adolescents also face difficult moments when they must either claim allegiance to an absent friend and risk the scorn of the group or remain silent and ignore, or even laugh along with, the ridiculing of their friends. When a friend learns of a friend's betrayal, the friendship may be at risk of ending abruptly.

If your daughter has bowed to social pressure and refrained from defending her friend, listen to her as she shares what happened. Let her talk about the reasons why she gave in to the group. Invite her to share what she might have done differently or would do differently in the future. If you believe it might help, encourage your daughter to come clean to her friend and let her know that she realizes that she misstepped by not coming to her friend's defense.

If your daughter learns that her friends did not stick up for her in the group, provide a healthy dose of emotional support and acknowledge the feelings that she is experiencing. Let her talk about her assessment of the situation and how she feels about the friends who didn't come to her defense. She may have empathy for their situation or determine that it is time to cut them loose. Sharing your own assessment of the situation in a way that she can understand—and that highlights her strengths and self-worth—may help her stretch her own perception of the incident. She may recognize the intense social pressure that some groups exert on non–group members and be more willing to make allowances for her friends, depending on the situation and what she herself might have done.

RULE #8: DO NOT "BRING DOWN" OR INTENTIONALLY ANNOY YOUR FRIENDS (CHAPTER 10: BRING JOY TO YOUR FRIENDS)

Seeing your daughter being "ragged on" by a friend about her choices or preferences can be painful. As young girls turn into young women, they are going to be increasingly guided by peers in how they define their identities and choose their activities. When a friend seems to be constantly telling your daughter what she should do, what she should wear, how she should act, and whom she should befriend, it is distressing. Some young women seem to assume the power of leadership in their cliques and take pleasure in creating rules and expectations for belonging. The movie *Mean Girls* provides quite an illustrative example of this dynamic among adolescents. Unfortunately, group cohesion and group acceptance rest on the willingness of members to do and be what is expected of them by the group leader. When a young woman feels that interactions with her friends are bringing her down, it may be time to reevaluate the pleasures and benefits gained through the relationship.

As a parent, you can encourage your daughter to recognize her unique strengths as an individual and to take pride in who she is and what she does. If a friend is nagging her to ditch the volunteer duty at the local food pantry to hang out with her on Thursday nights, remind your daughter of the difference she is making to so many people through her commitment to caring. If another friend is encouraging your daughter to blow off the study session for the ACT because she needs her to give her a ride to the mall, remind your daughter that her commitment to her future is more important at the moment than being a taxi service for her friends.

Helping our daughters recognize and enact healthy boundaries with friends can be a challenge, but it is a labor of love that can enhance your daughter's self-love and self-respect. Encouraging her to pursue her goals, her interests, and her dreams—regardless of friends who may want to distract or derail her—is also a valuable path for a parent to follow. However, it is important for both you and your daughter to bear in mind that even high-quality friends might ask her to do things that unintentionally derail her. This is part of the lifelong learning process in developing skills in setting healthy boundaries. While parents have some ability to control the friends with whom their daughters associate, it is much more effective when you help your daughter make her own well-planned and well-thought-out decisions. She must determine which friends bring happiness and value to her life and which friends weigh her down with their own unhappiness or efforts to control her decisions. Again, help her to understand that even good friends may present challenging opportunities in which she must set her personal boundaries.

And if your daughter is seeking to share her angst and dissatisfaction with friends, let her know that she is really limiting the type of friends she will attract. Encourage her to explore what she is seeking in her friendships and where she may be able to find those experiences without holding back or dragging down another. Also, ensure that you are not the role model that she is using to guide her relationship behaviors. Sometimes parents model distance, nagging, lamenting, complaining, and criticizing as acceptable relational behaviors. Make sure to provide a more altruistic and productive friendship and relationship model that inspires your daughter to practice healthy friendship behaviors. Children learn what they live, and when negative interactions are what they see modeled, they may not realize the difference that a positive outlook and exchange can make.

RULE #9: DO NOT CRITICIZE A FRIEND IN FRONT OF OTHERS (CHAPTER 11: CRITICISM IS NOT OKAY)

Just as there is a rule about sticking up for friends when others are putting them down, we also do not want our daughters to be criticized by their friends when others are around, or in private. We definitely don't want our daughters to insult or poke too much fun at their friends in front of others. For some young women, social pressure leads them to make comments or exhibit behaviors that they would never do on their own. When some young women have an audience, they may also be led to cross the line between "gentle teasing" and "blatant digs" at a friend.

As women mature, they develop a stronger sense of identity that comes from deep within; adolescents define their identities from the outside in. Earning acceptance by their desired social group is essential to their self-identities, so metaphorically stepping on the toes of a friend to cement their own place in the social pecking order is not as unexpected as it would be for adults. We all have heard that insecurity is what drives many bullies to pick on others, and it is also why many young women may be willing to put down a friend in front of a group. Through naming another as "less than" others, especially herself, she is attempting to anchor her own social status.

Informal feedback from a friend can be helpful if it is seen as constructive criticism and is delivered privately between the friends. Criticizing friends in public is not acceptable. If your daughter has been a victim of another girl's critical remarks, let her know that her friend's criticisms say more about the friend than they do your daughter. Remind your daughter that not everyone matures at the same rate and that some young women may be slow to recognize the childishness of their behaviors. Encourage your daughter to communicate her feelings about the incident to the friend who created the problem. Encourage your daughter to evaluate the friendship and determine the value of continuing the relationship as opposed to letting it go. If you learn that your daughter has been putting down friends and leveling criticism at them, you may need to initiate a dialogue with her to determine what is motivating her to engage in these negative behaviors. You may choose to encourage her to imagine how it would be if she had been the target of a friend's public criticism. Open a dialogue with her about what she feels should be "okay" behaviors between friends. She may need to be educated on the potential power of her words and how friends might be especially sensitive to criticism in group settings.

RULE #10: DO NOT CRITICIZE OR BE JEALOUS OF A FRIEND'S OTHER RELATIONSHIPS (CHAPTER 12: JEALOUSY IS NOT OKAY)

Little girls and not-so-little girls are often too liberal with their opinions about others. Sometimes young girls are just having fun in a blow-for-blow insult battle that gets sillier and louder with each name-calling slam. They can trade highly creative slurs that may go from absurd to unintentionally profane in a number of rounds. Mothers may need to break into the game and call a halt while reminding the girls that it is unkind and hurtful to call each other names. If they are on a roll, encourage them to play a different game—trade the insults for compliments. It can be just as entertaining to tell your friend, "You are sweeter than the best, most chocolatey-ist cookie ever baked!" and be told back, "You are prettier than the prettiest pretty flower in the world!" It's never too early to start young girls on the right path toward using words as instruments of kindness, not as weapons.

When you overhear much more intentional slams between your daughter and a friend, it is imperative that you step in and let them know that it is not acceptable to say unkind things about a friend. If your daughter lets you know that a friend has been saying things that have hurt her feelings or if she seems "different" after being with a friend, check in closely with her. Assess whether something is going on in the relationship that needs an adult's perspective or, perhaps, intervention.

Sometimes jealousy can be handled in a way in which everyone comes out a winner, as evidenced in the experience shared by Sarah, a mother of one daughter and three sons. Sarah shared a story about one of her daughter's friends who felt jealous of the large, close, and engaged family that Sarah and her partner had created with their kids. Sarah's daughter, Gigi, confided that this friend, Brittani, often commented on how lucky Gigi was to have parents who enforced family mealtimes, took them to the children's museum, and made time for Gigi and her brothers. Brittani's parents clearly adored her, but they had divorced before Brittani was out of diapers. They also both led high-profile professional lives that left Brittani often feeling in the way. Sarah recognized that flavor of jealousy pretty quickly, as she had often felt that way as a child herself about her friends' larger families, so she invited Brittani to accompany them on day trips that summer and allowed Gigi to have Brittani sleep over on a fairly regular basis. Although Sarah didn't know either of Brittani's parents well enough to discuss the girl's jealousy with them, she did make a point of letting them know how much Gigi and the whole family enjoyed having Brittani spend time with Gigi.

Friends may be jealous of one another for many different reasons. It is best if parents get the complete story before rushing in and trying to resolve the situation without fully understanding the core concern. However, if your daughter is showing signs of being hurt by the comments of others or has become less actively engaged with friends or is complaining about how others treat her, please do not hesitate to find out more. Young girls begin to show aggressive behaviors much earlier today than even a decade ago,[3] so if you suspect that your daughter is at risk of emotional or physical harm from peers, investigate and step in as needed. If your daughter is saying hurtful things to others, discuss her behaviors in a calm and open manner. Remind her that words have the power to hurt others and to imagine what it would be like if her friend used words as weapons with her.

Part III

Toxic Environments Outside the Home

14

SOCCER MOMS AND CARPOOL DIVAS

Parents spend an enormous amount of time ferrying kids from place to place during the first eighteen years of their children's lives. Whether you load up the kids into the SUV at exactly 7:45 every weekday morning for school or before daybreak on Tuesday and Thursday mornings for ice hockey practice, you likely pick up another child or two along the way as part of a carpool arrangement. And when it is not your day to drive, you may sometimes find yourself anxiously looking out the kitchen window wondering where your children's ride might be, especially if you are running late for something yourself. While most mothers appreciate the village's assistance in the raising of their children, you might wish all "villagers" ran on the same schedule and held the same values you do. A shared interest in keeping children on the fast track to school and assorted extracurricular activities is not always enough.

PRESSURE COOKER OR STEAM VALVE?

An ongoing, polarizing debate surrounds the value of children's involvement in extracurricular activities. In books like *The Overscheduled Child*,[1] parents are warned against filling every waking moment of their children's lives with structured enrichment activities. Not only do children have little free time to create their own entertainment, to experience the unrest of boredom, or to discover which activities they actually enjoy, but researchers have linked highly structured, busy schedules with depression, anxiety, and substance abuse among adolescents.[2] It turns out, though, that *parental pressure* on children to be super achievers in those mandatory leisure time obligations creates the pressure cooker effect, not simply involvement in the activity itself.

WHO'S ON THE ROSTER?

Evidence indicates that when kids are involved in a variety of extracurricular activities, they will become well rounded and better adjusted.[3] They are exposed to new situations and new behavioral expectations. They learn the value of community engagement. They also develop an appreciation for teamwork and being part of something larger than themselves. It is good to know that these activities have intrinsic benefits beyond parental satisfaction derived from getting the kids out of the basement or bedroom, as a huge number of kids are involved in structured programming for athletics, performing arts, academics, activity clubs, and service opportunities like scouts or junior docents at museums. In fact, regarding athletics alone, over 50 percent of high school seniors are engaged in school athletics[4] and over three million kids aged four to nineteen are registered members of the United States Youth Soccer Association.[5] One report indicated that almost a quarter of a family's time together was spent in children's sports-related activities.[6]

Whether a creative, athletic, academic, or socially responsible pursuit interests you—or more importantly, your child—a sign-up sheet is probably somewhere just waiting for your names. From the earliest "BYOB (Bring Your Own Baby) swim class" to local and regional high school "all-star" teams, children need taxi service to and from the pool, gym, field, school, community center, banquet hall, museum, and innumerable stopping points in between. In addition to the "captive time" with your own child, you will likely be spending a significant number of those hours in the company of her teammates, cast mates, fellow scouts, and so on. Add in even more time for coordinating, collaborating, commiserating, communicating, and contending with their mothers.

SOCCER MOMS A.K.A. HOCKEY MOMS A.K.A. DANCE MOMS

Would you believe that there are numerous research studies on the "soccer mom" phenomenon?[7] The moniker was originally coined to describe, as a group, mothers who had the twin luxuries of time and economic resources to extensively invest in their children's active pursuits. Many women reject being labeled soccer moms for a variety of individual reasons. However, one prevalent reason is that the term typically implies a single-minded, competitively flavored dedication to winning[8] . . . within a world in which we prefer to believe that in the case of children, at least, it's not whether they win or lose, but how they play the game. But the real world of parents as spectators does not always reflect such high-minded and principled beliefs and behaviors. Following are descriptions of a few types of parents who are least likely to earn the "Good Sportsmanship" or "Most Congenial" award at the end-of-year banquet. These types may show up in the gym, at the dance studio, on the court, on the field, or anywhere children gather in competitive situations.

The Sidelined Coach

This parent believes she has better knowledge of each team member's skills than the coach—as well as confidence that she'd do a much better job if she could call the shots. She has the roster memorized, can tick off the stats for each player, and has a game plan for how to sew up this year's championship. During the games, she is always one step ahead of the coach, trying to suggest plays, call time-outs, and suggest substitutions. Before the game, she tries to "brief the coach" on her strategies for winning. After the game, she barges into the team huddle. She also likes to connect with each player individually after the game to offer feedback and a pat on the back. Her knowledge of the game and of the players may impress you if you are just glad that you finally understand the difference between offense and defense or turkeys and spares. Her interest in the team's success is a shared interest, for sure. When children are given conflicting advice, however, it can be confusing for them in a game they may just now be mastering.

Team coaches can often encourage parents to step back and let them do their job, although there are, sadly, increasing reports of physical altercations between parents and coaches or referees.[9] If your team's sidelined coach is really just a distraction and not a potential disaster, you can laugh about her sideline coaching when you are at home, keep your child focused on the coach's directions at the game, and gently distract her with questions about the game or the players if she's getting in between the coach and the kids. If you decide to address the issue yourself, you may want to use the "Oreo Cookie" feedback model: Compliment + Critique + Compliment. First, provide a positive comment about something your friend does well, then add the constructive feedback, and then end with another upbeat message about your friend. This may not work and she may not change, so then you may have to decide if your child is better off on this team or on another after the season runs its course.

The Megaphone Mom

Similar to the sidelined coach, this mother is deeply invested in the outcome of the game, and her enthusiasm is often heard far across the field or high in the stands. She is likely jumping up and down at the edge of the playing field, shouting encouragement to the team members on the field. When the enthusiasm is upbeat, positive, and contagious, megaphone moms get everyone feeling good. But, depending on the ages of the players, it can be particularly problematic when parents are calling out insults or expressing frustration with the children on "their team" or cheering too boisterously when the opponents make mistakes. Parents may feel uncomfortable if the "trash talking" goes too far, and young players may be distracted by the feedback. If this is your friend, you can try to speak with her about how painful it might be for the kids whose mistakes are called out in public. Encouraging empathy for the kids who are still young and still learning the game is the best avenue for change. Calling out the parent in public is just following her poor example.

The Offensive Defender

This is the parent who "flips out" when her child is called for a penalty, a rule violation, or misbehavior off the field. Offensive defenders refuse to believe their children could do anything wrong and are quick to challenge anyone who says otherwise—including referees, coaches, and other parents who may try to help clarify the situation. Depending on the sport and the age of the players, it can be wise to sit back and steer clear when this parent goes on the attack. Just like parents who confront teachers when their children are disciplined at school, the offensive defenders may confront anyone who tries to prove their child is in the wrong on the field.

If you are friends with this soccer mom variation (and they are unfortunately growing in their prevalence), you may already have witnessed her disbelief that her child is in the wrong on the field or in the classroom. In fact, one study showed that public school teachers say one of their biggest problems in the schools is pushy parents who force the administration to back down when children's behavior is censured.[10] While creating an uncomfortable situation on the field, these parents are also training their children to become offensive defenders. The aforementioned study indicated that more than three-quarters of the teachers surveyed had experienced a misbehaving student arguing with them about student rights and threatening that parents would sue if the student was punished. Similar altercations occur between parents and other authority figures as well. Whether it's a child who is not given first chair in the school orchestra, does not get a speaking part in the class play, must sit out the first half of a game, or is in a similar situation, some parents overpersonalize the decision and place the blame on the decision maker.

For some parents who grew up in a culture that promised "everyone's a winner," being told their children are *not* always winners can create internal dissonance. Additionally, many parents live vicariously through their children and overidentify with their children's successes and failures. When competition and winning take priority over fun for parents, hostility can result between the adults and confusion results for the players.[11] Depending on team dynamics, parents may be able to remind the offensive defenders that youth sports are about recreation, not altercation, and that modeling good sportsmanship is the best way to instill positive behavior in the kids. If the drama isn't manageable, finding a new team or a new league for your child may be necessary. Physical safety is the real priority, and if you feel that it is at stake, leaving the arena is a wise decision.

CARPOOL DIVAS

Shifting gears, the focus now is on those friends who *literally* help us get our kids from point A to point B, but with a bit more attitude than we might like. These are the *carpool divas*, or the other parents who share the responsibility of seeing that your child arrives at key points on time and, most importantly, safely. Some mothers find themselves engaged in carpools for their children well before the first birthday and swapping out car seats on the fly. Other mothers, though, may be hesitant to allow even their teenagers to hitch rides with their friends' parents. Whatever a mother feels is right probably is right for *her* child. Based on some of the types of carpool divas described by respondents, many mothers might wish that they had decided against shared ride systems for their kids as well.

A while back, two sociologists, Adler and Adler, explored the world of children's carpooling from the children's perspective.[12] Their research indicated three basic types of drivers: moderators, who engaged the passengers in conversation and led group discussions; interventionists, who limited interaction to overseeing potential passenger discord and squabbling; and laissez-faire drivers, who left it up to the passengers to work out any problems on their own. Beyond driver-passenger interactional styles, described below are three other categories applicable to some carpool drivers.

Tempus Fugit—Backward and Forward!

This particular driver can drive you crazy with her lack of attention to the time; she may be either consistently late or persistently early. It can be a challenge to teach children about the value of punctuality and being ready to roll on time when other carpoolers are much more laissez-faire about the time. And when the late arriver makes you late for your own appointment or to work, it can be a potential powder keg. Alternately, when the carpooler is hanging out in the driveway, racing the motor, and laying on the horn as you try to find your daughter's second blue sock and get the cat off her science project, it can be just as irritating. The necessity of punctual pickups should be communicated as soon as a carpool arrangement is made. Reminders that increase in intensity over time from gentle to urgent may need to be a part of the strategy if a friend is lax and you want to keep her in the group. Reminding drivers that both the children and their parents rely on timely pickups may be useful in some groups.

My Car Is My Temple

If you have children or have a reason to carry them about in your vehicle occasionally, you know that kids don't travel lightly. Babies and toddlers have diaper bags stuffed with toys, snacks, bottles, books, and backup clothing in addition to the expected diapers and wipes. Young children tend to have grubby hands, "blankies," favorite toys, picture books, and an imaginary companion or two. Team members have soccer cleats, soccer sandals, shoulder pads, helmets, basketballs, hockey sticks, tennis rackets, lacrosse sticks, and the possibility of bloody cuts and left-behind Band-Aids. Hauling kids is a messy business! Yet some carpool drivers pull up into the driveway in freshly washed, waxed, and vacuumed kid-transporters. One woman shared the fury she felt when her child was berated by a driver for "sweating on her leather seats, for crying out loud!" And towels alone under wet bathing suit bottoms are never enough to keep some of the swim team carpool drivers satisfied.

When your friends give you grief because your kids are just kids, it can put you in a quandary as to how to respond when you need that mom in the carpool rotation. Let your children know that just like some families have different rules and expectations about behavior in their homes, the same applies to their vehicles. While you may not be able to keep your child from sweating or getting a gash in her knee, encourage her to alert the driver to any potential critical incidents that might require special care.

Detour Delight

Do you know the shortest route from your house to the next closest carpool rider? Do you know the shortest route between the last house and the destination? This may seem basic to most of the carpool drivers, but one driver typically can find a million reasons to make quick stops when she's en route to her final destination with the car loaded with kids. When you are waiting for your son's arrival so that you can get him to the orthodontist or get the family to their next event, checking "Find My Friends" only to find out that he is wandering through the mall with the rest of the carpool crew can be maddening. The detour delight driver drives other parents crazy by running errands or making side trips with their children in tow. For the parents of younger children, the fear of the driver running into a business and leaving the riders alone for just a second can be overwhelming. For parents of older kids, the thought of them wandering through parking lots or trailing after the driver on her errands can generate fear and anger, too. Emergency stops when a real emergency exists (carsickness?) can be understood, but expectations about "nonstop, express commutes" should be voiced and upheld by the group.

Tips for a Smooth Ride

Most parents recognize that carpools are both a necessary evil and a potential lifesaver when the kids have to be somewhere at some time that they just cannot make happen. Some carpool families have taken steps to ensure a smoother ride for everyone by having clear expectations and limitations in place from the outset of the year. Other parents think that "carpool protocols" are unnecessarily dictatorial. However, if you have ever had your daughter call you at work for a ride to school because she was two minutes late getting out the door for the carpool or if a parent has let an obviously sick child climb into your car, get into the middle seat, and buckle in tight, leaving you to race to the nearest gas station restroom, carpool protocols might be viewed in a very positive light. Creating ground rules early on and taking the kids (and parents) involved on a metaphorical "test run" in the backyard with a family barbecue will allow everyone to get to know each other beyond the classroom rosters and neighborhood streets. Seeing everyone interacting in the wide, open spaces of a backyard or park can also help you determine exactly the types of ground rules that need to be hammered out before the carpool rotation begins.

Sharing the Ride with Coworkers

What happens when adults enter a carpooling relationship? Trying to regulate the rider rules for children presents one set of challenges, but carpool rules for adults present another. Negotiating points can range from snack stops, errand running, and cell phone usage to smoking, just to name a few.

One of our interviewees shared a story about her own efforts at reaching "carpool diplomacy" with two neighbors with whom she began sharing rides. These three women were eager to cut their expenses by sharing rides to the multibusiness complex where they all worked. They were looking forward to reduced gas costs as well as time to relax and unwind on the ride two out of every three weeks.

After the initial discussion began, one of the new carpool members was adamant that she would participate only if they could make a stop at Starbucks—each and every morning. In the interest of the greater group, the demand was met and the coffee run became a part of the carpool culture. Another member of the group was chronically and reliably late. Group members tolerated this for the good of the group. The third member of the group made no demands, was willing to go the extra mile to get along with everyone, actively negotiated points of potential tension, and was about to leave the area for a new position. When the carpool tried to find a replacement rider, they ended up with a smoker, and that was where the line was drawn in the sand—and the ashtray. The original members of the group both pulled out, and the carpool disbanded once and for all.

CONCLUSION

While raising children is a lot easier with assistance from the village, it can also require unexpected patience with those friends who view the process a little differently than you do. Learning how to handle the "other" parents in your child's life can be a challenge, but remember that you are setting the example that your kids will follow. At the end of the game or in the home stretch, playing to win does have its place, but good sportsmanship always comes in first.

15

CHURCH AND CIVIC GROUP FRIENDS

Participation in churches, synagogues, temples, or chapels, as places to gather and for fellowship with others, can play a significant role in people's overall well-being.[1] While studies suggest that churchgoers are healthier and happier than those who don't attend church, the key difference is regular social involvement. If you choose not to attend faith-based services, it's important to your overall well-being to get involved in some form of regular social engagement over the long haul. Unfortunately, every social institution, even faith based or altruistically focused, seems to have its share of in-groups and out-groups, leaders and followers.

KEY PLAYERS

One of our respondents, Lee, now in her mid-forties, recalled an earlier transformation of her own perspectives on the inner workings of churches and other, similar organizations. When she first moved out on her own, she quickly found a church home. She affirmed, "I was raised that you just go to church, there wasn't a question." As her involvement increased, she was asked to take on greater responsibility within the organization. Lee soon found herself serving on the church council, and that was when her understanding of the functioning of the church changed dramatically. She recounted her surprise: "I never realized church was a business. I thought Bible study was important and we could never learn enough to stop going. I didn't realize the church is also in the business of keeping the doors open, the coffee machine full, and calculating how to increase the membership rolls as a means to financial success." As she spent more time working with a larger number of other members, she realized that people brought tremendously variable levels of commitment to the church. She also discovered that a number of strong personalities among the membership were like caricatures of "real people." It was a very challenging lesson in organizational effectiveness as she observed the political and personal maneuvering of a somewhat disappointing cast of supporters trying to work together for the common good.

As adults, we must learn how to navigate the social waters of churches, clubs, civic organizations, and even the PTA. It might feel like we are once again amid a cast of characters who leaped right out of the local high school social scene into adulthood. Following are descriptions of a few roles that people might play in civic organizations.

The Do-Gooder

It feels great to do a good turn for someone—helping others helps us feel better about ourselves and our fellow humans, whether it is doing a favor or donating money.[2] However, some friends can't seem to get enough of helping others and seek out causes and charity projects with fervor and devotion. While the work done has unquestionable value, some do-gooders also have a way of making some of us feel bad. In fact, research has shown that when we are in the midst of exceptionally generous people, within situations where exceptional generosity isn't the norm or exactly necessary, we have a tendency to view them as "rule breakers" and likely harbor a desire to expel them from the group.[3] Tacit agreements overlay most of the social exchanges in which we participate, and when people do too little or do too much, we feel that they are breaking the unspoken rules that govern a situation. We may also fear that their exceptionally benevolent behavior may raise the bar for all of us who long to belong to the group.

Some do-gooders can leave us feeling like the Grinch, with our hearts two sizes too small. How do you handle it when the paragon of virtue leaves you feeling uncomfortably selfish? If she is giving because she is just that good-hearted, share your admiration of her service and acknowledge that she is making a difference for many. She might not need the pats on the back, but it might leave you feeling good to provide them. If she is giving to impress, it may be tiresome to hear of her many good deeds. The easiest response might be to simply commend her virtue and get on with the tasks at hand.

The Hypocrite

In some settings this friend might be referred to as the "Saturday Sinner/ Sunday Repenter." She is the friend who sees two sides to every rule. Side one includes the rule-driven expectations of members' behaviors; side two is how far she feels justified in bending the rule to excuse her own behavior. These women may be the friends who can offer you a smile, a quick embrace, and a blessing on Sunday morning even when they have spent the prior evening tearing down your reputation with another group of friends.

One woman, Vinnie, shared a story about a group of church friends that she felt were cruelly hypocritical at a time when she most needed support. Vinnie and her husband had been having difficulties within the marriage. Their arguments were growing increasingly frequent and intense, and Vinnie was fearful that violence might erupt. She turned to her church leader and her women's circle for counsel. Unfortunately, both provided the same suggestion for ending the conflict: Vinnie should submit to her husband's wishes and do whatever he asked, since the husband is the ultimate ruler of the family. This directive left her furious for many reasons, but one of the most offensive was the hypocritical stance taken by her friends. Vinnie's honesty about her situation led them to pretend that not a one of them had ever had any type of marital discord or conflict. They blamed Vinnie for creating the problems in her marriage, and the group left her feeling somewhat ostracized after voicing her request for input and assistance. Friends and fellow group members who preach tolerance and love, but are motivated by hypocrisy and exclusion, are better left off the friends list. Authentic friends do not marginalize others and they intentionally avoid behaviors that compromise a friend's self-worth or self-esteem.

The Social Director

This enthusiastic organization member is always encouraging social get-togethers beyond the auspices of the group. Whether it's trying to drum up karaoke singers, trivia teams, or bowling buddies, she is always encouraging group participation as she tries to get people to be more "sociable" or "closer." When you enjoy the company of the social director, she can be a great person to know. She keeps things moving and keeps life interesting. However, if you favor a quieter and more reflective life, the persistent entreaties to "come join us, just this once!" can be tiresome.

For women who would prefer to direct their own social activities without outside assistance, this person can be an obstacle instead of a blessing. One woman, Chris, shared that she had a social director in her life who suggested weekly dinners for the church school class group in addition to the regular Sunday class meetings. The couples had great chemistry, but schedules were too tight to add a weeknight dinner gathering to most families' schedules. Chris encouraged the social director to suggest monthly, not weekly, extracurricular get-togethers, which worked for many but not for all. Although some organizers try to make nonparticipants feel guilty about their absences, keeping your own boundaries clear is essential to a long-term, amicable relationship.

The Volunteer Coordinator

For this member, a good cause is always just waiting for the organization to assist. The volunteer coordinator likely has a list of roles that people can play and a roster of potential volunteers that she is happy to solicit for assistance. The good works this member can organize are definitely substantial and worthy of support, but the energy required from the other members to meet the needs may be lacking.

For some of us, the easiest way to respond to her requests for assistance is simply to agree and sign up for duty. The satisfaction that many feel through service to others is reward in itself, and the intrinsic benefits of service continue to increase as we grow older.[4] For others, offering to provide financial assistance is infinitely easier than trying to eke out time or labor for the cause. When a volunteer coordinator reaches your name on the list, offer to do what works best for you, whether you decide to help cover the bake sale for an hour or two, bake the cookies to be sold at the bake sale, buy a dozen cookies while running by the bake sale, or ask for a pass until next time. Only you know your own skills, availability, and boundaries, so you may need to speak up for yourself and protect your resources. Every organization needs someone willing to put a plan in place, but everyone needs to feel comfortable deciding when and where their places should be.

The Clique Maker

Many large organizations seem to spawn multiple subgroups through which some members create their own microcosms of power or control. The clique maker is the leader who drives the formation and composition of the group and creates a sense of "in-group/out-group" politics within the larger organization. Depending on a group's structure, these clique makers may function independently within the overall group or develop committee-based cliques. These might include the budget committee, leader search committee, youth education committee, and so on.

For some in-group members, the mission of the committee may be in close alignment with their own interests and strengths. For instance, placing an accountant on the finance committee is a logical choice. Other groups may have leaders who choose members in a less equitable manner that involves favoritism or organizational politics. Unfortunately, when an out-group member expresses interest in joining a subgroup, it can be frustrating when her efforts to join are met with resistance. If the goal is one for which you care passionately, perseverance may be worth the effort. If you are a member of the in-group and feel uncomfortable due to the attitude or behaviors of other subgroup members, you may want to get involved in other groups or focus on friendships within the larger organization. In addition, if you know of others trying to gain entry into your committee/group, offer support and help them break through the invisible, but effective, barriers.

The Martyr

Only the martyr herself usually does not realize the discomfort her self-sacrificing behaviors can cause in a relationship. Unfortunately, martyrs see themselves only as "humble servants." They would not hesitate to offer to bear a burden in the service of others. If you need someone to sew up eight costumes overnight for a holiday cantata, she will volunteer. If you need someone to clean up after the annual bazaar, her name is first on the list. Someone needs to come in early to make sure the heat is on an hour before the special Saturday brunch? She will be unlocking the door at dawn.

While the world is often a better place due to the service of selfless others, some people extract compensation in the form of public acknowledgment, accolades, and metaphorical or literal pats on the back. Expressing genuine appreciation for their work isn't really difficult, but their persistent earnestness and air of sacrifice *for others* can bog down otherwise-healthy relationships. Friendship with a martyr can be difficult and is somewhat akin to relationships with do-gooders. Do-gooders encourage us to join in their altruistic service and leave us feeling guilty if we don't. Martyrs, however, are happy to shoulder their burdens solo but often leave us feeling guilty for not doing the things that they vehemently affirm they do not want us to do.

Martyrs show up in every sphere of daily life—work, family, friendships, and primary romantic relationships. They can potentially drain your emotional well-being if you allow yourself to feel guilty about what they accomplish that you therefore do not have to do yourself. Reminding yourself that you are doing what is expected and giving your fair share can help you to maintain a healthy attitude toward yourself and others. In churches, clubs, and social organizations, martyrs may be especially likely to find appreciation from others due to the number of collective tasks that a group might have on its plate. Weighing the good that martyrs accomplish against having to do everything by yourself can quickly change the lens through which you view them.

CONCLUSION

Bear in mind that the overarching topic of this book is friendships that present difficulties and show the *least best* side of humans in their relationship with others. Churches, synagogues, clubs, and other institutions are brimming with hardworking, warm, and altruistic members, but the focus of this chapter has been those types of members who tend to get under the skin of other members. Social connection is essential to well-being—especially as people mature—so it can be valuable in many ways to learn to *work around* or *work with* those other members with whom you clash.

Perhaps there is some consolation in knowing that many of the types of individuals that get under your skin are getting under the skin of others around the globe. Just as psychological archetypes have been described as universal and present in the collective unconscious, our "church friend" types are also universal. It might be said that these types find their way into our own lives to help us learn a lesson or two. C. G. Jung described us as having both a *persona* self, the side of our identity that we show to others, and a *shadow* self, the side we like to keep hidden.[5] Often the personality type that drives us mad actually reflects a piece of our own shadow self that we would prefer not to acknowledge. As one young woman shared as we discussed "church friend" types, "I think those types are the kind of people we dislike because they are too much like a part of ourselves we don't like . . . or a type that we may actually secretly want to be." Reflecting on the types that create the greatest emotional response on your part may actually offer you the opportunity to gain deeper self-knowledge and self-awareness that you may not have otherwise discovered.

In closing, no matter what our comembers' shortcomings might be in any of the organizations and institutions to which we belong, the majority of us are there to belong, to serve, and to be a part of something bigger than ourselves, which provides a sense of purpose and meaning in our lives. Learning how to accept your fellow members for whatever they contribute to the greater good can be challenging, but this commitment to the group provides enhanced well-being from early childhood throughout the rest of our lives.

16

DOWN THE STREET AND ON THE JOB: GETTING ALONG WITH NEIGHBORS AND COWORKERS

People often describe their friends as a "family of choice." We are free to choose whom we want to befriend. Neighbors and coworkers, however, are more like our families of origin. We may have little influence over who is in the apartment or the cubicle next door. When a neighborhood feud develops, however, moving out is not always feasible. In terms of the workplace, the scarcity of alternative career opportunities may require that you find a way to peacefully get along with even the most aggravating of coworkers. In this chapter, we explore these two environments, the neighborhood and workplace, and offer suggestions for shifting perspectives and relational dynamics when conflicts appear.

LOVE THY NEIGHBOR?

No matter where you grew up, you were likely reminded to "love thy neighbor." This directive has been conveyed throughout history and around the globe. Around 500 B.C., Confucius[1] asked that his fellow citizens "never impose on others what you would not choose for yourself." In ancient Greece, Pittacus[2] entreated others, "Do not do to your neighbor what you would take ill from him." Although these requests refer both to literal and metaphorical neighbors, research shows that get-

ting along with the people on your street and in your community is good
for you.[3]

When you feel a sense of belonging within your community, you
benefit tangibly and intangibly.[4] Getting along with our neighbors gives
us peace of mind that our home is a little more secure when we are not
present, that we can call on someone if we need that proverbial cup of
sugar or packet of Splenda, and that the walk to the mailbox isn't something to dread when our neighbors are outside. When you have healthy
ties with your neighbors, even if you live in a less-than-ideal neighborhood, the social connections buffer the negative aspects of the community.[5]

Getting along with neighbors, unfortunately, is not always as easy as
we might like. Not every woman has an "Ethel" in the apartment down-
stairs to help make her own "Lucy moments" a little more amusing. Two
iconic television neighbors and best friends, Mary Richards and Rhoda
Morgenstern, might also be a dream neighborhood pairing you'd like to
re-create in your own life. Unfortunately, your own neighbors may be the
stuff of *Stepford Wives* nightmares.

Many of us may have learned about the importance of getting along
with neighbors through family-oriented, gentle television storylines from
The Waltons to *Rugrats*. Fast-forward from shows from your childhood
and you now see news accounts of neighborhood disputes that arise over
property boundaries, backyard fences, unruly dogs, disruptive children,
and even poorly manicured lawns. Contemporary neighborhood disputes
seem more likely to end up on Court TV than Nick at Nite. A heartwarm-
ing, sixty-minute packaged solution might be preferred, but some neigh-
bor-to-neighbor conflicts require stronger interventions.

A Neighborhood Disaster All Too Real

Neighbors are in a unique position to observe and be more familiar with
your daily life than almost anyone else who does not live under your roof.
One woman we heard from, Deborah, felt that one neighbor was too close
for comfort. Her neighbor frequently stopped by to complain about Deborah's kids, Deborah's yard, the outdoor lights being left on too late, and
any other points of potential contention she could dredge up. Deborah
was overwhelmed by the complaints and the neighbor's efforts to intimi-
date her, especially as they had once been good friends.

Deborah noted that she was so surprised and perturbed by the neighbor's behavior that she "studied adult bullying on the Internet and realized that [her] neighbor was the complete epitome of the adult bully. Nobody stopped her as a child; therefore she became very skilled at bullying as an adult." As Deborah described how the friendship actually reached its end, it was startling to learn that it was a natural disaster, a forest fire, that gave rise to the change. This resulted in a more dramatic and traumatic ending than normal circumstances would predict. However, when friendships end poorly with neighbors, the proximity factor can create long-term difficulties if both former friends plan to stay put. Deborah went on to say, "Circumstances changed. I no longer have anything to do with this person. It took a forest fire and tremendous loss to get away from it. When my home burned down and hers did not, I did not even care. It was so liberating that it was all finally over."

When a neighbor is constantly belittling or complaining about you, your family, those you care about, or how you live your life, it can be very difficult. You may want to heed the reminder that "good fences make good neighbors." Choosing to move out of your home is seldom the ideal solution. However, if close neighbors exert a sufficiently negative force and intimidating presence on our lives, finding a simple and effective method to limit their destructive influence can be difficult. Clarifying boundaries, modeling respect for others, and making sure you don't lower yourself to retaliation are the best ways to respond to unpleasant neighbors. However, some relationships cannot be salvaged, as evidenced in Deborah's story in which a wildfire provided the opportunity for positive transformation.

SAFE AT HOME

As the mortgage lending commercials remind us, a home is often the most expensive single purchase you will ever make. However, the emotional investment in your home—whether a studio apartment, lake estate, or anything in between—is substantial as well. One woman shared that she had to make the choice to stay or go when neighborhood drama and extramarital affairs between neighborhood friends were revealed. She felt that she was constantly being placed in unbearable situations in which even casual neighborhood get-togethers were more stressful than she could tolerate. As noted earlier, satisfaction with your home and your community plays a significant role in your overall well-being. Being a good neighbor may mean taking a stand on some issues and backing down on others.

A mother of two children, Christine has lived in the same neighborhood since her older child was born eleven years ago. She shared her thoughts on dealing with neighborhood drama:

> I love my neighbors. Even though they park in the street and that makes it less safe for the kids. Even though neighbors on both sides of me do not mow their lawns up to the end of their property line and I am out there pushing a half-dead, 200-pound mower. Even though a few complain about wonderful events like Halloween. But I do love my neighborhood! The good neighbors outweigh the bad. We chat, we drink, we gripe, we watch kids run wild together. So it is not that I don't care that there are people unwilling to do minimal yard maintenance, because I sure as heck do—I just care about the agreeableness of the neighbors more than the beauty of the neighborhood.

Christine's words hopefully sum up the sentiments of many readers. Looking for the good in our communities can be much more satisfying than cataloging the bad. However, when the bad seems to outweigh the good, and as advised in all potentially toxic, long-term relationships, weigh the *consequences* of your actions against the potential for lasting misery before taking action. While a "geographical cure" is always a possibility, ideally you can find a workable solution to neighborhood conflict before boxes would need to be packed. Similarly, learning how to get along with difficult coworkers can be a better solution than looking for a new job.

WORKPLACE DRAMA

If you are like the majority of women in the United States, you are spending over thirty-six hours each week on the job.[6] This is equivalent to about two and a half full months, day and night, of your life each year. We spend a lot of time with our "workplace families," and much like the family into which we were born, we have little choice about how these groups are peopled. We have to work at work relationships, sometimes much harder than we feel is fair.

Working Relationships

Researchers have been studying the relationships between coworkers for decades. These relationships have been examined for a variety of reasons, but most relate to productivity and efficiency.[7] Some organizations bring in external consultants to administer personality assessments, such as the Myers-Briggs Type Indicator or the Enneagram Type Indicator, in the hope that employees will understand better and get along more easily with one another. Happy coworkers usually mean a more productive staff. In fact, positive relationships with coworkers play a strong role in employee retention.[8] Yet workplace cultures can also provide opportunities for employees to regress to a less evolved set of rules and behaviors than their off-the-clock and out-of-the-office social interactions might suggest.

In social relationships, we typically measure a new friend's commitment and investment in the relationship on an exchange-by-exchange basis.[9] As we get more invested in the relationship and the "friendship credits" we deposit are matched equally by the new friend, we eventually stop counting and let the shared history of mutuality suffice. In work relationships, however, you may spend years or even decades sharing office space and organizational resources with individuals whom you may not like much or respect. How these situations are handled varies widely across individuals.

What Color Is Your Frustration?

A continuing favorite book for those with career path questions and concerns is *What Color Is Your Parachute?*[10] This book is designed to help readers find the job that most closely aligns with their skills, goals, and passion. Unfortunately, even dream careers may require that you work with difficult people who can create frustrating situations that can squeeze the joy out of the job.

When faced with daily contact with coworkers who rub them the wrong way, some people respond with a simple "emotional check-out." They will function on the job at the minimal accepted performance level.

Others might try to "go along to get along" and bring in a cheerfully sunny disposition each day, hoping that things might be better. Some might ignore the object of their frustration or annoyance and continue doing their job with passion and commitment because they can see beyond the cubicle walls and their current situation. Others might take a more direct route to changing the situation and confront individuals whose behavior they find unappealing. Still others might resort to passive-aggressive tactics in which they subtly try to make work life more difficult for others. Others might seek sabotage, whether by bringing down the efforts of another overtly or by stealthily "working the crowd" or "working the boss" to discredit their targeted colleague. Still others build alliances with coworkers they believe share their feelings. Once banded together, they may quietly stand apart from the others and keep their focus on their jobs or quietly (or not-so-quietly) pursue rebellion and achievement at the expense of others' success.

Many readers may recognize themselves in more than one of the types described above. As has been highlighted in earlier chapters, different situations elicit different responses from people, depending on the circumstances. Unfortunately, you can do little about who ends up in the office next to yours, sometimes even if you are the boss.

BEWARE: COLLEAG-EMIES ARE EVERYWHERE

The following stories illustrate just a few of the many types of frustrating and toxic coworkers. We are using the term *colleag-emies*, a combination of *colleague* and *enemies*, to describe these coworkers. We provide suggestions for dealing with them that won't leave you standing in the unemployment line or a police lineup. Keep in mind, too, that these workplace nightmares could be your coworker, your supervisor, or your supervisee.

Colleag-emy #1: The Diva

The diva believes that she is the most important person in an organization. She enjoys drawing attention to herself and expects others to show enthusiastic support of her ideas. When a diva is in charge, it can be frustrating for her employees when they realize that there is no choice but to meet her needs or satisfy her whims to ensure job security. When the diva is your equal, it is best to steer clear as much as possible. It is unlikely that a diva recognizes or cares about the negative effect her behavior has on the overall organization. When a diva reports to you, sit down with her and revisit job descriptions, organizational expectations, and what are and are *not* acceptable workplace behaviors. Unfortunately, by the time a diva has joined the workforce, her behaviors and attitudes are likely well ingrained. Patience at work, patient friends with whom you can kvetch, and the ability to keep a firm work/life balance are all helpful in handling the veteran workplace divas you encounter.

Colleag-emy #2: The Stealth Bomber

Stealth bombers can be dangerous colleagues, as they can be ruthless in their efforts to get ahead. They spot weaknesses, plan attacks, and seek revenge for even imagined slights by coworkers. When a stealth bomber reports directly to you, be wary of what you share, how you share it, and when you share it. Be just as careful in your listening as well. Don't directly or indirectly reward her attempts to bring down her coworkers or your colleagues. She may try to earn your praise and approval through her efforts to blow up others, but don't allow yourself to buy into this danger-ous game. Imagine yourself as her target and use this perspective as a guideline in handling this type of behavior.

If she is your colleague, keep yourself from giving her the power to demoralize you with her words. People can only upset you if you allow them to do so; maintain a strong personal boundary and recognize her tactics as a form of insecurity. If this person is your supervisor, it is essential that you keep your eyes on the prize and your work ethic clearly in mind. When an employer tries to set up in-fighting within a team, don't allow yourself to be drawn into the ring. Show your colleagues respect, give your best on the job, and find ways to build up team morale and group cohesion outside of the workplace, if possible. When a team is united, it is a lot more difficult for stealth bombers to isolate one member to target for a strike.

Colleag-emy #3: The Whiner

Working alongside a whiner potentially wears on the nerves and crushes the joy you would normally feel for the job. While it seems undeniably true that "misery loves company," a workplace whiner has the power to alienate even those colleagues who are as miserable on the job as she is. Whiners "wind up" their colleagues by making them come unglued! Martina, a counselor with a legendary amount of patience for her clients, but a fierce and assertive manner with her colleagues, shared her thoughts about her experience working alongside a whiner:

> First, you try to be kind and empathic, "yes that sounds like you're having a tough time with that." But if the whiner assumes that you've opened the door for more whining, you've got to try a tougher tactic, such as "holding up the mirror" to the whiner. Say something like "It seems that you have a lot of frustration on the job. You might not realize this, but you really are coming across negatively to others here in the office."
>
> When that doesn't work, you might need to try and beat them at their own game—times ten! Match their every whine or complaint with an even bigger, more intense whine. Really show them what their whining is like. Whining back can be effective, but it can also be fun if you get in the spirit and do it like the "exaggerating technique" in counseling. Make it big and make it ludicrous. And if none of those work, you must confront the whiner with your other coworkers for a full-scale intervention.

Dealing with whiners is trying, but trying some of the solutions above might be a good place to start with supervisees or colleagues. If your supervisor is the whiner, you may need to practice smiling meditation when she is on a roll. This form of meditation is easy to master. Just smile gently and focus on your breath, keeping your mind clear of clutter or external frustrations. If you know what sets her off and have any power to minimize the triggers, do what you can to make everyone's life easier. Remember, no matter how crazy a boss might drive her employees, she is still the boss. Doing what you can to contribute to overall operational success will help everyone look good.

Colleag-emy #4: The Pleaser

On the surface, it would seem that this coworker might be a dream employee because she wants to do everything right and fears disappointing the people for whom she works. Pleasers may blame themselves for delays or obstacles to progress over which they have no real control. Pleasers never realize that they may be creating trouble and assume that obedience and self-deprecation are the keys to approval.

If you supervise a pleaser, you may need to have a one-on-one discussion of how "pleasing the boss" differs from "groveling and kowtowing to the boss." Pleasers usually come from a place of extreme helpfulness and deference to their employers, but it can grate on your nerves when you have an employee groveling at your feet or begging for forgiveness for minor mistakes. If the pleaser in the office is on one of her very first jobs, a little tough love may deepen her value as an employee throughout her career. If she's on her fifth or sixth job in her career, it may be fear of disapproval that motivates her desire to please. This may be especially difficult to change if she has been fired from a job in the past.

Seldom would this type of worker move very far up the chain of command; she does not usually show management skills, since she spends her time trying to please the managers around her. However, if she is a colleague and you can't spend another day witnessing her self-abasement in her efforts to please the boss, then you might want to have a one-on-one, heart-to-heart conversation with her. Letting her know how she is coming across may provide her with insight into her behaviors that she might not be able to muster on her own. Pleasers *want* to please and may actually take the constructive feedback to heart.

Colleag-emy #5: The Gossip

While it can be useful to have a contact in the organization who acquires the latest information with ease, if the "inside connection" is simply a gossip, it may compromise her value to you and to the group. When someone becomes the office gossip, she has crossed into the "organizational no-fly zone," and you will want to limit the scope of your conversations with her. She may have the latest news flash about the company, but she also may be sharing someone's secrets that she was asked to keep confidential. If you have shared your own updates with her, the news she is sharing with others may very well be yours.

If you are supervising the office gossip, and she shares information that affects you or your team, use the information appropriately and carefully. If you feel that she is repeating rumors to get a reaction, simply do not react. Gossips often enjoy getting a rise out of people; do not be one of those people. Be highly circumspect in what you say to her, what materials she is allowed to peruse, and the conversations you have in her presence. If she is your coworker, do not take everything she shares as truth. Do not let her stir up your emotions, especially if that is her goal. Do not let her revelations about others pique your interest or boil your blood. Disinterest is the best way to disarm a gossip. Keeping your opinions to yourself will give her less ammunition to use with others.

Lastly, if the gossiper is your supervisor, this can be a double-edged sword. If she really does have inside information about future organizational developments, her willingness to provide confidential updates can be professionally useful. Knowing what is coming down the pike can help you plan for career moves that propel you closer to your overarching professional goals. However, she may also be pumping you for updates on what is going on at your level or, perhaps even more risky, in your life. You may feel torn between being candid with your boss and being cautious with what you share. Choose the path that protects your own long-term investments over those of others or the organization. Do not share information that you would not want others to attribute to you as its source.

Colleag-emy #6: The Outright Bully

In the past couple of decades, research studies addressing bullying have expanded exponentially. We have finally acknowledged the long-term danger of allowing schoolyard bullying to blossom into harmful adult behaviors. In the workplace, bullying of women by other women is rampant, although women have often learned to use much more "defensible" or "subliminal" methods of bullying colleagues.[11] Women know how to be mean in such a way that men might not even recognize a bully shot was fired. Facial expressions, glares, passive-aggressive actions, and backhanded compliments are examples of how women bully their coworkers.[12]

Dealing with workplace bullies can be exhausting and can lead to physical as well as emotional stress. Unfortunately, many women are not trained to confront those who have harmed them, and this makes them easy targets for their tormentors. If you feel you are being bullied, the first step should be to document what is happening between you and the bully. Dates, times, locations, behaviors, and so on—log these as soon as you realize that you may be a target of bullying. Next, you need to go against traditional, gendered behavioral patterns of avoiding confrontation and actually speak up to the bully. Many women assume that others will refrain from taking action if bullied, so simply speaking up and calling out the bully for her actions may be adequate to tame the situation in some cases. If this doesn't work, you will need to move up the chain to your supervisor or the human resources department. *Caveat: If you feel that sexual harassment is even a small part of the bullying from the onset, immediately file a complaint with your human resources department.* Left unchecked, bullies typically do not stop on their own—they may move from target to target, but the bullying tends to continue. Lastly, if no interventions are successful in getting the bully off your back, you may want to consider a transfer within the company or a departure, if no other solution is viable.

Colleag-emy #7: The Brawler

This final type of toxic workmate is the most rare and distressing, but she can show up unexpectedly at almost any site. This is the brawler, the person who moves from verbal to physical aggression against others. While research indicates that verbal aggression is much more frequent that physical aggression,[13] we have heard several stories about women who turned their frustrations into physical assaults. If this happens where you work, your first concern is your own physical safety. If you are in management, handling the aftermath may also fall onto your shoulders, and how you handle the incident may very well shape your reputation in the organization.

Dealing with a brawler on-site may require immediate intervention from security or police personnel, depending on the nature of the aggression. However, knowing the potential risk factors for workplace violence may raise awareness and, ideally, aid in prevention. According to a Rutgers University report on workplace violence,[14] the following are the most common risk factors involved in employee violence: history of violent behavior, being upset with assigned low-level tasks, bitterness and unhappiness, absence of job security, difficulties during childhood and adolescence, and substance use/abuse. And although white, middle-class men were noted as the most likely to perpetrate workplace violence, women are more likely to engage in "workplace mobbing," in which targeted enemies are increasingly victimized by gossip, passive-aggressive behaviors, and increasingly hostile climates. [15]

THE FIVE O'CLOCK WHISTLE

We typically spend more waking hours with the people with whom we work than with families, loved ones, or friends. Women fought long and hard to earn the right to spend forty hours a week dedicating themselves to professional pursuits. Unfortunately, whether you are working in the fields, the schools, the office, or the forest, women are actively involved in keeping down other women and can make each other miserable through a variety of workplace behaviors. Whining and pleasing may grate on your nerves, but stealth bombers and bullies may sabotage your success. Even women who do their best to get along with their workmates, their supervisors, and their supervisees may find themselves behaving in ways that reflect the environmentally supported competitiveness between women. When you find yourself behaving in ways that are pulling you or others down, it's time to step back and take a look at the damage you might be doing to yourself, your colleagues, and your organization. Being a part of the problem—or refusing to seek a solution—will not serve to advance your career or your best interests. Negative relationships at work are toxic to your emotional health. [16]

CONCLUSION

In summary, when you are on the job, remember that it is *just* a job. No job should be the measure of your worth and no job should come before your own well-being. When coworkers drive you crazy, train yourself to tune out and let it go. Focus on doing the best job that you can and find ways to "control your controllables" as you do what you can to contribute to operational excellence of your organization. As a counselor often tells her clients, you cannot change anyone's behavior but your own—neither coworkers', neighbors', nor family members'. Therefore, direct your energy toward maintaining your positive relationships and developing ways to minimize the negative influence of the toxic neighbors or coworkers who populate your life.

Part IV

Taking Stock and Cutting Back

17

PLAYING BY THE RULES

While this book was organized around a set of basic rules that have been found to function in social relationships across cultures,[1] thirteen key personality traits have been identified as essential in maintaining healthy friendships.[2] These traits fall into three distinct groups: traits of integrity, traits of caring, and traits of congeniality. Serving as the building blocks of the rules of friendship, if a woman is short on these qualities, she will have difficulty "playing by the rules." Below we will describe these qualities and the roles they play in friendship, and provide an example of how each one's absence or presence may influence a friendship.

INTEGRITY IS ESSENTIAL

Five interconnected qualities comprise the group of integrity-related traits: trustworthiness, honesty, dependability, loyalty, and ability to trust others. In sum, the presence of these qualities allows people to follow what some consider the Golden Rule—to treat others as you would like to be treated. In the social landscape, these five characteristics are the glue that bonds a relationship.

Trustworthiness

As noted by Degges-White and Borzumato-Gainey, trustworthiness is one of the "make or break" elements, and may be the most important, in a healthy friendship.[3] Without credibility, a person has little authenticity to offer a friend, and healthy relationships cannot develop. Trustworthiness is also essential in honoring promises to respect a friend's confidences and being true to your word.

When inviting women to share about their toxic friendship experiences, betrayal of trust was hands-down the most frequently mentioned relationship breach. It is important to note that the *magnitude* of the betrayal may have little influence on the *impact* of the betrayal. For many women, a friend who steals a dollar is considered as toxic as a friend who steals a boyfriend. One woman affirmed that she ended friendships when she discovered a friend "stealing from me—either a thing of monetary or sentimental value, or my spouse." Another woman noted, "The breaking point for a friendship would be breaking trust. Breaking trust comes in a lot of forms: not keeping a secret, gossip, two-faced behavior, or passive aggressive behavior." Trustworthiness relies on the presence of honesty, dependability, and loyalty.

Honesty

Each of us knows what honesty entails. As a virtue, it is instilled in most of us from early childhood onward. Honesty between friends is expected. Having someone in our lives who is genuine, authentic, and transparent can be a welcome relief from those who are deceptive, phony, or fake.

Depending on the issue at stake, however, being 100 percent honest with friends can be a challenge. In some situations, fear may keep someone from offering full disclosure to a friend. If honesty could jeopardize your own reputation, you may be hesitant to offer the truth. In altruistically motivated cases, you may avoid honesty to avoid wounding the reputation or feelings of another. In quality friendships, or in relationships you want to see grow into friendships, honesty is a requisite. It is the cost and the benefit of authentic relationships. One interviewee reminded us, "Always tell the truth, even if you know it's going to be argued against or it's going to hurt someone. The closer you are, the more that person values your opinion and you can't keep your mouth shut when [something] important [needs to be shared] just because it can rock the boat." But when laying out the truth for your friends, communicate it in a way that makes it easy for them to hear. The "Oreo Cookie" approach, as described in chapter 14, works well. Provide a positive comment, then add your constructive feedback, and then end with something upbeat and positive about your friend. This can protect your relationship while still getting your message across.

The significance of the identified concern is key, and the possibilities for correction and adjustment are also relevant. For instance, when a friend asks if a particular pair of jeans makes her "tush" look big—and they do!—circumstances and the geographical location of the "denim inquisition" dictate the best response. If she is trying on the jeans in the fitting room and has not yet purchased them, this is the perfect time for honesty. However, if the two of you are standing in front of the full-length mirror in the ladies' room at a club and she asks the same question about a similarly fitting pair of jeans, there is no way the current situation can be altered. A little hedging in your response now is fine. Something along the lines of "Well, they aren't my favorite jeans on you, but . . ." or "Maybe, just a bit, but not enough to worry about," or "No, they make you look hot" might be the best answer at that moment. If life, limb, or lifelong commitments are at stake, absolute honesty is the only choice and probably what you would want from your own friends: "Just be honest about everything, have fun, make good memories, be loyal, and overall follow the Golden Rule."

Dependability

It is also important to say what you are going to do and do what you said you would do. Dependability is one of the most valued characteristics of a friend, in fact.[4] If you fail too often to deliver on promises, you may be pushing the relationship to its end. One young respondent bemoaned her experiences with a toxic friend who "changed her mind" about shared plans for the evening of their high school graduation. This was the biggest achievement of her young life, and when her friend backed out, the much-anticipated celebration mutated into a miserable, lonely night. Another woman, in her sixties, affirmed that she had ended friendships with women who let her down by "being flaky and not fulfilling promises."

Unfortunately, we do not always realize the negative impact of our behaviors. Describing a friendship that ended, an interviewee shared that the cause was a "lack of reciprocation—I had to try so hard just to get my friend to respond to a phone call or invitation. To make it worse . . . the friend was blind to the ways that I was being hurt emotionally." If a friend becomes increasingly difficult to reach, perhaps it is time to give the relationship a time-out and see if your friend makes a move to reconnect. On the flip side, some women express frustration with friends who judge them because "life happened" and plans were canceled. To keep a friendship vibrant, do your best to follow through on your promises. Life does sometimes "happen," so cut your friends some slack if this is an occasional thing. However, if a friend's habit of being out-of-pocket has turned into a pattern, you may need to initiate a conversation about this concern or rethink the status of the relationship.

Loyalty

Loyalty is another make-or-break expectation between friends. Many readers may even have created "blood brothers" rituals with their closest friends. When loyalty disappears, so can a relationship, as one woman pointedly noted in describing her personal friendship breaking point: "It is a lack of loyalty. One thing that ruins friendships for me is when so-called friends are happy to talk about you behind your back, share your secrets with others, or simply use you when they have nothing better to do." Disloyalty can be especially painful if it involves public humiliation. One person summed up an experience of betrayal by lamenting, "So, with one quick act of betrayal, I ended up losing three friends who I had previously considered to be my best friends." In some unpleasant situations, friends are left to choose sides, and the betrayed often fares worse than the betrayer.

More often than some expect, betrayal involves cheating with a friend's romantic partner. One woman shared that she ended a friendship when she learned that "my best friend developed an intimate relationship with my husband. They had been growing close over the past year. They both keep saying they were 'just friends,' but everything pointed to more." Another revealed that a friendship and a budding romance ended on the same night. A good friend slipped a business card into the back pocket of the interviewee's new boyfriend—and the now ex-boyfriend followed up with a phone call to the now ex-friend later that week.

Loyalty should be a given in any significant relationship—whether romantic or platonic. It is the bond between family members, teammates, and partners in crime. Loyalty is about honoring the relationship by sticking up for friends, having their backs, and protecting their interests. Without loyalty, friendships lose their value.

Ability to Trust

How do you respond when you are asked to trust someone? Does trust come easy for you, or do you feel anxious at the thought of putting your faith in another person? Some women trust others far too easily and far too early in a relationship. Others have a hard time opening up and being vulnerable for fear of being hurt.

It may not be a surprise that the ability to trust is partially grounded in your biology,[5] much like many of our social behaviors. Oxytocin, which is commonly referred to as the love hormone, also plays a part in our willingness to trust others. While early interaction with our caregivers teaches us a lot about trust, our physiological makeup provides an incentive to build trusting social relationships with others. When we call on friends for help and they provide it, that good feeling or rush that we get is the biologically based reward for taking a chance on friendship.

However, when we place our trust in a friend and that trust is betrayed, we may experience a physical reaction. Some people call it a "bitter pill to swallow" or "a blow to the gut." No matter how it is phrased, we all understand the emotional/physical combination pain that results from a betrayal of trust. An interviewee recounted the relationship fallout from an incident in which a friend had lied to her, not once, but twice: "I told a friend that I can't be friends when being lied to more than once. The trust in the relationship is null and void." Friends want to give friends the benefit of the doubt. One mistake is often forgivable, but a second one can be the breaking point. For others, a single failure to respect the sanctity of the relationship can be the friendship death knell.

Regardless of where your personal breaking point is positioned, you may be confronted with a situation that leads us to the same conclusion as this interviewee, who emphatically believes that "loss of trust is my ultimate 'breaking point' in a friendship; most others things are fixable.

Losing trust is nearly impossible to recover from." Without the ability to increasingly deepen your trust and faith in an acquaintance, a friendship cannot develop or endure.

CARING FOR YOUR FRIENDS

This next group of traits consists of empathy, being nonjudgmental, good listening skills, and the provision of support in both the good and bad times for your friends. Each of these qualities speaks to a different way to show care, concern, and open acceptance of your friends. These are also the qualities that make friendships feel more "warm and fuzzy" than a typical business relationship would. These qualities, by the way, are also the ones that counselors and therapists provide to allow us to feel so safe in therapeutic relationships. When we accept our friends for who they are, make it known that we understand their experiences, and listen to their experiences, we are building a relationship on a solid foundation.

Empathy

Some people confuse empathy with sympathy. If you have sympathy for a friend going through a hard time, you are "feeling sorry" for your friend. If you have empathy for her, then you really understand what she is experiencing and can really "get" what she is feeling. It's seeing the world *as if* you were in her shoes. It is like that feeling of joy you get deep inside when a friend is telling you about something wonderful that happened to her. Or that heavy feeling in the pit of your stomach when a friend is describing a frightening or heartbreaking situation she experienced. Sympathy has its own place in relationships—but it involves a separation of self from other, whereas empathy is the joining of two minds and hearts. And this empathetic connection is essential. In fact, its absence was mentioned by a number of women as a reason to end a friendship. One woman clearly stated that she has no tolerance for those who "have no real empathy and can't feel for others."

Studies suggest that empathy develops over time and that it shapes our prosocial behaviors.[6] As we develop our ability to understand another's experiences both cognitively and emotionally, we can bring greater maturity to our interactions with others. It's been suggested that our music preferences are associated with our ability to engage in empathetic, pro-social behaviors.[7] This might be one of the reasons that some performers reach specific demographic groups so effectively. Their lyrics and musicality reflect the emotions and experiences of the audience so well. When we "get" our friends, it's as if there is harmony between our hearts.

Ability to Be Nonjudgmental

The second trait of caring is the ability to accept your friend and all of her shortcomings without judgment; this is akin to unconditional positive regard, which is a loving acceptance that we see modeled by our parents, in the best of cases. While we are not expected or required to approve of everything a friend does or says, genuine friendships will endure many differences along the way. When friends accept us as we are, it actually increases our self-esteem.[8]

Unfortunately, not every friend will be capable of withholding judgment about your choices. One woman noted that she had to end a relationship with a former friend who spent too much time "belittling my choices and judging me for my feelings about things." Uncensored honesty, a trait we generally desire, can sometimes lead to hurt feelings or frayed friendships. It is important to focus on the friend, not the friend's choices, in order to keep the relationship strong. Open-mindedness and tolerance are important in getting along with others. Accepting your friends and their quirks is essential for healthy relationships. Of course, there are always caveats to blind acceptance. If someone's well-being is in danger (and this can be financial, physical, emotional, or even spiritual well-being), then a good friend's insights and perspective may be just what is needed to prevent disaster. If she is a good friend, though, you will need to accept that she may follow a different faith tradition; date men with whom you wouldn't want to share an elevator; choose fashion statements you consider fashion questions; or use tarot cards to make career decisions. In some instances, your differences are part of what brings fun to the relationship! Relationships are complicated, and good friends can be hard to find; don't sacrifice a solid friendship just because your friend is trying on new ideas or new behaviors that you would never consider exploring yourself.

A Good Listener

Sometimes all we need is a shoulder to cry on and a friend to listen. Although there are times we may need advice, a serious talking-to, or a threat or two to keep us from making a bad decision, we often most need a safe space to speak our mind. Girls and women forge and solidify their friendships through increasingly intimate sharing. Listening well is an art and one that is even more valuable today, as the technology that brings us together also creates more distortion and distraction. Good listeners do not try to put words in their friends' mouths. They make eye contact and observe body language, if face-to-face. Good listeners give their friends their undivided attention and focus on the words and the *metamessage*, or the larger, overarching message. They also check in with their friends to make sure they "hear" what a friend is really saying. Good listeners do not jump in and start talking as soon as their friends take a breath. Counselors use the 80/20 rule with their clients. The client is expected to speak approximately 80 percent of the session and the counselor gets the other 20 percent. Furthermore, good friends do not tell friends what they *should do* or try to fix the problem unless a friend is truly asking for suggestions or advice.

Some friends listen the old-fashioned way, face-to-face with one another, but many other modes of communication can be just as affirming. Due to the prevalence of geographical relocations for so many women today, multiple methods of communication are very beneficial. Moving up the corporate or military ladder can result in moving around the globe. Best friends separated by a thousand miles may still share their daily run before work, but it may be a hands-free phone that now keeps them in sync.

Text messaging, Snapchat, and Instagram are just a few of the innovative methods available for reaching our friends. At the heart of this technological explosion is the need for connection. When asked how her friendships could be improved, one woman shared, "With mutual understanding and what is more important . . . being good listeners." That about sums up this trait. It is the key to stronger relationships. A million pictures of your cat may fill your Facebook time line, but a Skype or smartphone call lets you share your deeper feelings with the friends who matter most.

Supportive in Tough Times

Everyone will face tough times in life, and as you have probably been reminded all too often, life isn't fair. When you are feeling beaten up by the world, you want friends there to help bolster you. You need someone to listen and commiserate with you that your boss is impossible, that you are desperately underpaid, that bankruptcy is a terrible thing, or that your new love interest forgetting your birthday is disappointing. (Caveat: Do not go too far in verbally beating up the potential lifelong partner of your best lifelong friend!) Friends listen and offer as much support as they are able.

When friends are not there when the going gets tough, you may need to get going without that friend. One woman shared her indignation with us as she recalled how one past friendship ground to a halt: "I was speaking with a friend and I revealed that I was still upset over what had happened with my family awhile back. My former friend shocked me as she responded, 'I was going to say it's probably a full moon, that's why you're feeling upset.'" With insufficient empathy and without support, friendships offer little of emotional value.

Unfortunately, when one friend is doing all the supporting and the other is doing all the needing, friendships become unbalanced. Resentment can erupt, depending on one friend's tolerance for another's neediness. If you are feeling overwhelmed by a friend, you may need to encourage her to seek professional help. For instance, suggestions may include counseling, medical care, government agencies, or twelve-step support groups. Friendship involves the provision of support, not the orchestration of salvation.

Supportive in Good Times

We all know that friends should support us when we are down, but do your friends support you when you are riding the twin tides of happiness and success? In a study with elementary students, researchers found out that children were unlikely to share news of academic success with friends who were less successful.[9] The children likened it to bragging or implying that they were better than their friends.

Hard work combined with the unpredictability of life may create situations in which some of us reach pinnacles of success financially, socially, professionally, or relationally as if by magic. When you soar, you may want to let everyone know of your achievements. It can be like a shot of endorphins, and you want to share your high. Unfortunately, our competitive culture may leave some of us feeling like those elementary school children who were afraid of being seen as boasters or show-offs. Some people's responses to a friend's success give credence to that concern. One woman shared that she had ended a friendship because her ex-friend "always appeared to seem envious of her friends' good luck and always appeared to be actively jealous of any other friends' success." With authentic, heart-to-heart friends, this should not be the case.

True friends can share in your joy through a connected empathy and authentic concern for your welfare. Jealousy, envy, and other negative emotions may fleetingly arise, because human nature can be like that. In the long run, however, most recognize that a friend's good fortune only adds to the mutual pleasure found within the relationship. Smiles and good moods are contagious, so revel in the happiness of those close to you. If you have a friend who consistently dismisses your success, perhaps you will need to consider dismissing her as a friend.

TRAITS OF CONGENIALITY

These final three traits speak to the pleasure that you bring in the company of others. While some friends offer all of the ten traits above, if someone is less than a joy to be around, we are unlikely to spend as much time with her as we would with more congenial friends. Self-confidence, being fun to be around, and finding the humor in life are also components of general well-being and happiness, [10] and they make our paths through life a little easier.

Self-Confidence

Because we choose friends whom we consider to "be like us," it is only natural that we prefer friends who have a strong level of self-confidence and who like who they are. Further, research on leadership has shown that self-confidence is *contagious*. [11] Your own self-esteem rises when in the company of friends who feel good about themselves.

Most of us know how disheartening it can be, as well as exhausting, in the company of friends who think little of themselves. Constantly having to shore up a friend's ego can get in the way of deeper, more salient dialogues. You may ask yourself just how many iterations of confidence-building affirmations you must provide, such as *Yes, your potato salad is absolutely the best at the potluck. No, you are definitely not going to be unemployed forever. Yes, you do look amazing in that wrap dress. No, you do truly deserve to be happy.* The list could go on and on.

A young woman in her twenties shared her own recognition regarding the role her own sense of self played in friendships: "If I allowed myself to be more compassionate with myself and not so judgmental and self-deprecating, I believe I would open up more and friendships would be easier." Knowing that she lacked self-confidence, she felt that she had little to offer others and had needs too great for others to fill. Turning to friends for support and validation when life knocks the stuffing out of you is perfectly acceptable and absolutely expected. Expecting friends to be a 24/7 cheer squad or pep team is asking too much. If this is what you consistently seek from your friends, it might be helpful to work with a counselor to help you find and focus on your own inner strengths and support skills. If a friend seems to constantly need this type of support, you may want to encourage her to explore counseling as a way to help her become her own full-time cheerleader.

Fun to Be Around

Similar to the quality above, being around friends who know how to have fun in life is much more inviting than being around friends who are consistently too serious or too downhearted. When a friend is down, we naturally try to boost her spirits, mitigate the negative situation, or "revive" her to the joy of living. Providing emotional support is what friendship is all about. If a friend, however, wallows in her misery or refuses to do what is necessary to get back on the upside of down, we tend to draw away.

Just as self-confidence is contagious, misery can be as well. While misery does love company, few of us like to hang out with misery indefinitely. Happiness with your lot in life is much more likely to bring positive and rewarding friendships.[12] One young woman voiced frustration with an ex-friend when asked to describe her friendship breakup decision:

"If a person doesn't feel good about themselves, they can sometimes make people feel bad to feel better within themselves. If that is the case, I have to ask myself if I can help them; if not, is it worth hurting myself to continue the friendship?" Friends don't make friends feel bad. Their role is to bring happiness, not bitterness, into others' lives.

Appreciates the Humor in Life

All of us have probably heard the saying "It is as easy to laugh as to cry," and especially in these unpredictable times, laughing makes a lot more sense. From economic booms to economic busts, life takes everyone on a roller-coaster ride, whether or not you buy a ticket. It should go without saying that most people would rather share the ride with those who can find the joy and the humor in a situation. No one is immune to rocky times, but if someone can keep her sense of humor, she is more likely to keep her forward momentum. And nothing improves a bad day like a liberal dose of laughter.

Expert words of wisdom regarding how to make friendships last were succinctly shared by one survey respondent: "Never judge. Never lie. Laugh often." Taking time for a good laugh—either at life or at yourself—might even help you get a good night's sleep.[13] People pay good money to laugh—movies, plays, books, comedy clubs, and even laughter yoga sessions, in which laughter is intentionally elicited. Being the friend who helps others see the lighter side of life will leave more cash in your pockets for group treats!

FRIENDSHIPS ARE A HEALTHY MIX

Integrity, caring, and congeniality are integral to healthy relationships—whether platonic friendships, romantic relationships, or any familial or relational bonds. While everyone may have a bad day, a bad week, or a bad habit that keeps her from adding all thirteen of these traits to the relationship soup on occasion, *toxic* friends tend to substitute their own brand of poison for one or more of these prized relationship ingredients. The most important measure of a relationship's value is whether the traits you need most in a friend are the traits that she can most reliably provide.

Or at least she can provide enough of the relevant traits at a pivotal moment.

Friendships can change over time as a friend's needs and resources shift. However, friends who consistently bring little to the relationship equation but expect much in return may not be lasting friends, in truth. Developing your own set of standards, or code of conduct, for the behaviors that are or are not okay in a friendship is the best way to ensure that your friendscape remains healthy and vibrant. In the next chapter, we provide suggestions for writing your own set of friendship rules.

18

WRITING YOUR OWN
RULES OF RELATIONSHIP

The starting point for creating healthier, more balanced friendships is increased awareness of the following areas: what a healthy relationship should look like, knowledge of what you are bringing to the relationship, and clear ideas about your personal expectations and boundaries. A healthy friendship begins with a healthy dose of honest self-reflection. Unless you understand the role that you are playing in any relationship, you are unable to initiate positive, *intentional* change within the relationship.

Clients often enter counseling without a clear idea of where they want their paths to lead them. They may voice nebulous goals such as "a more fulfilling life," "a faithful partner," "authentic relationships," or "self-confidence." Married or partnered clients may desire better relationships but believe that the absent partner must change. Lonely clients may desire more friends or better friends but place the responsibility on others to make this happen. Counselors offer empathy and support as they encourage a client to acknowledge that she can control or transform only her *own* behavior.[1]

Some clients may believe that they are somehow *unfit* for friendship. Their parents or caregivers may have been unable to establish healthy relationships within the home, socially, or professionally, and so they have no model of how a healthy relationship might work. When counselors model empathy, congruence, and unconditional positive regard, ideally a client can learn to look to other role models beyond her mother/

parent for one who may be more socially successful. Until you know
what a successful relationship looks like and feels like, you will have a
very difficult time establishing and maintaining one.

THE RIPPLE EFFECT

When it comes to changing the dynamics of any relationship—whether
friendship, familial, romantic, or professional—transformation only begins when one member of the pair changes her own behaviors and responses within the dyadic structure. Luckily, all it takes to change the
pattern of a larger system's functioning—including family, friendship,
and work settings—is for one member of the system to shift, and the
whole system will necessarily shift in response.[2] That is the ripple effect
at work. When you throw a pebble into a pool, it lands in one spot but
generates ripples that affect a larger and larger portion of the body of
water. If you can change just one single aspect of your *own* relational
behavior, you can potentially transform all of your relationships as a
result of that one small change. For instance, if you seldom send texts or
call just to say hello to your friends, switch up this behavior by reaching
out first. Send a friend a "good morning" text just to brighten her day.
This is an easy way to strengthen the sense of connection between you
and a friend.

CHOOSING TO ENGAGE

Another important aspect of relationships is that it takes two to create one
and two to maintain one. Even when you feel that a friend's behavior is
not "okay" and borders on intolerable, so long as you remain engaged in
the friendship and continue your same behaviors, you are giving silent
assent to the way the relationship is working. As the saying goes, "If you
are not part of the solution, you are part of the problem." If you would
like to reset a relationship balance, it is up to you to begin the change
process.

GETTING READY TO ASSESS AND REFINE YOUR RELATIONSHIPS

To change your existing relationships and reshape your friendscape, you will need to determine the qualities that you need most from friends and the specific rules you want your relationships to follow. Each of your friends may be bringing something very different to a relationship. Seldom can one person meet 100 percent of a woman's friendship needs, and this is really the healthiest situation. For instance, some friends are there for you to confide in; others are there to sweat through Zumba with you each week. Variety is healthy. In addition, each woman values different traits more than others in their acquaintances. And a friend whom you love dearly for all of her warmth and kindness may be just too "clingy and touchy-feely" for someone else. Therefore, as you complete the following exercises, remember that there is not one single correct profile or right answer. A friend who is "perfect" for you may be another woman's toxic friend nightmare.

PREFERRED TRAITS

Starting with the list of traits (found in figure 18.1) that are considered highly valuable in a friend,[3] reflect first on which ones you feel confident that you offer in sufficient quantities to your friends. Check off those you feel confident that you can provide to friends. Next, focusing on a friend with whom you have been having difficulties, objectively assess her ability to exhibit those traits with you. Note examples of times when she failed to bring any of these to your relationship. Reviewing the list of traits again, circle the ones you believe are absolutely essential to your friendships. What needs do you have, personally, that are not being met in this current relationship?

Reflecting on your needs and what your friend cannot offer, ask yourself if what you are hoping to find in this friend are traits that this friend is even reasonably capable of providing to you—or even others. We heard from women who expressed disappointment that some friends are never there for them when they are going through difficult times, but seem to jump to assist other mutual friends as they are needed. In cases such as this, you may need to objectively assess a couple of factors related to the

Me	Quality	My Friend:
	Honest	
	Supportive of others in their good times	
	Supportive of others in their bad times	
	A good listener	
	Trustworthy	
	Fun to be around	
	Able to see the humor in life	
	Empathic	
	Loyal	
	Non-judgmental	
	Self-Confident	
	Dependable	

Figure 18.1.   Essential Traits for Quality Friendships

relationship. First, have you been willing to assist your friend under the same circumstances in which you expect her to be there for you? And, if not, is it actually reasonable to expect more from a friend than you are willing to provide? Second, if you have been there and given support, yet the friend is unwilling to do the same for you, you may need to ask yourself if the friendship is worth your continued investment.

Not every friend can be "super dependable," and maybe that is not even something you can be for others. If you are a carefree, "life happens" type of person whose schedule changes as the wind shifts, then perhaps you do not value this trait highly in others. When friends have extremely strong values regarding religion, politics, or child-rearing practices, it may be very hard for them to withhold judgment of choices you make that go against their personal values. Yet their honesty may be appreciated, and they may be the friends who will help out when the plumbing fails or the kids need to be picked up unexpectedly from school.

Understanding the mismatch between what you need in a friend, what you offer a friend, and what you and the friend seem willing to bring to the relationship may provide all of the information and confirmation needed to decide how you want to proceed. If the relationship clearly has little value to you now or you feel that there is little potential for a transformation, it may be time to let go of the relationship.

KNOW YOURSELF AND KNOW YOUR VALUES

The values you hold most dear may also play a role in your decision to repair or release a friendship that is not as satisfying as you would like it to be. Researchers continue to show that similarity of values, attitudes, and beliefs is essential to the success of long-term romantic partnerships.[4] In friendships, there is a little more room for diversity between friends, but there may be some values you hold so dear that a friend who challenges or disparages them may not be kept as a friend for the long haul.

When most of us think of values, our minds go to religious or spiritual, faith-based values, obedience to laws, and responsibilities as a partner/parent/professional/friend. One woman shared that she had recently set in place a brand-new rule for her friendships: "Stay away from people who drink and get nasty when they are drunk." Before one of her friendships recently went toxic, she shared that she had never cared whether her friends drank alcohol, but after numerous ugly incidents, she realized that this was a rule she needed to add to her list. Another woman shared that she was a recovering alcoholic, but she had friends who were still struggling with sobriety. To respond to the negativity that one of her struggling friends was bringing to her new life, she had to create a new friendship rule: "Friends can only call me when they are sober. I am sober and a mother now. I can still be here for them, but I can't be THERE for them." She noted that this rule may lead old friends to believe she is not compassionate, but she affirms that sometimes the best way to help a friend is to step away, even if it is painful for both parties.

When you think about the values you hold, do any of them create significant conflicts with your friends? Does a friend's unwillingness to accept or embrace one of your values lead you to believe the friendship is at risk of ending or has already turned toxic? Some areas that seemed to be of special concern for interviewees included friends who had undergone abortions, betrayed their partners, stolen from or lied to them, withheld important information from them for too long (e.g., a partner who was cheating on them), or were involved in illegal drug use, among others.

Take a few moments and reflect on the behaviors that you consider "right behaviors." These are those actions that are in accordance with our deepest beliefs. While not all of us hold exactly similar values, those we hold generally center on the following seven areas: achievement, enjoyment, maturity, prosocial, restrictive conformity, security, and self-direction.[5] In the worksheets in figures 18.2–4, we have listed the value category and provided a brief description of each. In addition, two examples of value statements are listed for each value. We invite you to use these categories as a stimulus to help you to identify and then reflect on the specific values you cherish. Next, create value statements reflecting the categories you believe friends should not disregard.

After you have completed the values and beliefs reflection worksheet, you may be able to more clearly assess the problems in a currently unsatisfying relationship, as well as more easily determine its prognosis. When strongly held and unlikely-to-be-relinquished values clash, you may want to open a dialogue with your friend to explore her own perspective on the issue that has created the rift. For some values, compromise is possible. Sometimes friends must "agree to disagree" and stick to this agreement to maintain their friendship. It can actually be personally enriching to learn about different perspectives and diverse views when mutual respect is present between friends. One woman with whom we spoke, who was very much pro-life, noted that she had a friend who had an abortion some thirty years prior. Our interviewee affirmed that she had consciously chosen to accept her friend wholeheartedly, something that was a challenge for her due to her pro-life beliefs. However, when the friendship ended due to a recent incident that was totally unrelated to the "hot-topic value clash," she acknowledged that she could not be sure that the friend's past decision did not play some small, subconscious role in the ending of the friendship. Sometimes we need to objectively assess our beliefs, our values, our behaviors, and our relationships. When these entities are congruent and in alignment, our lives will feel more on track. When our behaviors or relationships are out of sync with our values and beliefs, reflection may need to lead to action. Although we can only change our own behavior, as we change, so, too, will our relationships.

Research shows that there are specific value types that are universally acknowledged around the globe. These seven areas are listed and described below. Reflect on your own personal experiences and expectations and write down the values that you hold most dear.

Value Category	My Personal Values
Prosocial (Caring about others) *Ex: Friends should call to check in when a friend is ill.* *A good friend lets you cry on her shoulder when you lose your job.*	
Restrictive Conformity (Avoiding harm to others) *Ex: Friends do not lie to each other.* *Friends would not spread rumors about you.*	
Enjoyment (Seeking pleasure) *Ex: We should be able to laugh and joke with our friends.* *Friends help us forget our troubles when we are down.*	

Figure 18.2.   Personal Values Self-Assessment

Achievement (Personal success in life) Ex: We all should work hard to do well in school or on the job. Friends should not ask to borrow money for things they really cannot afford on their own.	
Maturity (Understanding, accepting self and others) Ex: Adults should not expect others to cover up their mistakes for them. When a friend cannot be everything you need them to be, you should accept them as they are.	
Self-direction (Independence in thought and action) Ex: People should take responsibility for their own actions. Friends should be willing to accept and support you even when your goals are not the same.	

Figure 18.3.   Personal Values Self-Assessment *(continued)*

TESTING YOUR LIMITS

In some unhealthy relationships, it is almost as if friends are trying to take control of the relationship and your own freedom to make choices about

Security (Safety and stability of self, relationships; belongingness in groups) *Ex: Friends don't put your well- being in danger.* *A true friend would never ignore me or exclude me from a group conversation.*	

Figure 18.4. Personal Values Self-Assessment *(continued)*

how you spend your time and with whom you interact. You may go along with a friend's suggestion about an activity or her choices about whom to include at an event even if you would rather be doing something else with someone else. You may *go along to get along* and convince yourself that you are really having fun, even if you actually are not. Other friends may ask you to pick up the tab when they are waiting for a paycheck or cosign a loan when their own credit is not as shiny as your own. In fact, financial boundaries are one of the most mentioned limits that can be pushed too far by toxic friends. Other friends may assume that their presence in your life is payback enough for any favors that they have requested from you. They may have no awareness of pushing your limits in terms of requests or expectations of your support. If you feel you are being pushed past reasonable limits or your boundaries are being disrespected, it is time to assess the need for personal friendship rules related to honoring your limitations. These limits may address time, money, energy, personal choice, or independence.

On a blank piece of paper, draw a circle and label it "My Time." Imagine another circle, labeled "Her Decisions," that you are going to place on top of your time. Which one of the illustrations in figure 18.5 best represents how willing you are to let your friend make decisions about how and with whom you spend your time?

If you feel that each of you still offers "give and take," as in column A, with neither one of you co-opting any decision making unfairly, then your relationship is relatively healthy in its boundaries. If you find that column B or C is a better illustration of your relationship, you may be losing ground or may have set up the "social exchange" in this lopsided way without realizing it. If you are growing uncomfortable with the lack of independence, a conversation with your friend may be the way to initiate a resetting of your boundaries. And if column D, "Total Pushover," describes the relationship, you may need to practice flexing your boundaries and finding your limits. When a relationship has grown increasingly unhealthy in terms of personal boundaries, not only has the overbearing friend been pushing your limits, but you may also have allowed this to happen through poor limit setting. Friends can only push us as far as we are willing to go.

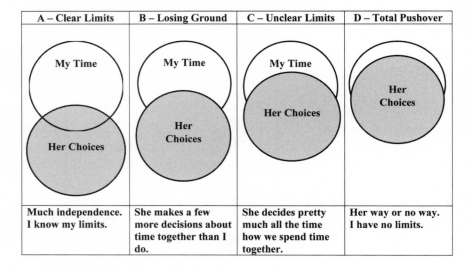

A – Clear Limits	B – Losing Ground	C – Unclear Limits	D – Total Pushover
Much independence. I know my limits.	She makes a few more decisions about time together than I do.	She decides pretty much all the time how we spend time together.	Her way or no way. I have no limits.

Figure 18.5.   Testing Your Limits?

If you feel that you are often being controlled or subsumed by your friends, it may be time to introduce or reinforce a rule regarding personal boundaries. One woman shared that learning to "kindly set limits" was something that she was still working on with her friends, but a past experience with a controlling friend underscored the value of this personal friendship rule. Another woman shared how her limits were tested by a friend who was subtly manipulative. As she described it, she now honors a personal friendship rule in which she is attuned to any signs of "manipulation, possessiveness, over-smarmy 'warmness' or smothering with kindness, gifts." Sometimes your personal "limits rule" may include not only how far you will go for a friend but also how far you let a friend "barter" for your time in a manipulative, possessive way.

In terms of personal boundaries, what rules do you need to put in place? Would you want to create rules addressing friends who try to control your activities or rules that limit who can spend time with the pair of you, the amount of money you would be willing to lend, the number of favors you would do before having a favor repaid? Many transactions may transpire between friends that could encroach on your limits. Everyone's experiences in prior uncomfortable situations vary in nature and degree. Use prior experiences and current concerns to shape the rules that govern just how far you are willing go to accommodate a friend who is treading too close to your personal boundaries.

BALANCING ACT

Friendships should be mutually satisfying to be enduring. However, if you spend more time meeting your friend's needs than she spends meeting yours, it is likely that the imbalance will eventually negatively affect the relationship. One of the top rules of friendship, addressed earlier in chapter 8, is that favors should be repaid in a timely manner, with neither friend having to mention the debt of the other. Beyond favors, other commitments and resources need to be balanced over the course of the relationship. While every friend is unique and you likely do not expect an identical investment in a friendship from one friend as you do from another, the need for balance in the give-and-take is essential.

If you feel like a friendship is currently a little bit wobbly on the tightrope, you may want to complete the following exercise. It can help you determine if you have a rule already in place that needs acknowledging and solidifying. Take a moment to list the things that you do for this friend (using the model in figure 18.6). You may have more than five items to list, so you will want to use your own blank sheet of paper. Next, on a subjective scale of 1–10, rate the level of "discomfort" or "burden" you feel in doing each favor or obligation to your friend. For instance, you may volunteer to babysit her children once a week for a few hours. You might rate that as a 2 on the 1–10 scale, if you have children the same age as hers, they are good playmates, and they keep your own children occupied for a while. If you don't have children and you have to baby-proof your home and remember to purchase special snacks, this weekly favor may be something more like an 8 on the 1–10 scale for you. If she gives you a ride to work every day, but you live in the same apartment building and you cover more than half the gas money each week, you might rate this favor she provides you as a 1 for your friend. If you live ten miles out of her way, she is a night owl, and she dislikes having to get up twenty minutes early each morning to pick you up to make it to work on time, this might weigh her down at a 10. Bear in mind, of course, that you are only guessing at how another measures the subjective discomfort or commitment. However, if you believe there is a definite imbalance, this exercise can provide you with a concrete list of talking points to begin a conversation about the friendship.

As you reflect on your assessment of the balance in the relationship, you may recognize that you already know where your personal "balance rule" stands. Having a visual or a list may help those who are trying to determine if something about the relationship just seems a little off. In life, seldom is any relationship consistently at a true balance point. Sometimes we are a little needier than we are at others. If the imbalance, however, has left you feeling like you are keeping your friend afloat, articulating a personal friendship rule will allow you to determine how to proceed with this relationship and be more proactive in future relationships when the weight of a friendship starts to feel a bit too heavy.

ECHO OR SILENCE?

When you call for assistance, are you met with a resounding "I'm there!" or are you put off with an "Umm . . . let me check my calendar"? When

What I Carry for my Friend:

What it Weighs:

(On a Subjective Scale of 1-10)

_____   _____

_____   _____

_____   _____

_____   _____

_____   _____

Total Weight: _____

What My Friend Carries for Me:

What it Weighs:

(On a Subjective Scale of 1-10)

_____   _____

_____   _____

_____   _____

_____   _____

_____   _____

Total Weight: _____

What She Carries for Me

What I Carry for Her

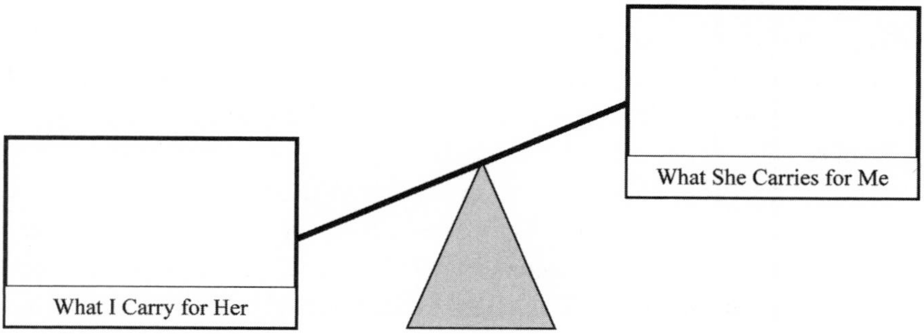

Figure 18.6.   Balancing Act

something good happens in your life and you call up your friends to join you for a "happy me" party, do they pick up or pass on the call? If something falls through on you—the job went to someone else, the biopsy came back positive, or the relationship is over—and you send out an

SOS, do the troops rush in, or do you feel as if you are flying a white flag of surrender, all alone?

Today many people use social media to spread news and personal updates. Some women we spoke with noted that the online response—likes or comments—were a measure of how deeply their friends cared for them. It is likely that you have friends who are constantly bombarding social media with updates about their progress in life, happy or not so happy. As a good friend, you may respond by clicking "Like," posting "Congrats" or "I'm there for you," and so on. However, if your friend is noticeably absent from these activities on your own page, this may be a warning that the friendship is less mutual than assumed if you both are active users of the site. As a reminder, however, not everyone is a Facebook fan, LinkedIn lover, or frequent user. Therefore, bear in mind that Facebook responses are not the best measure of the value of every friendship. Look to other means to assess friends' willingness to engage and be present in the relationship if they seldom check in to the social network sites.

While some women may continue reaching out to their friends, some women consider a persistent silence or consistent offering of regrets to invitations as an indication of a faltering friendship. Are there rules you need to have in place to protect yourself from allowing others to make you feel rejected through their lack of availability or show of interest in your life? One interviewee, Dana, shared that she enforced a "three strikes and you're out" rule. Dana stated that the third time a friend refuses an invitation or cancels out of a meeting, she takes her off the roster and waits for the friend to contact her if the friendship is going to continue.

When you experience an event that encourages you to call a friend to share the news about it, empathy is one of the things you are most likely seeking. When you need to complain about a bad day, a good friend may echo back an empathic acknowledgment of your feelings. A toxic friend might respond with silence, rather than an echo, or immediately say, "Yeah, I hear you. But let me tell you what happened to me today." Creating a personal rule regarding friends' availability and responsiveness may help you determine if friends are worth their place in your life or if their silence and distance warrant a decision to exit the relationship.

RECIPROCITY REVIEW

Beyond the exercises listed in this chapter, there are several other ways to reflect and review the status of your friendships. Journaling is one of the most accessible and satisfying activities for this purpose. Half a century ago, writing in a pastel-colored, locking diary was the common method of journaling for adolescents and even young adults. Now, social media and blogs provide new means for tracking your experiences and reactions in life. However, the value of the journaling process has not diminished with time. In fact, having a set space and time to allow yourself the luxury of logging your experiences and reflecting on your life can be even more valuable today, as technology and on-demand entertainment and communications negatively affect our powers and moments of self-reflection for self-knowing.

If you do not already have a journal, you can use a spiral notebook, a blank piece of copy paper, the back of an envelope, or whatever scrap of paper you can find. However, you may want to purchase something designed for just this purpose. If you are totally averse to the process of handwriting your thoughts and feelings on paper, creating an electronic journal is also a possibility, but handwriting is often considered the most effective way of connecting your words to your heart.

LETTING GO WITH GRATITUDE

Some of the most common journal prompts include the gratitude list. To create a gratitude list, you write down all of the things in your life for which you are grateful; the list might include the people you appreciate (e.g., family, romantic partners, friends, and teachers/mentors), skills you possess, positive circumstances in your life, pets, and so on. This is a useful tool for working with feelings of depression, dissatisfaction, or envy, or when facing an unpleasant transition.

Gratitude lists can be helpful when you are ending a relationship. If you are moving toward the end of a friendship or if you are trying to work through an ugly ending of a relationship, you can create a journal entry that is focused on the positive aspects or learning experiences that arose out of the relationship. Even when a relationship has run its course, chewed you up, and spat you out, there are still possibilities for positive lessons from the experience. In friendships, as in all relationships, some benefit is derived from even negative interactions. By exploring and deconstructing the satisfaction and attraction found in these toxic relationships, you will better know what your personal needs were that were met in such a difficult situation.

For instance, social acceptance by others can sometimes be so valued that we allow ourselves to experience significant humiliation and pain. Whether you are pledging a sorority in college or being assigned the most menial tasks in an elite civic organization, you may be willing to pay institutionalized "personal dues" for acceptance in the group. In one-on-one relationships, you may allow yourself to be treated poorly, just for the crumbs of friendship that are offered. While these are somewhat extreme examples, when you feel yourself on the losing end of a friendship and resentment is building toward the toxic friend—and perhaps toward yourself for allowing the relationship to go too far—it is a good time to engage in a gratitude review.

1. Label the journal page "Gratitude for (Friend's Name)."
2. Write the following prompt: "I am grateful for the experience of this relationship because I learned that I enjoy the following activities."
3. List the new things you learned you enjoyed as a by-product of this friendship. These can include new experiences you had. For instance, did you try new activities because of the friendship, such as karaoke singing or swing dancing or hang gliding or preparing Vietnamese fusion cuisine? Did you explore a new part of town? Did you meet over a classroom project and discover how much you loved saltwater marine biology? List all of the new experiences that you had and found to be pleasurable.
4. Write the prompt "I am grateful for the experience of this relationship because I learned that I do not enjoy the following activities."
5. You may list things such as having learned that you actually do *not* like singing karaoke or dining on Vietnamese cuisine.
6. Write the prompt "I am grateful for this relationship because it taught me that I do not like being treated in the following manner."
7. List the negative experiences within this friendship that have created disappointment, unhappiness, or other negative emotions and responses. This list may include such things as "I learned that I do

not like being stood up by a friend because she gets a better offer." Or "I learned that I do not like being around a friend who brags about her accomplishments but couldn't care less if I won the Nobel Peace Prize."

8. Write the prompt "I am grateful for this relationship because it taught me that I expect the following behaviors from true friends."

9. This list is actually part of your own personal set of "friendship rules." These are the rules that this friendship has taught you to value among those you hold most dear. By creating a list of expectations, you will be more consciously aware of what you need from a friendship. Unless we know what we are seeking in a relationship, we will have difficulty determining whether the relationship is a good fit.

CONTRACTING WITH YOURSELF

These activities can help you determine exactly what you need and what you do *not* need in a friendship. While ten basic, universally endorsed rules for friendships were addressed in individual chapters in this book, the exercises above guide you through the process of creating your own personal set of friendship rules. Writing these down by hand in a journal will help you fully connect to them and affirm them. Typing them up, printing them out, and posting the list on your bathroom mirror or your refrigerator—or, in some cases, even framing them and hanging them on your wall—will help you keep your "code of friendship ethics" in mind. If you have suffered from more than one breach of friendship ethics in recent times, this may be what is needed to help you avoid similar future toxic friendships.

The most effective relationship rules and the ones that will be most effective in shaping future relationships are those that are born out of your own experiences and self-knowing. Each of us will have unique limits, tolerance levels, and friendship flashpoints. This makes it essential that you create and adhere to your own personal friendship code or relationship contract. While you cannot control the behavior of others, sticking to the contract you make with yourself will produce shifts in relationships that continued inaction simply cannot generate.

YOUR PERSONAL PLAYBOOK

In this chapter, several exercises have been presented to help you determine the rules you would prefer your relationships to follow. First, methods of determining the traits and values you most need in a friend were presented as a way to lay out your ground rules for friendships. These should be the foundational playbook for any future friendship you pursue, as well as the litmus test for any current friendship that is a source of discomfort or significant dissatisfaction. Also presented were a variety of activities that can be used to explore specific relationships that may need additional nurturing, reworking, or terminating. There is great value in developing a diverse friendscape, but this requires attentive maintenance to each of your relationships. Very few enduring friendships are ever totally conflict free. Therefore, if you can step back and assess the incident, the relationship, and the potential long-term effect of the current conflict, you will be able to more intentionally shape the friendscape you desire.

19

TAKING STOCK AND LETTING GO

Everyone has a different breaking point in their relationships. Some of us will tolerate a great deal more pain for a lot longer than others might choose to endure. Some might inflict a great deal more heartache on friends than others might choose to dish out. As noted throughout this book, friendships are social exchanges, and the currency values fluctuate depending on the overall stability and alternative resources of each member of the relationship. It is likely that you have known someone, if not yourself, who made a romantic match with someone whose temperament or personality seemed so different that the relationship defied logic. This match may last a lifetime or just until the thrill is gone in a week, a month, or a year. Sometimes friendships defy logic as well, and these relationships can be as difficult to comprehend or disentangle as some love matches can be.

MAKING THE CHOICE: STAY OR GO

In the previous two chapters, we explored personality traits that contribute to healthy friendships as well as provided opportunities for self-exploration and self-assessment of the expectations you hold regarding friendship behavior. Hopefully, you have greater clarity about the resources you bring and those you need others to bring for friendships to be sufficiently satisfying. If you completed the exercises, you will have created a framework for interactions that could be considered akin to a code of ethics for friendships. This may help you assess where problems truly lie in relationships that you find less than ideally satisfying. And if you are facing a crossroads in a relationship, you will need to determine if the next step is to correct or conclude its progress. It is essential to commit fully to whatever course of action you take; it is not always as easy to repair or end a relationship as we might hope.

Working It Out

Investing energy in cleaning up a toxic situation may be the best choice if you still value the friendship and the current circumstances are the exception, not the norm. If you believe your own behavior is detrimental to the friendship, changing the way you behave or engage with your friend is the first step in relationship repair. In addition to shifting the interactions, it is important to openly address any relationship concerns with your friend. Perhaps you have been dealing with difficult issues unrelated to the relationship but have allowed these to bleed over into the friendship. Perhaps your behaviors or words have been misunderstood. Perhaps you have simply been a poor friend. While it can be difficult to have an honest conversation about your own shortcomings, this is essential to putting the relationship to rights.

If you are confident that your friend is at fault but feel committed to working through this current issue, tread carefully as you approach the matter. While your friend may hold the responsibility for the conflict, it is counterproductive to play the "shame and blame" game. Anger (even righteous anger), accusations, and blaming will not improve your relationship. Taking ownership of your own feelings, however, can be helpful. Communicating with "I" statements, a practice long taught in couples' communications workshops, is a more effective method of getting your point across.[1] And your point should be that you are in distress and the friendship needs attention. For example, if a friend did not text back when you invited her to get together:

- Do say "I did not hear back from you yesterday when I texted you. I miss you! Can we get together sometime soon?"
- If the friend has been ignoring texts/calls for longer than a day or two, you might say something like "Hey, I am concerned about you

and our friendship. It has been too long since we got together—let's get together and catch up."
- Do not say "You really ticked me off when you blew me off yesterday. You are so toxic."

As has been suggested in earlier chapters, speaking in a way that your friend can hear your message is essential to effective communication. To rebuild a bridge within the friendship, be sure to choose words that support this intention. Do not resort to passive aggression in your communication, such as "I know you probably don't realize how mean you can be, but I am willing to forget what happened last month . . ." Choosing a neutral place to have this discussion can be helpful, as can avoiding any unnecessary distractions. For starters, these might include not having your children present, not meeting up where alcoholic beverages are served, and not choosing a place where conversations are easily overheard.

Even more important, perhaps, is how you handle communication *after* the discussion. As many women know, the awkwardness that can show up between friends *after* this type of conversation is most difficult to navigate. If you are the initiator of the conversation, it can be as uncomfortable for you at your next meet-up with your friend as it can be for the friend who received your feedback. This is totally normal. By laying the groundwork during the initial discussion, you may be able to proactively deal with the situation.

After opening up and sharing your concerns about the friendship and providing your friend the opportunity to share her own perspectives, you will want to plan for future emotional responses at your next meeting. Even sharing with your friend something like "Don't you hate it when you have a fight with your boyfriend/mother/girlfriend/significant person and even though you both cleared the air, it still feels uncomfortable around them for a while? Lucky we are friends and that makes it easier to cut each other some slack!" can help. This will not necessarily prevent the discomfort, but you and your friend have both acknowledged it might show. This prior conversation may pave the way for you both to joke about it or admit you feel it when you next meet. Saying something like "Well, we knew it might be awkward, didn't we? We need a 'Thelma and Louise' moment right about now, don't we?" might ease the tension when you are next in each other's company.

In counseling, often what a client or family refuses to name creates the greatest obstacle to healthy functioning. By naming the invisible barrier between you and your friend, you gain the upper hand in overcoming it. An extra measure of friendship protection might be to make plans to do something you both enjoy as soon as schedules permit. One woman shared that when she and a good friend had a falling out, they quickly held a feedback session, and when the awkwardness lingered after their meeting, she picked up the phone, called her friend, and started the conversation with the question, "Can we just kiss and make up? I miss you!" Her honesty and clear appreciation for the friendship won over the friend, and they immediately set up a football tailgate get-together for their families for the coming Sunday. This acknowledgment of the discomfort and the desire to get things back on track can be highly effective in soothing lingering feelings of anger or hurt associated with friendship conflicts.

In summary, while it is not necessarily easy to initiate these types of feedback conversations with friends, openness and honesty are key components of being a good friend. If you are willing to fight for the friendship, it is essential that you bring your own "best self" to the relationship. Unfortunately, even your best intentions may not be enough to improve your relationship. One woman summed up her experiences in working to save relationships: "I did fight for each of those friendships for as long as I could, and tried to work things out . . . but, in the end, none of them wanted what I had to offer, so all I could do then was leave each one." If you have reached the point where you know you are ready to let go of the relationship, the following information may help you plan for and achieve as healthy a break as possible.

TRUTHS ABOUT (EVEN NECESSARY) FRIENDSHIP BREAKUPS

1. Breaking up a toxic friendship is not always easy to do

There is a classic, golden-oldies record called "Breaking Up Is Hard to Do."[2] The song's title conveys the difficulty that can accompany the effort required to end a relationship. No matter how confident you are that it is time for a friendship to end, a fair amount of pain can be associated with the process of cutting yourself loose from a friend.

Counselors, therapists, and just about anyone else knows that the hardest thing in this world for people to do is change.[3] Most everyone appreciates the familiar—whether it is seeing the same people on the train each day, enjoying a cup of coffee every day at the same time and in the same place, or coming home each day to the routine welcome of our pets, our kids, or our families. We take comfort in what we know and have a sense of hesitation or anxiety about what we do not yet know. Who is not familiar with butterflies in the stomach the first day of school or on a new job, before a blind date, or before a wedding? Even positive changes can provoke anxiety, and for most of us, dealing with anxiety is difficult.

Extenuating Circumstances

For some women, physical safety may be the concern that produces the greatest anxiety at the end of a relationship, as unfortunate as this is. Some toxic friends are also thoroughly toxic people who take satisfaction in having power over others. Other individuals wrestle with unmanaged emotional and mental disorders and may wreak havoc on your physical and emotional well-being. We heard more than a few stories about past friends who lashed out through threats, vandalism/property damage, stalking-like behaviors, and attempts to sabotage other relationships or professional success. In cases like these, you may need to involve other friends in the relationship breakup if they are at risk, too. You may also need to involve law enforcement agencies, if there is a risk for harm. We heard stories from a large number of women who did not realize just how dangerous or mentally ill their friends were until they tried to sever their ties. As one woman related regarding the termination of a friendship, "When the ex-friend threatened me with violence, I filed a police report. You need to protect yourself. . . . You really need to protect yourself." Do what is necessary to keep yourself and those about whom you care from harm's way.

2. It can hurt when the friendship is ended—a lot

While many of us may be extremely relieved to see a friendship take its last gasp, some may feel acute pain when we end a friendship that we know has run its course. As one woman shared, "The decision to end the friendship was like a death that I mourned for months. I still miss her, but know a true best friend wouldn't hurt me that way." True friends should keep one another's best interests at heart, and when you sever the friendship—no matter how well grounded the reason for this may be—not only has a friend been lost, but your own assumptions about this person and beliefs about the future relationship have been lost as well. If a friend has humiliated you, let you down, or damaged the relationship in some other way, not only might you be reeling from the loss of a friend, but some of us also suffer the pain of knowing that we let ourselves be hurt and that our assumptions about the relationship have been compromised. Both of these latter beliefs can be particularly painful, as they reflect our own mistaken ideas. In addition, if the friend has been cut out of a group of friends, her absence may be noticed and keenly felt, even if it is only because the evening is less drama-filled or more tranquil for all. It can be helpful to know that pain sometimes accompanies even necessary break-ups and emotional gains.

Women are born and raised to tend and befriend[4] as a survival mechanism, and when you are unable to maintain a friendship, you may feel disappointed in yourself, not just your toxic friend. Some women believe they should be the consummate peacekeepers, friend makers, and diplomats within their social networks. If they can't keep a relationship on track, even if the other friend is to blame, they perceive it as a personal failure. When a woman has few friends or only a single friend, this loss can represent a virtual shutdown of her entire support system. This may lead to a knee-jerk response, and she may rush to build friendships that turn out to be ill fated; if you recognize yourself in this situation, remember that being a friend to yourself first is an essential prerequisite to establishing healthy friendships with others. "Rebound friendships" may be every bit as risky in the long term as "rebound romances." Stick to your personal expectations about a potential friend's traits and values before investing too much into a new relationship.

3. Mutual friends may be lost in the breakup

Just as it can happen when a marriage or romantic relationship is dissolved, a broken friendship may also cause "collateral damage" within intersecting friendscapes. This can be especially difficult when the sacrifice of a toxic friend leads to the loss of a mutual friend that you had cherished as a companion and a confidante. When friendships or romantic relationships fall apart, one of many women's first instincts is to find a sympathetic ear. When a former confidante shows allegiance to the friend with whom you've fallen out, it can lead to a double dose of emotional fallout. You may be angry at the friend whose behavior led to the breakup and sad and confused that another friend sided with her over you.

Being aware of and planning for the potential rifts in your social circle may help you better handle any friendscape mutinies. The first step is figuring out which friendships might be affected by this change. Most of us have a sense of the inner allegiances within our friendship groups. It is just human nature that some people are more drawn to others and that some friendships are stronger and more intense than others. Therefore, you will benefit from thinking about which friends might be more sympathetic to your side or your friend's side of the conflict and mentally preparing yourself for their reactions to the event. You may also want to let your friends know what is happening shortly after the friendship breakup. This could be done via phone calls or when you next connect in person; texting and e-mailing leave too much room for misinterpretation. When you share the news, do so diplomatically and with as much consideration of the former friend's reputation as possible. Remember that you are sharing this news with women who consider themselves her friends, too. However, bear in mind that sometimes even preparing for an eventual loss does not necessarily make it totally pain free or allow us to remain unaffected by the loss.

4. You may be lonely for a while once the friendship has ended

When you learn a new sport or physical skill, you often are building up "muscle memory." Thus, when you are on the court, on the track, or in Zumba class, your body "knows" what is coming next, even if your mind is a million miles away. When you have spent years going out for dinner every Thursday night with a friend, on that first Thursday night after the breakup, you may suddenly realize that your body is still moving toward the train that takes you down to the favorite restaurant where you met up each week. If you do not have a substitute activity already in place, realizing that you will be dining alone may leave you feeling acutely lonely, although you are glad to be free of the toxic relationship. You may try texting other friends to see if someone is available, but that sense of loneliness may linger for a while. This is normal and not necessarily a sign that you made a mistake in breaking off the friendship. However, if the loneliness feels more like the climate than the weather, a distinction described in chapter 6, you may want to speak with a counselor to help you work through this emotional response if it affects your daily functioning. Missing companionship is normal; obsessing or dwelling on your misery is not.

5. As time passes, it will get easier and life will be better

While many might say that time heals all wounds, it is probably more true to say that distance allows us to keep our focus on other, more current concerns and events. Humans are remarkably resilient, and while the longing for a friend's presence may not evaporate completely, it will take up less space in your head and heart with time. When a friendship ends on an unpleasant note, you may experience anger *and* sadness, relief *and* disappointment. Luckily, our hearts and minds can tolerate sensory overload only for a limited period of time, so the red-hot anger will begin to fade and the lingering sadness will recede eventually. However, if you find the anger burning red-hot too long or the thoughts of revenge or retribution growing stronger, this suggests that you might benefit from speaking with a counselor or other helping professional to assist you in handling these unproductive and potentially dangerous feelings.

Termination of a friendship can affect women similarly to how they are affected by someone's death. Your normal pattern of interactions and your support system now have a void where once there was a friend. As this loss becomes the "new normal" and you establish new relationships and shift your friendscape to fill this space, the loss will begin to feel more like your history, not your present.

6. If you have followed the steps in the prior chapter for writing your own friendship rules or code of friendship ethics, your future relationships stand a much stronger chance of *lasting*

Some friendships begin after you have known an acquaintance for quite some time. You may finally strike up a conversation with the person whom you run into every morning at the coffee shop, and a friendship begins to bloom. Or you might be introduced to a new colleague at work and hit it off immediately. No matter how the budding friendship has begun, it is important to move the relationship forward in alignment with your own personal code of friendship ethics. Providing the same level of respectful behavior that you expect from a friend is essential. In addition, being aware of any red flags that pop up early will allow you to identify potential fault lines in the friendship before things go too far. Addressing any concerns early is beneficial in a couple of ways. First, you model the practice of clear and honest communication from the outset, which is necessary for authentic relationships to thrive. Second, you can find out early if this is just a "hiccup" or a full-blown viral threat to the health of the friendship. Correcting the course of the friendship is much easier at the earliest stages than after having allowed poor behaviors to become an accepted norm.

Clearly, ending even a difficult or unsatisfying friendship can create another set of emotional challenges for you. However, freeing yourself from a relationship that is holding you back from enjoying life to the fullest or feeling as good as you can about yourself is well worth the short-term difficulty. In fact, research suggests that relationships that are unsatisfying or marred with unpleasant interactions are worse for your emotional well-being than an absence of friendships.[5] As you begin the process of ending a friendship, the following section provides ideas for making the break as smoothly and compassionately as possible.

SUGGESTIONS FOR THE CLEANEST OUTCOME WHEN LETTING GO

1. Do not let toxic relationships go on for too long

The longer you allow a poor relationship to drag on, the longer your period of suffering will last. This is just a logical truth. In addition, the longer you delay, the more deeply entrenched the two of you become in the unhealthy system. The deeper the hole you dig, the higher you have to climb and the harder you have to work to get out of it. Many women recognize that their kinder, gentler, forgiving natures put them in positions to care too long and hope too optimistically that the toxic friends will change. Additionally, one woman shared her acknowledgment that she might have been much more capable of quickly ending a toxic friend-ship that she allowed to go on too long if she had "more experience, judgment, and better self-esteem." Feeling more confident about the types of friends you want in your life will put you in a position to recognize and terminate unsatisfactory relationships more expediently and more effec-tively. Another woman said that her best advice for ending a toxic rela-tionship was to "check out of new friendships the moment toxic traits begin to appear."

2. Weigh your words carefully

This suggestion is important to follow for a couple of reasons. First, if a friend has shown any evidence of a lack of trustworthiness, then remem-ber that anything you share with her may be shared with others. In the event that your conversation, e-mail, or texts should go public or viral via social media, having been discreet and mature in your communications may save you a lot of headaches down the road. Second, you never know if this current friendship fissure is going to be a temporary break or a permanent solution. The flashpoint issue today may be totally inconse-quential a month or a year from now. Make sure that you say nothing that could jeopardize any rebuilding of the relationship if the opportunity were to present itself in the future.

3. If you will likely still run into her in the neighborhood, at work, on campus, or at the gym, make sure that you end the relationship on as positive a note as possible

Cold glares, pointedly avoiding looking in her direction, or cringing when she unrolls her yoga mat next to yours are more subliminally damaging to you than they might be to her. Save yourself the long-term suffering and include her in your "loving kindness meditation." In this form of medita-tion, you ask for wellness, happiness, and freedom from suffering for yourself, a loved one, a neutral person, and then an enemy.[6] She may need to be acknowledged as the "enemy" at first, if need be, but work to include her as a "neutral person" as soon as you can. If you are not likely to practice meditation, it can be beneficial to your emotional well-being to mentally wish her well or make a list of her past kindnesses to you. Research shows that positive activities, whether making a gratitude list or listing positive qualities, actually protect our mental health.[7] In spite of your good intentions, the relationship may still end in a drama-filled, voices-raised disagreement or all-out fight. If this is how your situation unfolds, it can be especially important to take steps to let go of any anger or strong negative energy that remains. This is about protecting your own emotional well-being and taking away any power you have given your former friend to control your thoughts or feelings.

Many reasons support the value of ending relationships as cleanly and kindly as possible, but perhaps the need to avoid any future or collateral shame might be one of the most personally motivating reasons. In small towns, big cities, campuses, or workplaces, word can travel quickly. Web connections and cell phone towers only expedite the latest gossip's progress between people. Thus, the less fodder you offer others, the more glowing your reputation will remain.

4. Technology issues may need consideration

Facebook, Instagram, Snapchat, and other forms of electronic communication have brought our intimate relationships onto a whole new stage. A few years ago, the number of women who detailed the role that social media played in their friendship breakups would have been significantly lower and more age-specific than it is today. Women all across the life span are now creating Facebook profiles, sending e-mails, and texting friends.

One midlife woman shared that an incident involving social media was the catalyst for ending one of her friendships. She related that "a friend showed me part of a private Facebook message that someone had sent to her and that was the end for me; to me she was no longer a trustworthy person." While this was the case of confidential information being shared with others in an unethical manner, there are also stories in which technology is used to disparage and denigrate friends.

One respondent shared, perhaps unknowingly so ironically, that she was shocked by a former friend who turned to Facebook to belittle some and gather sympathy from others: "She . . . is filling her Facebook page with posts about how ill she is, how some people are just bitter and jealous, and imploring people not to be unkind to others . . . and is racking up love and sympathy comments by the hundred!" Her own comment suggested that the toxic friend had been at least partially successful in drumming up negative feelings and bitterness in this particular friend.

Another woman in her thirties shared that Facebook was the vehicle that led to the breakup of a friendship: "I texted her after being disrespected via Facebook and told her not to talk to me anymore. I wish she'd told me to my face what her problem was. I'm not sure what I would do differently." In listening to her story, there is perhaps more than a little bit of irony in her wish for a face-to-face discussion, as she used a text message to terminate the relationship.

The wide variety of ways that technology can be used to establish or terminate friendships was illustrated in this comment: "I confronted the toxic friend and told her outright how I felt and then I backed off from the friendship 100 percent. On Facebook, I unfriended her. On my cell phone, I spammed her messages." Being unfriended or doing the unfriending can be an effective way to keep yourself from ruminating on the failed relationship. Blocking e-mails, blocking/spamming texts, and unfollowing a friend on Twitter also may facilitate the process of distancing yourself from the relationship. Further, putting distance between you and your former friend in cyberspace can be a proactive move, especially if you are prone to poring over others' updates and profiles and wishing your own life were more exciting.[8] When you make negative comparisons about your own life to those of friends—or worse yet, ex-friends—via Facebook and Twitter feeds, you increase your own risk for depression. Making a clean break is best for your own mental health.

5. Make it about yourself and your needs, not her wrongs

Too often, an individual will rush in and place blame on the friend who had wronged her when she is making the decision to terminate a friendship. Next, the person being blamed will then immediately jump in to defend herself from the verbal assault. A conflict may erupt that can transition quite rapidly from a serious discussion to a flat-out fight when blaming begins. Regardless of who might actually deserve the label of victim or perpetrator, avoid beginning any sentences with "fighting words" such as "You made me . . ." or "You should never have . . ." or "You are such a . . ." and so on. While letting her know what you think may seem like a cleansing and cathartic choice, you are more likely to be setting yourself up for an unexpectedly ugly scene.

Owning your own feelings and taking responsibility for how the relationship has unfolded or unraveled can actually be a much more freeing experience. By stating, "I really felt _____ when _____ happened," you are affirming your own personal reactions and needs. By acknowledging your own feelings, you are recognizing what you do and do not want to experience within a friendship. By describing the action that created the negative feeling, you are acknowledging the behaviors you will need to see as red flags in future relationships. Shaming and blaming may provide a very temporary feeling of victory, but being open and honest about what you will and will not tolerate in relationships will yield a longer-lasting sense of satisfaction.

Unfortunately, no matter how well you work to keep the discussion on an even keel, your friend may choose to escalate the intensity and volume of the interaction. If you feel that things are getting out of hand and your efforts to keep the discussion productive have failed, you may need to diplomatically end the conversation and remove yourself from the scene. Let the person know that you appreciate her feelings, but it is not in anyone's best interest to engage in an unproductive and hurtful exchange. She may not hear the message you are sending, but you will know that you have done the best you can, given the current set of circumstances.

6. Acknowledge the benefits that the relationship has offered over time and express appreciation for the role she has played in your life in the past

After you have owned your feelings and acknowledged to your friend that you feel that the relationship is not working out for you, if there is something positive to share about her or the friendship, offer this information to her. Let her know that you have enjoyed having a gym buddy, or a lunch buddy, or a Saturday-night-no-date buddy, or neighborhood walking buddy, and so on. If she shared taxi rides or carpooled with you, mention these. If she listened to you complain in the past or helped plan your wedding or held your hand as you dealt with the loss of someone you loved, let her know. Most of us want to be let down easy. You can model this kindness and thoughtfulness for your friend, and she may actually learn something about the value of exhibiting the traits of a good friend.

Through your willingness to share what was positive in the relationship with your former friend, you are also sending a message to her about behaviors that others might value in her other relationships. You are also affirming to yourself the behaviors that are of value to you. Friendships are social exchange microsystems, so at some point you received some form of benefit from your original investment in the relationship. If she was just someone to speak to at work, then acknowledge that she helped you feel more comfortable on the job. If she was willing to watch your pets one weekend or water your flowers or accompany you to a wine tasting or book club meeting, acknowledge her past kindness. While this may not be easy, it will leave you feeling so much better about how you chose to manage the breakup.

7. Do not allow yourself to dwell on negative thoughts about revenge or punishment of the former friend

While some people enjoy getting caught up in the conflict at hand and even "wallow" in anger and negativity, this is not the best choice for optimal well-being. If you have been the victim of intentional hurt, offense, or disrespect, it is normal to feel anger and, for some, to desire to see the perpetrator face consequences for her behavior. Obsessing about this desire, however, is extremely detrimental to your own well-being. Researchers have revealed some interesting things about the anticipated joy that is expected to occur through inflicting punishment/revenge on others.[9] It turns out that the pleasure in plotting revenge actually diminishes your psychological well-being, and engaging in punishment is further detrimental to your state of mind. Imagining retribution against your former friend causes you to hold on to negative feelings and engage in rumination much longer than if you just let the transgression go and move on in your life. While forgiveness may be suggested by some as the key to a peaceful heart, not everyone is capable of forgiving those who have hurt them. However, consciously reminding yourself to "let it go" when you find yourself replaying the conflict in your head and actually "letting it go" is an achievable goal. The saying that living well is the best revenge may actually be true. It is important to keep yourself from allowing your former friend to have further control of your thoughts and feelings once the "friendship expiration date," as one respondent termed it, has passed.

MOVING FORWARD

In summary, each of us possesses an individual code of friendship ethics, or set of friendship rules, that reflects what we believe to be honorable behavior between friends. While we may not have conscious awareness of these beliefs, we may be quick to recognize when friends cross our lines of acceptable behavior. In the previous two chapters, we have shared material to help you recognize and clarify your personal expectations regarding healthy and satisfying friendships. While many of us learn through the loss of a relationship just where our boundaries had been drawn, we hope that you feel more prepared to define and defend your boundaries before a toxic friendship has gone too far. In addition, we hope that, as you move forward, you can let go of lingering disappointment and other negative emotions that have resulted from past toxic friendship conflicts. A better use of this energy would be to focus on fortifying your relationships with existing friends and establishing supportive relationships with new friends as you move forward.

We invited women to share the stories of toxic friendships they had experienced as well as the lessons they had learned from these challenging relationships. We will end this book with a concise summary of lessons that were not explicitly highlighted in earlier chapters addressing friendship rules but positively influence the maintenance of strong interpersonal ties. We hope you can integrate these lessons into your own personal code of friendship ethics:

- Communicate openly and honestly to keep the relationship on track.
- Set clear boundaries; these are essential components of any healthy relationship.
- Acknowledge the value of the relationship through word and thoughtful deed.
- Make time to spend one-on-one and face-to-face with your friends.
- If distance keeps you apart, check in with texts or phone calls to stay current.
- Celebrate your friends' successes and help them to recognize their own strengths and accomplishments.
- Expect disagreements to occur on occasion, but do not "go to bed angry."

- Accept that not every friendship is going to last a lifetime and not every friend is going to be a best friend.

Few and far between are the individuals who have not been hurt by someone they considered a friend. Whether the pain inflicted was intentional or inadvertent, the resulting damage can leave a person reeling. Willingness to speak up for your own best interests, address the conflict, and initiate a discussion about the incident will allow you to make a sound decision about the future of the friendship. By determining your boundaries and your personal code of friendship ethics, you will be better prepared to establish and maintain thriving relationships that bring satisfaction and joy. Remember that when you are faced with a friendship that brings pain or displeasure, you should treat yourself with the kindness with which you would treat your good friends. Be willing to take stock, let go, and move on when a relationship has clearly run its course.

NOTES

1. THE NEED FOR COMMUNITY

1. Pew Research Center. (2013). Internet Project Survey, August 7–September 16, 2013.

2. Ibid.

3. The Beatles. (2000). *The Beatles anthology*. San Francisco: Chronicle Books.

4. Baumeister, R. F., & Leary, M. R. (1995). The need to belong: Desire for interpersonal attachments as a fundamental human motivation. *Psychological Bulletin, 117*(3), 497–529.

5. Denissen, J. J. A., Penke, L., Schmitt, D. P., & van Aken, M. A. G. (2008). Self-esteem reactions to social interactions: Evidence for sociometer mechanisms across days, people, and nations. *Personality and Social Psychology, 95*(1), 181–96.

6. Hagemann, J. A. (1986). Confucius say: Naming as social code in ancient China. Paper presented at the 37th Annual Meeting of the Conference on College Composition and Communication, New Orleans, LA, March 13–15, 1986.

7. Wischniewski, J., Windmann, S., Juckel, G., & Brune, M. (2009). Rules of social exchange: Game theory, individual differences and psychopathology. *Neuroscience and Biobehavioral Reviews, 33*(3), 305–13.

8. Blau, P. M. (1964). *Exchange and power in social life*. New York: Wiley.

9. Ibid.

10. Broszormenyi-Nagy, I., & Spark, G. M. (1973). *Invisible loyalties: Reciprocity in intergenerational family therapy*. Hagerstown, MD: Harper & Row.

11. Snyder, R., Shapiro, S., & Treleaven, D. (2012). Attachment theory and mindfulness. *Journal of Child and Family Studies, 21*(5), 709–17.

12. Ainsworth, M. D. S., Blehar, M. C., Waters, E., & Wall, S. (1978). *Patterns of attachment: A psychological study of the strange situation.* Hillsdale, NJ: Erlbaum.

13. Ogden, P., Minton, K., & Pain, C. (2006). *Trauma and the body.* New York: W. W. Norton.

14. Siegel, D., & Solomon, D. (2003). *Healing trauma: Attachment, mind, body, and brain.* New York: Norton Publishing Group.

15. Maner, J. K., DeWall, C. N., Baumeister, R. F., & Schaller, M. (2007). Does social exclusion motivate interpersonal reconnection? Resolving the "porcupine problem." *Journal of Personality and Social Psychology, 92*(1), 42–55.

2. FRIENDSHIP PATTERNS FROM GIRLHOOD THROUGH OLDER ADULTHOOD

1. Letters, *Time*, U.S. edition, September 16, 2000, and Australian edition, October 9, 2000.

2. See Degges-White, S., & Borzumato-Gainey, C. (2011), *Friends forever: How girls and women forge lasting relationships* (Lanham, MD: Rowman & Littlefield), for a detailed exploration of the early social development of young females.

3. Niffenegger, J., & Willer, L. (1998). Friendship behaviors during early childhood and beyond. *Early Childhood Education Journal, 26*, 95–99.

4. Hallman study (as cited in Hartup, W., & Stevens, N. [1997]. Friendship and adaptation in the life course. *Psychological Bulletin, 121*, 355–70).

5. Lindsey, E. W. (2002). Preschool children's friendships and peer acceptance: Links to social competence. *Child Study Journal, 32*, 145–55.

6. Ibid.

7. Castelli, L., Amicis, L., & Sherman, S. (2007). The loyal member effect: On the preference for ingroup members who engage in exclusive relations with the ingroup. *Developmental Psychology, 43*, 1347–59.

8. Reddy, S. (2014). Little children and already acting mean: Children, especially girls, withhold friendship as a weapon. Retrieved June 11, 2014, from http://online.wsj.com/news/articles/SB100014240527023048111904579586331803245244.

9. Shin, H., & Ryan, A. M. (2012). How do young adolescents cope with social problems? An examination of social goals, coping with friends, and social adjustment. *Journal of Early Adolescence, 32*(6), 851–75.

10. U.S. Department of Health and Human Services. (n.d). Age Trends in the Prevalence of Bullying. Retrieved July 1, 2014, from http://www.prevnet.ca/

sites/prevnet.ca/files/fact-sheet/PREVNet-SAMHSA-Factsheet-Age-Trends-in-the-Prevalence-of-Bullying.pdf.

11. Potenza, G. M., Konukman, F., Yu, J., & Gumusdag, H. (2014). Teaching self-defense to middle school students in physical education. *Journal of Physical Education, Recreation, and Dance, 85*(1), 47–50.

12. Ojanen, T., Sijtsema, J. J., Hawley, P. H., & Little, T. D. (2010). Intrinsic and extrinsic motivation in early adolescent friendship development: Friendship selection, influence, and prospective friendship quality. *Journal of Adolescence, 33*(6), 837–51.

13. Jones, R. M., Vaterlaus, J. M., Jackson, M. A., & Morrill, T. B. (2014). Friendship characteristics, psychosocial development, and adolescent identity formation. *Personal Relationships, 21*(1), 51–67.

14. Dijkstra, J., Verhulst, F., Ormel, J., & Veenstra, R. (2009). The relation between popularity and aggressive, destructive, and norm-breaking behaviors: Moderating effects of athletic abilities, physical attractiveness, and prosociality. *Journal of Research on Adolescence, 19*, 401–13.

15. Ojanen et al. (2010).

16. Richards, T. N., & Branch, K. A. (2012). The relationships between social support and adolescent dating violence: A comparison across genders. *Journal of Interpersonal Violence, 27*(11), 1540–61.

17. Sheehy, S. (2000). *Connecting: The enduring power of female friendships.* New York: William Morrow.

18. Hamilton, B. E., Martin, J. A., & Ventura, S. J. (2013). Preliminary data for 2012. *National Vital Statistics Report, 62*(3). Hyattsville, MD: National Center for Health Statistics.

19. United Nations, Department of Economic and Social Affairs, Population Division (2013). World Fertility Report 2012 (United Nations publication).

20. Taylor, P., Passel, J. S., Wang, W., & Velasco, G. (2011). *For Millennials, parenthood trumps marriage.* Washington, DC: Pew Social and Demographic Trends. Also available at http://www.pewsocialtrends.org/files/2011/03/millennials-marriage.pdf.

21. Ibid.

22. Kim, T. H. M., Connolly, J. A., & Tamim, H. (2014). The effect of social support around pregnancy on postpartum depression among Canadian teen mothers and adult mothers in the maternity experiences survey. *BMC Pregnancy and Childbirth, 14*, 1–15. Negron, R., Martin, A., Almog, M., Balbierz, A., & Howell, E. (2013). Social support during the postpartum period: Mothers' views on needs, expectations, and mobilization of support. *Maternal and Child Health Journal, 17*(4), 616–23.

23. Kawano, S. (2014). A sociocultural analysis of childrearing support for mothers of preschoolers living in Tokyo. *Japan Forum, 26*(1), 46–64.

24. Alles-Jardel, M., Fourdrinier, C., Roux, A., & Schneider, B. H. (2002). Parents' structuring of children's daily lives in relation to the quality and stability of children's friendships. *International Journal of Psychology, 37*(2), 65–73.

25. Stevens, A. (1994). *Jung: A very short introduction*. Oxford: Oxford University Press.

26. See Degges-White, S., & Borzumato-Gainey, C. (2011).

27. Ibid.

28. Birditt, K. S., Antonucci, T. C., & Tighe, L. (2012). Enacted support during stressful life events in middle and older adulthood: An examination of the interpersonal context. *Psychology and Aging, 27*(3), 728–41.

29. Gurung, R. A. R., Taylor, S. E., & Seeman, T. E. (2003). Accounting for changes in social support among married older adults: Insights from the MacArthur Studies of Successful Aging. *Psychology and Aging, 18*, 487–96.

30. Antonucci, T. C., Lansford, J. E., & Akiyama, H. (2001). Impact of positive and negative aspects of marital relationships and friendships on well-being of older adults. *Applied Developmental Science, 5*, 68–75.

31. Pew Research Center. (September 2013). *Social networking fact sheet*. Retrieved July 14, 2014, from http://www.pewinternet.org/fact-sheets/social-networking-fact-sheet/.

32. Arling, G. (1976). The elderly widow and her family, neighbors and friends. *Journal of Marriage and the Family, 38*, 757–68.

33. Matthews, S. (1986). *Friendships through the life course*. Beverly Hills, CA: Sage.

34. James, W. B., Witte, J. E., & Galbraith, M. W. (2006). Havighurst's social roles revisited. *Journal of Adult Development, 13*, 52–60.

35. Argyle, M., & Henderson, M. (1984). The rules of friendships. *Journal of Social and Personal Relationships, 1*, 211–37.

36. Argyle & Henderson as cited in Samter, W., & Cupach, W. R. (1998). Friendly fire: Topical variations in conflict among same- and cross-sex friends. *Communication Studies, 49*, 121–38.

3. IT'S A MATTER OF TRUST

1. Blieszner, R. (2014). The worth of friendship: Can friends keep us happy and healthy? *Generations, 38*(1), 24–30.

2. Blair, B. L., Perry, N. B., O'Brien, M., Calkins, S. D., Keane, S. P., & Shanahan, L. (2014). The indirect effects of maternal emotion socialization on friendship quality in middle childhood. *Developmental Psychology, 50*(2), 566–76.

3. Bigelow, B. J. (1977). Children's friendship expectations: A cognitive-developmental study. *Child Development, 48,* 246–53.

4. Schwarzwald, J., Moisseiv, O., & Hoffman, M. (1986). Similarity versus social ambition effects in the assessment of interpersonal acceptance in the classroom. *Journal of Educational Psychology, 78*(3), 184–89.

5. Morry, M. M. (2005). Allocentrism and friendship satisfaction: The mediating roles of disclosure and closeness. *Canadian Journal of Behavioural Science, 37*(3), 211–22.

6. Strohmaier, H., Murphy, M., & DeMatteo, D. (2014). Youth sexting: Prevalence rates, driving motivations, and the deterrent effect of legal consequences. *Sexuality Research and Social Policy: A Journal of the NSRC,* June 2014, no pagination specified. doi:10.1007/s13178-014-0162-9.

7. Ibid.

8. Flashman, J., & Gambetta, D. (2014). Thick as thieves: Homophily and trust among deviants. *Rationality and Society, 26*(1), 3–45.

9. Spock, B., & Rothenberg, M. B. (1992). *Dr. Spock's baby and child care* (7th ed.). New York: Simon & Schuster.

10. Roberto, K. A. (1996). Friendships between older women: Interactions and reactions. *Journal of Women and Aging, 8*(3–4), 55–73.

11. Blieszner (2014).

4. JUST THE WAY YOU ARE

1. Rogers, C. R. (1957). The necessary and sufficient conditions of therapeutic personality change. *Journal of Consulting Psychology, 21,* 95–103.

2. Taylor, Z. E., Eisenberg, N., Spinrad, T. L., Eggum, N. D., & Sulik, M. J. (2013). The relations of ego-resiliency and emotion socialization to the development of empathy and prosocial behavior across early childhood. *Emotion, 13*(5), 822–31.

3. Van Lissa, C. J., Hawk, S. T., de Wied, M., Koot, H. M., & van Lier, P., et al. (2014). The longitudinal interplay of affective and cognitive empathy within and between adolescents and mothers. *Developmental Psychology, 50*(4), 1219–25.

4. Lemay, E. P., & Clark, M. S. (2008). "Walking on eggshells": How expressing relationship insecurities perpetuates them. *Journal of Personality and Social Psychology, 95*(2), 420–41.

5. Smithyman, T. F., Fireman, G. D., & Asher, Y. (2014). Long-term psychosocial consequences of peer victimization: From elementary to high school. *School Psychology Quarterly, 29*(1), 64–76.

6. Bauman, S., & Newman, M. L. (2013). Testing assumptions about cyberbullying: Perceived distress associated with acts of conventional and cyberbullying. *Psychology of Violence, 3*(1), 27–38.

7. Shrum, W., & Cheek, N. H. (1987). Social structure during the school years: Onset of the degrouping process. *American Sociological Review, 52*(2), 218–23.

5. ANY FRIEND OF HERS
IS A FRIEND OF MINE

1. Feld, S. L. (1991). Why your friends have more friends than you do. *American Journal of Sociology, 96*(6), 1464–77.

2. Hodas, N. O., Kooti, F., & Lerman, K. (2013). Friendship paradox redux: Your friends are more interesting than you. *ICWSM, 13*, 8–10.

3. Selfhout, M., Denissen, J., Branje, S., & Meeus, W. (2009). In the eye of the beholder: Perceived, actual, and peer-related similarity in personality, communication, and friendship intensity during the acquaintanceship process. *Journal of Personality and Social Psychology, 96*(6), 1152–65.

4. Ibid.

5. Goel, S., Mason, W., & Watts, D. J. (2010). Real and perceived attitude agreement in social networks. *Journal of Personality and Social Psychology, 99*(4), 611–21.

6. Degges-White, S., & Borzumato-Gainey, C. (2014). *Mothers and daughters: Living, loving, and learning over a lifetime.* Lanham, MD: Rowman & Littlefield.

7. Schaefer, D. R., Simpkins, S. D., Vest, A. E., & Price, C. D. (2011). The contribution of extracurricular activities to adolescent friendships: New insights through social network analysis. *Developmental Psychology, 47*(4), 1141–52.

8. Antonucci, T. C., Lansford, J. E., & Akiyama, H. (2001). Impact of positive and negative aspects of marital relationships and friendships on well-being of older adults. *Applied Developmental Science, 5*, 68–75.

6. BEING THERE WITH
EMOTIONAL SUPPORT

1. Rose, A. J., Carlson, W., & Waller, E. M. (2007). Prospective associations of co-rumination with friendship and emotional adjustment: Considering the so-

cioemotional trade-offs of co-rumination. *Developmental Psychology, 43*(4), 1019–31.

2. Stone, L. B., Hankin, B. L., Gibb, B. E., & Abela, J. R. Z. (2011). Co-rumination predicts the onset of depressive disorders during adolescence. *Journal of Abnormal Psychology, 120*(3), 752–57.

3. Rose, A. J., Schwartz-Mette, R. A., Glick, G. C., Smith, R. L., & Luebbe, A. M. (2014). An observational study of co-rumination in adolescent friendships. *Developmental Psychology, 50*(9), 2199–2209.

4. Copen, C. E., Daniels, K., & Mosher, W. D. (2013). First premarital cohabitation in the United States: 2006–2010 National Survey of Family Growth. National health statistics reports, no. 64. Hyattsville, MD: National Center for Health Statistics.

5. Kreider, R. M., & Ellis, R. (2011). Number, Timing, and Duration of Marriages and Divorces: 2009. Current Population Reports, P70-125, U.S. Census Bureau, Washington, DC.

6. Davila, J., & Kashy, D. A. (2009). Secure base processes in couples: Daily associations between support experiences and attachment security. *Journal of Family Psychology, 23*, 76–88. doi:10.1037/a0014353.

7. Jones, E. E., & Harris, V. A. (1967). The attribution of attitudes. *Journal of Experimental Social Psychology, 3*, 1–24. doi:10.1016/0022-1031(67)90034-0. Sullivan, K. T., & Davila, J. (2014). The problem is my partner: Treating couples when one partner wants the other to change. *Journal of Psychotherapy Integration, 24*(1), 1–12.

8. Robbins, M. L., Focella, E. S., Kasle, S., Lopez, A. M., & Weihs, K. L. (2011). Naturalistically observed swearing, emotional support, and depressive symptoms in women coping with illness. *Health Psychology, 30*(6), 789–92.

7. A FRIEND IN NEED

1. Reddy, S. (2014). Little children and already acting mean: Children, especially girls, withhold friendship as a weapon. Retrieved June 11, 2014, from http://online.wsj.com/news/articles/SB10001424052702304811190457958633 1803245244.

2. Wiseman, R. (2002). *Queen bees and wannabees: Helping your daughter survive cliques, gossip, boyfriends and other realities of adolescence.* New York: Three Rivers Press.

3. Erikson, E. (1959). *Identity and the life cycle.* New York: International Universities Press.

4. Rubia, K. (2013). Functional brain imaging across development. *European Child and Adolescent Psychiatry, 22*, 719–31.

5. Clarke, S. A., Booth, L., Velikova, G., et al. (2006). Social support: Gender differences in cancer patients in the United Kingdom. *Cancer Nursing, 29*, 66–72.

6. Friedman, L. C., Baer, P. E., Nelson, D. V., et al. (1988). Women with breast cancer: Perception of family functioning and adjustment to illness. *Psychosomatic Medicine, 50*, 529–40.

7. Lauer, C. S. (2007). A friend in need: Character counts when someone near and dear is ill. *Modern Healthcare, 37*(48), 37.

8. KEEP THE "FRIENDSHIP FAVORS" BALANCE IN CHECK

1. Le, B. M., Impett, E. A., Kogan, A., Webster, G. D., & Cheng, C. (2013). The personal and interpersonal rewards of communal orientation. *Journal of Social and Personal Relationships, 30*(6), 694–710.

2. Miller, J. G., Bland, C., Kaillberg-Shroff, M., et al. (2014). Culture and role of exchange vs. communal norms in friendship. *Journal of Experimental Social Psychology, 53*, 79–93.

3. Fiske, A. P. (1992). The four elementary forms of sociality: Framework for a unified theory of social relations. *Psychology Review, 99*(4), 689–723.

4. Hartup, W. W., & Stevens, N. (1997). Friendships and adaptation in the life course. *Psychological Bulletin, 121*, 355–70.

5. Roberto, K. A. (1996). Friendships between older women: Interactions and reactions. *Journal of Women and Aging, 8*(3–4), 55–73.

6. Ibid.

7. Dew, J., Britt, S., & Huston, S. (2012). Examining the relationship between financial issues and divorce. *Family Relations, 61*(4), 615–28.

8. Dew, J., & Dakin, J. (2011). Financial disagreements and marital conflict tactics. *Journal of Financial Therapy, 2*(1), article 7. http://dx.doi.org/10.4148/jfft.v2i1.1414.

9. DEFENDING YOUR HONOR

1. Theran, S. A. (2010). Authenticity with authority figures and peers: Girls' friendships, self-esteem, and depressive symptomatology. *Journal of Social and Personal Relationships, 27*, 519–34.

2. Taylor, M., Carlson, S. M., Maring, B. L., Gerow, L., & Charley, C. M. (2004). The characteristics and correlates of fantasy in school-age children:

Imaginary companions, impersonation, and social understanding. *Developmental Psychology, 40*(6), 1173–87.

3. Dunbar, R. I. M. (2004). Gossip in evolutionary perspective. *Review of General Psychology, 8*(2), 100–110.

4. Kuttler, A. F., Parker, J. G., & La Greca, A. M. (2002). Developmental and gender differences in preadolescents' judgments of the veracity of gossip. *Merrill-Palmer Quarterly, 48,* 105–32.

5. Spears, B., Slee, P., Owens, L., & Johnson, B. (2009). Behind the scenes and screens: Insights into the human dimension of covert and cyberbullying. *Journal of Psychology, 217*(4), 189–96.

6. Talwar, V., Gomez-Garibello, C., & Shariff, S. (2014). Adolescents' moral evaluations and ratings of cyberbullying: The effect of veracity and intentionality behind the event. *Computers in Human Behavior, 36,* 122–28.

7. Shrum, W., & Cheek, N. H. (1987). Social structure during the school years: Onset of the degrouping process. *American Sociological Review, 52*(2), 218–23.

8. Taylor, S. E., Klein, L. C., Lewis, B. P., Gruenwald, T. L., Gurung, R. A. R., et al. (2000). Biobehavioral responses to stress in females: Tend-and-befriend, not fight-or-flight. *Psychological Review, 107*(3), 411–29.

9. Ibid.

10. Feinberg, M., Willer, R., Stellar, J., & Keltner, D. (2012). The virtues of gossip: Reputational information sharing as prosocial behavior. *Journal of Personality and Social Psychology, 102*(5), 1015–30.

11. Fingerman, K. L., Miller, L., & Charles, S. (2008). Saving the best for last: How adults treat social partners of different ages. *Psychology and Aging, 23*(2), 399–409.

10. BRING JOY TO YOUR FRIENDS

1. Kaniasty, K. (2012). Predicting social psychological well-being following trauma: The role of postdisaster social support. *Psychological Trauma: Theory, Research, Practice, and Policy, 4*(1), 22–33.

2. Lemay, Jr., E. P., Overall, N. C., & Clark, M. S. (2012). Experiences and interpersonal consequences of hurt feelings and anger. *Journal of Personality and Social Psychology, 103*(6), 982–1006. doi: 10.1037/a0030064.

3. Ranney, J. D., & Troop-Gordon, W. (2012). Computer-mediated communication with distant friends: Relations with adjustment during students' first semester in college. *Journal of Education Psychology, 104*(3), 848–61.

4. Jung, C. G. (1938). *Psychology and religion.* Binghamton, NY: Vail-Ballou Press.

I I. CRITICISM IS NOT OKAY

1. Blieszner, R. (2014). The worth of friendship: Can friends keep us happy and healthy? *Generations, 38*(1), 24–30.

2. Blieszner, R., & Roberto, K. A. (2004). Friendship across the life span: Reciprocity in individual and relationship development (pp. 159–82), in Lang, F. R., & Fingerman, K. L. (eds.), *Growing together: Personal relationships across the lifespan.* New York: Cambridge University Press.

3. Piehler, T. F., Veronneau, M. H., & Dishion, T. J. (2012). Substance use progression from adolescence to early adulthood: Effortful control in the context of friendship influence and early-onset use. *Journal of Abnormal Child Psychology, 40*(7), 1045–58.

4. Weaver, J. J., & Ussher, J. M. (1997). How motherhood changes life: A discourse analytic study with mothers of young children. *Journal of Reproductive and Infant Psychology, 15*(1), 51–69.

5. Sneed, R. S., & Cohen, S. (2014). Negative social interactions and incident hypertension among older adults. *Health Psychology, 33*(6), 554–65.

6. Smith, H. M. (2007). Psychological service needs of older women. *Psychological Services, 4*(4), 277–86.

7. Hunter, M. L. (1975). A report on the proceedings of the first and second symposia on education, training, and aging (Springfield, MA, November 1974, and Portland, ME, February 1975). Durham, NH: New England Gerontology Center. Mandell, F., & Jordan, K. (2010). *Becoming a life change artist: 7 creative skills to reinvent yourself at any stage of life.* New York: Penguin.

8. Yalom, I. (2009). *The gift of therapy.* New York: Harper Perennial.

I 2. JEALOUSY IS NOT OKAY

1. Benenson, J., & Heath, A. (2006). Boys withdraw more in one-on-one interactions, whereas girls withdraw more in groups. *Developmental Psychology, 42,* 272–82.

2. Lansford, J., & Parker, J. G. (1999). Children's interactions in friendship triads: Effects of gender and relationship intransitivity. *Developmental Psychology, 35,* 80–93.

3. Parker, J. G., Low, C. M., Walker, A. R., & Gamm, B. K. (2005). Friendship jealousy in young adolescents: Individual differences and links to sex, self-esteem, aggression, and social adjustment. *Developmental Psychology, 41*(1), 235–50.

13. A RULE-BY-RULE GUIDE FOR PARENTS

1. Taylor, Z. E., Eisenberg, N., Spinrad, T. L., Eggum, N. D., & Sulik, M. J. (2013). The relations of ego-resiliency and emotion socialization to the development of empathy and prosocial behavior across early childhood. *Emotion, 13*(5), 822–31.

2. Barry, C. M., & Wentzel, K. R. (2006). Friend influence on prosocial behavior: The role of motivational factors and friendship characteristics. *Developmental Psychology, 42*(1), 153–63.

3. Reddy, S. (2014). Little children and already acting mean: Children, especially girls, withhold friendship as a weapon. Retrieved June 11, 2014, from http://online.wsj.com/news/articles/SB10001424052702304811190457958633 1803245244.

14. SOCCER MOMS AND CARPOOL DIVAS

1. Rosenfeld, A., & Wise, N. (2000). *The overscheduled child: Avoiding the hyper-parenting trap.* New York: St. Martin's Press Griffin.

2. See Luthar, S. S., Shoum, K. A., & Brown, P. J. (2006). Extracurricular involvement among affluent youth: A scapegoat for "ubiquitous achievement pressures"? *Developmental Psychology, 42*(3), 583–97.

3. Fredricks, J. A., & Eccles, J. S. (2006). Is extracurricular participation associated with beneficial outcomes? Concurrent and longitudinal relations. *Developmental Psychology, 42*(4), 698–713.

4. Bachman, J. G., Johnston, L. D., & O'Malley, P. M. *Monitoring the future: A continuing study of American youth* (8th, 10th, and 12th-Grade Surveys), 1976–2011 (computer files). Conducted by University of Michigan, Survey Research Center. ICPSR ed. Ann Arbor, MI: Inter-university Consortium for Political and Social Research (producer and distributor).

5. U.S. Youth Soccer. "Key Statistics." Retrieved July 6, 2014, from http://www.usyouthsoccer.org/media_kit/keystatistics/.

6. Gutierrez, K. D., Izquierdo, C., & Kremer-Sadlik, T. (2010). Middle class working families' beliefs and engagement in children's extra-curricular activities: The social organization of children's futures. *International Journal of Learning, 17*(3), 633–56.

7. Swanson, L. (2009). Complicating the "soccer mom": The cultural politics of forming class-based identity, distinction, and necessity. *Research Quarterly for Exercise and Sport, 80*(2), 345–54.

8. Ibid.

9. Fiore, D. K. (2003). Parental rage and violence in youth sports: How can we prevent soccer moms and hockey dads from interfering in youth sports and causing games to end in fistfights rather than handshakes? *Villanova Sports and Entertainment Law Journal, 10*, 103–30.

10. Public Agenda. (2004). *Teaching interrupted: Do discipline policies in today's public schools foster the common good?* New York: Public Agenda.

11. Thompson, K. A. (2010). *On and off the ice: A case study of the involvement of parents in competitive youth hockey.* UMI Dissertations Publishing.

12. Adler, P. A., & Adler, P. (1984). The carpool: Adjunct to the educational experience. *Sociology of Education, 57*(4), 200–210.

15. CHURCH AND CIVIC GROUP FRIENDS

1. See Krause, N. (2010). Receiving social support at church when stressful life events arise: Do Catholics and Protestants differ? *Psychology of Religion and Spirituality, 2*(4), 234–46.

2. Aknin, L. B., Barrington-Leigh, C. P., Dunn, E. W., et al. (2014). Prosocial spending and well-being: Cross-cultural evidences for a psychological universal. *Journal of Personality and Social Psychology, 104*(4), 635–52.

3. Parks, C. D., & Stone, A. B. (2010). The desire to expel unselfish members from the group. *Journal of Personality and Social Psychology, 99*(2), 303–10.

4. Kahana, E., Ghatta, T., Lovegreen, L., Kahana, B., & Midlarsky, E. (2013). Altruism, helping, and volunteering: Pathways to well-being in late life. *Journal of Aging and Health, 25*(1), 159–87.

5. Jung, C. G. (1938). *Psychology and religion.* Binghamton, NY: Vail-Ballou Press.

16. DOWN THE STREET AND ON THE JOB: GETTING ALONG WITH NEIGHBORS AND COWORKERS

1. Confucius & Waley, A. (1938). *The Analects of Confucius.* New York: Random House.

2. Laertius, D. (2009). *The lives and opinions of eminent philosophers.* Charleston, SC: BiblioBazaar.

3. Prezza, M., Amici, M., Roberti, T., & Tedeschi, G. (2001). Sense of community referred to the whole town: Its relations with neighboring, loneliness,

life satisfaction, and area of residence. *Journal of Community Psychology, 29*(1), 29–52.

4. Maurizi, L. K., Ceballo, R., Epstein-Ngo, Q., & Cortina, K. S. (2013). Does neighborhood belonging matter? Examining school and neighborhood belonging as protective factors for Latino adolescents. *American Journal of Orthopsychiatry, 83*(2, 3), 323–34. Wellman, B., & Wortley, S. (1990). Different strokes from different folks: Community ties and social support. *American Journal of Sociology, 96*(3), 558–88.

5. Ross, C. E., & Jang, S. J. (2000). Neighborhood disorder, fear, and mistrust: The buffering role of social ties with neighbors. *American Journal of Community Psychology, 28*(4), 401–20.

6. U.S. Census Bureau, Current Population Survey, 1975 to 2010 Annual Social and Economic Supplements.

7. Jepsen, D., & Rodwell, J. (2010). A social exchange model of the employment relationship based on keeping tally of the psychological contract. *Employment Relations Record, 10*(2), 20–45.

8. McGrath, D. (2012). Interpersonal contact at work: Consequences for wellbeing. *International Journal of Health, Wellness and Society, 2*(1), 33–47.

9. Blau, P. M. (1964). *Exchange and power in social life.* New York: Wiley.

10. Bolles, W. N. (2014). *What color is your parachute?* New York: Ten Speed Press.

11. Gottlieb, L. (2009). Mean girls at work. *Women's Health, 6*(9), 99–101.

12. Ibid.

13. Greenberg, L., & Barling, J. (1999). Predicting employee aggression against coworkers, subordinates and supervisors: The roles of person behaviors and perceived factors. *Journal of Organizational Behavior, 20*, 897–913.

14. Rutgers University has a website devoted to Crime Prevention Services for Business, and the traits listed were retrieved July 22, 2014, from http://crimeprevention.rutgers.edu/index.htm.

15. Shallcross, L., Sheehan, M., & Ramsay, S. (2008). Workplace mobbing: Experiences in the public sector. *International Journal of Organisational Behaviour, 13*(2), 56–70.

16. McGrath (2012).

17. PLAYING BY THE RULES

1. Argyle, M., & Henderson, M. (1984). The rules of friendships. *Journal of Social and Personal Relationships, 1*, 211–37.

2. Degges-White, S., & Borzumato-Gainey, C. (2011). Understanding who you are as a friend (pp. 143–54), in *Friends forever: How girls and women forge lasting relationships*. Lanham, MD: Rowman & Littlefield.

3. Ibid.

4. Cottrell, C. A., Neuberg, S. L., & Li, N. P. (2007). What do people desire in others? A sociofunctional perspective on the importance of different valued characteristics. *Journal of Personality and Social Psychology, 92*, 208–31.

5. Riedl, R., & Javor, A. (2012). The biology of trust: Integrating evidence from genetics, endocrinology, and functional brain imaging. *Journal of Neuroscience, Psychology, and Economics, 5*(2), 63–91.

6. Nantel-Vivier, A., Kokko, K., Caprara, V., Pastorelli, C., Gerbino, G., Paciello, M., & Tremblay, R. (2009). Prosocial development from childhood to adolescence: A multi-informant perspective with Canadian and Italian longitudinal studies. *Journal of Child Psychology and Psychiatry, 50*, 590–98. doi:10.1111/j.1469-7610.2008.02039.x.

7. Clark, S. S., & Giacomantonio, S. G. (2013). Music preferences and empathy: Toward predicting prosocial behavior. *Psychomusicology: Music, Mind and Brain, 23*(3), 177–86.

8. Cramer, D. (1987). Self-esteem, advice-giving, and the facilitative nature of close personal relationships. *Person-Centered Review, 2*(1), 99–110.

9. Heyman, G. D., Fu, G., & Lee, K. (2008). Reasoning about the disclosure of success and failure to friends among children in the United States and China. *Developmental Psychology, 44*(4), 908–18.

10. Lyubomirsky, S., King, L., & Diener, E. (2005). The benefits of frequent positive affect: Does happiness lead to success? *Psychological Bulletin, 131*, 803–55.

11. Lin, Y., & Forrest, B. (2012). Happiness, fear, and forced struggle (pp. 363–92), in *Systemic structure behind human organizations*. New York: Springer.

12. Myers, D. G. (2000). The funds, friends, and faith of happy people. *American Psychologist, 55*, 56–67.

13. Ko, H-J, & Youn, C-H. (2011). Effects of laughter therapy on depression, cognition, and sleep among community-dwelling elderly. *Geriatrics and Gerontology International, 11*(3), 267–74.

18. WRITING YOUR OWN
RULES OF RELATIONSHIP

1. Glasser, W. (1998). *Choice theory: A new psychology of personal freedom*. New York: HarperCollins.

2. Satir, V. (1988). *The new peoplemaking*. Palo Alto, CA: Science and Behavior Books.

3. Degges-White, S., & Borzumato-Gainey, C. (2011). *Friends forever: How girls and women forge lasting relationships*. Lanham, MD: Rowman & Littlefield.

4. Buss, D. M., Shackelford, T. K., Kirkpatrick, L. A., & Larsen, R. J. (2001). A half century of American mate preferences. *Journal of Marriage and Family, 63*, 491–503. doi:10.1111/j.1741-3737.2001.00491.x. Kuhle, B. X. (2012). It's funny because it's true (Because it evokes our evolved psychology). *Review of General Psychology, 16*(2), 177–86.

5. Schwartz, S. H., & Bilsky, W. (1987). Toward a psychological structure of human values. *Journal of Personality and Social Psychology, 53*(3), 550–62.

19. TAKING STOCK AND LETTING GO

1. Sullivan, K. T., & Davila, J. (2014). The problem is my partner: Treating couples when one partner wants the other to change. *Journal of Psychotherapy Integration, 24*(1), 1–12.

2. Sedaka, N., & Greenfield, H. (1962). Breaking up is hard to do. RCA.

3. Gallagher, P., Fleeson, W., & Hoyle, R. H. (2011). A self-regulatory mechanism for personality trait stability: Contra-trait effort. *Social Psychological and Personality Science, 2*, 335–42. doi:10.1177/1948550610390701.

4. Taylor, S. E., Klein, L. C., Lewis, B. P., Gruenwald, T. L., Gurung, R. A. R., et al. (2000). Biobehavioral responses to stress in females: Tend-and-befriend, not fight-or-flight. *Psychological Review, 107*(3), 411–29.

5. Antonucci, T. C., Lansford, J. E., & Akiyama, H. (2001). Impact of positive and negative aspects of marital relationships and friendships on well-being of older adults. *Applied Developmental Science, 5*, 68–75.

6. Many resources on the Web, such as https://thebuddhistcentre.com/text/loving-kindness-meditation, offer additional information on this form of meditation.

7. Layous, K., Chancellor, J., & Lyubomirsky, S. (2014). Positive activities as protective factors against mental health conditions. *Journal of Abnormal Psychology, 123*(1), 3–12.

8. Feinstein, B. A., Herschenberg, R., Bhatia, V., Latack, J. A., Meuwly, N., & Davila, J. (2013). Negative social comparison on Facebook and depressive symptoms: Rumination as a mechanism. *Psychology of Popular Media Culture, 2*(3), 161–70.

9. Carlsmith, K. M., Wilson, T. D., & Gilbert, D. T. (2008). The paradoxical consequences of revenge. *Journal of Personality and Social Psychology, 95*(6), 1316–24.

BIBLIOGRAPHY

Adler, P. A., & Adler, P. (1984). The carpool: Adjunct to the educational experience. *Sociology of Education, 57*(4), 200–210.

Ainsworth, M. D. S., Blehar, M. C., Waters, E., & Wall, S. (1978). *Patterns of attachment: A psychological study of the strange situation.* Hillsdale, NJ: Erlbaum.

Aknin, L. B., Barrington-Leigh, C. P., Dunn, E. W., et al. (2014). Prosocial spending and well-being: Cross-cultural evidences for a psychological universal. *Journal of Personality and Social Psychology, 104*(4), 635–52.

Alles-Jardel, M., Fourdrinier, C., Roux, A., & Schneider, B. H. (2002). Parents' structuring of children's daily lives in relation to the quality and stability of children's friendships. *International Journal of Psychology, 37*(2), 65–73.

Antonucci, T. C., Lansford, J. E., & Akiyama, H. (2001). Impact of positive and negative aspects of marital relationships and friendships on well-being of older adults. *Applied Developmental Science, 5*, 68–75.

Argyle & Henderson, as cited in Samter, W., & Cupach, W. R. (1998). Friendly fire: Topical variations in conflict among same- and cross-sex friends. *Communication Studies, 49*, 121–38.

Argyle, M., & Henderson, M. (1984). The rules of friendships. *Journal of Social and Personal Relationships, 1*, 211–37.

Arling, G. (1976). The elderly widow and her family, neighbors and friends. *Journal of Marriage and the Family, 38*, 757–68.

Bachman, J. G., Johnston, L. D., & O'Malley, P. M. *Monitoring the future: A continuing study of American youth* (8th, 10th, and 12th-Grade Surveys), 1976–2011 (computer files). Conducted by University of Michigan, Survey Research Center. ICPSR ed. Ann Arbor, MI: Inter-university Consortium for Political and Social Research (producer and distributor).

Barry, C. M., & Wentzel, K. R. (2006). Friend influence on prosocial behavior: The role of motivational factors and friendship characteristics. *Developmental Psychology, 42*(1), 153–63.

Bauman, S., & Newman, M. L. (2013). Testing assumptions about cyberbullying: Perceived distress associated with acts of conventional and cyberbullying. *Psychology of Violence, 3*(1), 27–38.

Baumeister, R. F., & Leary, M. R. (1995). The need to belong: Desire for interpersonal attachments as a fundamental human motivation. *Psychological Bulletin, 117*(3), 497–529.

The Beatles. (2000). *The Beatles anthology.* San Francisco: Chronicle Books. ISBN 0-8118-2684-8.

Benenson, J., & Heath, A. (2006). Boys withdraw more in one-on-one interactions, whereas girls withdraw more in groups. *Developmental Psychology, 42*, 272–82.

Bigelow, B. J. (1977). Children's friendship expectations: A cognitive-developmental study. *Child Development, 48*, 246–53.

Birditt, K. S., Antonucci, T. C., & Tighe, L. (2012). Enacted support during stressful life events in middle and older adulthood: An examination of the interpersonal context. *Psychology and Aging, 27*(3), 728–41.

Blair, B. L., Perry, N. B., O'Brien, M., Calkins, S. D., Keane, S. P., & Shanahan, L. (2014). The indirect effects of maternal emotion socialization on friendship quality in middle childhood. *Developmental Psychology, 50*(2), 566–76.

Blau, P. M. (1964). *Exchange and power in social life.* New York: Wiley.

Blieszner, R. (2014). The worth of friendship: Can friends keep us happy and healthy? *Generations, 38*(1), 24–30.

Blieszner, R., & Roberto, K. A. (2004). Friendship across the life span: Reciprocity in individual and relationship development. In Lang, F. R., & Fingerman, K. L. (eds.), *Growing together: Personal relationships across the lifespan.* New York: Cambridge University Press.

Bolles, W. N. (2014). *What color is your parachute?* New York: Ten Speed Press.

Broszormenyi-Nagy, I., & Spark, G. M. (1973). *Invisible loyalties: Reciprocity in intergenerational family therapy.* Hagerstown, MD: Harper & Row.

Buss, D. M., Shackelford, T. K., Kirkpatrick, L. A., & Larsen, R. J. (2001). A half century of American mate preferences. *Journal of Marriage and Family, 63*, 491–503. doi:10.1111/ j.1741-3737.2001.00491.x.

Carlsmith, K. M., Wilson, T. D., & Gilbert, D. T. (2008). The paradoxical consequences of revenge. *Journal of Personality and Social Psychology, 95*(6), 1316–24.

Castelli, L., Amicis, L., & Sherman, S. (2007). The loyal member effect: On the preference for ingroup members who engage in exclusive relations with the ingroup. *Developmental Psychology, 43*, 1347–59.

Clark, S. S., & Giacomantonio, S. G. (2013). Music preferences and empathy: Toward predicting prosocial behavior. *Psychomusicology: Music, Mind and Brain, 23*(3), 177–86.

Clarke, S. A., Booth, L., Velikova, G., et al. (2006). Social support: Gender differences in cancer patients in the United Kingdom. *Cancer Nursing, 29*, 66–72.

Confucius & Waley, A. (1938). *The Analects of Confucius.* New York: Random House.

Copen, C. E., Daniels, K., & Mosher, W. D. (2013). First premarital cohabitation in the United States: 2006–2010 National Survey of Family Growth. National health statistics reports, no. 64. Hyattsville, MD: National Center for Health Statistics.

Cottrell, C. A., Neuberg, S. L., & Li, N. P. (2007). What do people desire in others? A sociofunctional perspective on the importance of different valued characteristics. *Journal of Personality and Social Psychology, 92*, 208–31.

Cramer, D. (1987). Self-esteem, advice-giving, and the facilitative nature of close personal relationships. *Person-Centered Review, 2*(1), 99–110.

Davila, J., & Kashy, D. A. (2009). Secure base processes in couples: Daily associations between support experiences and attachment security. *Journal of Family Psychology, 23*, 76–88. doi:10.1037/a0014353.

Degges-White, S., & Borzumato-Gainey, C. (2011). *Friends forever: How girls and women forge lasting relationships.* Lanham, MD: Rowman & Littlefield.

Degges-White, S., & Borzumato-Gainey, C. (2014). *Mothers and daughters: Living, loving, and learning over a lifetime.* Lanham, MD: Rowman & Littlefield.

Denissen, J. J. A., Penke, L., Schmitt, D. P., & van Aken, M. A. G. (2008). Self-esteem reactions to social interactions: Evidence for sociometer mechanisms across days, people, and nations. *Personality and Social Psychology, 95*(1), 181–96.

Dew, J., Britt, S., & Huston, S. (2012). Examining the relationship between financial issues and divorce. *Family Relations, 61*(4), 615–28.

Dew, J., & Dakin, J. (2011). Financial disagreements and marital conflict tactics. *Journal of Financial Therapy, 2*(1), article 7. http://dx.doi.org/10.4148/jfft.v2i1.1414.

Dijkstra, J., Verhulst, F., Ormel, J., & Veenstra, R. (2009). The relation between popularity and aggressive, destructive, and norm-breaking behaviors: Moderating effects of athletic abilities, physical attractiveness, and prosociality. *Journal of Research on Adolescence, 19*, 401–13.

Dunbar, R. I. M. (2004). Gossip in evolutionary perspective. *Review of General Psychology, 8*(2), 100–110.

Erikson, E. (1959). *Identity and the life cycle.* New York: International Universities Press.

Feinberg, M., Willer, R., Stellar, J., & Keltner, D. (2012). The virtues of gossip: Reputational information sharing as prosocial behavior. *Journal of Personality and Social Psychology, 102*(5), 1015–30.

Feinstein, B. A., Herschenberg, R., Bhatia, V., Latack, J. A., Meuwly, N., & Davila, J. (2013). Negative social comparison on Facebook and depressive symptoms: Rumination as a mechanism. *Psychology of Popular Media Culture, 2*(3), 161–70.

Feld, S. L. (1991). Why your friends have more friends than you do. *American Journal of Sociology, 96*(6), 1464–77.

Fingerman, K. L., Miller, L., & Charles, S. (2008). Saving the best for last: How adults treat social partners of different ages. *Psychology and Aging, 23*(2), 399–409.

Fiore, D. K. (2003). Parental rage and violence in youth sports: How can we prevent soccer moms and hockey dads from interfering in youth sports and causing games to end in fistfights rather than handshakes. *Villanova Sports and Entertainment Law Journal, 10,* 103–30.

Fiske, A. P. (1992). The four elementary forms of sociality: Framework for a unified theory of social relations. *Psychology Review, 99*(4), 689–723.

Flashman, J., & Gambetta, D. (2014). Thick as thieves: Homophily and trust among deviants. *Rationality and Society, 26*(1), 3–45.

Foundation for Community Association Research. (2012). *Statistical review for U.S. homeowners associations, condominium communities, and housing cooperatives.* Retrieved July 29, 2014, from http://www.cairf.org/foundationstatsbrochure.pdf.

Fredricks, J. A., & Eccles, J. S. (2006). Is extracurricular participation associated with beneficial outcomes? Concurrent and longitudinal relations. *Developmental Psychology, 42*(4), 698–713.

Friedman, L. C., Baer, P. E., Nelson, D. V., et al. (1988). Women with breast cancer: Perception of family functioning and adjustment to illness. *Psychosomatic Medicine, 50,* 529–40.

Gallagher, P., Fleeson, W., & Hoyle, R. H. (2011). A self-regulatory mechanism for personality trait stability: Contra-trait effort. *Social Psychological and Personality Science, 2,* 335–42. doi:10.1177/1948550610390701.

Glasser, W. (1998). *Choice theory: A new psychology of personal freedom.* New York: Harper-Collins.

Goel, S., Mason, W., & Watts, D. J. (2010). Real and perceived attitude agreement in social networks. *Journal of Personality and Social Psychology, 99*(4), 611–21.

Gottlieb, L. (2009). Mean girls at work. *Women's Health, 6*(9), 99–101.

Greenberg, L., & Barling, J. (1999). Predicting employee aggression against coworkers, subordinates and supervisors: The roles of person behaviors and perceived factors. *Journal of Organizational Behavior, 20,* 897–913.

Gurung, R. A. R., Taylor, S. E., & Seeman, T. E. (2003). Accounting for changes in social support among married older adults: Insights from the MacArthur Studies of Successful Aging. *Psychology and Aging, 18,* 487–96.

Gutierrez, K. D., Izquierdo, C., & Kremer-Sadlik, T. (2010). Middle class working families' beliefs and engagement in children's extra-curricular activities: The social organization of children's futures. *International Journal of Learning, 17*(3), 633–56.

Hagemann, J. A. (1986). Confucius say: Naming as social code in ancient China. Paper presented at the 37th Annual Meeting of the Conference on College Composition and Communication, New Orleans, LA, March 13–15, 1986.

Hamilton, B. E., Martin, J. A., & Ventura, S. J. (2013). Preliminary data for 2012. *National Vital Statistics Report, 62*(3). Hyattsville, MD: National Center for Health Statistics.

Hartup, W. W., & Stevens, N. (1997). Friendships and adaptation in the life course. *Psychological Bulletin, 121,* 355–70.

Heyman, G. D., Fu, G., & Lee, K. (2008). Reasoning about the disclosure of success and failure to friends among children in the United States and China. *Developmental Psychology, 44*(4), 908–18.

Hodas, N. O., Kooti, F., & Lerman, K. (2013). Friendship paradox redux: Your friends are more interesting than you. *ICWSM, 13*, 8–10.

Hunter, M. L. (1975). A report on the proceedings of the first and second symposia on education, training, and aging (Springfield, MA, November 1974, and Portland, ME, February 1975). Durham, NH: New England Gerontology Center.

James, W. B., Witte, J. E., & Galbraith, M. W. (2006). Havighurst's social roles revisited. *Journal of Adult Development, 13*, 52–60.

Jepsen, D., & Rodwell, J. (2010). A social exchange model of the employment relationship based on keeping tally of the psychological contract. *Employment Relations Record, 10*(2), 20–45.

Jones, E. E., & Harris, V. A. (1967). The attribution of attitudes. *Journal of Experimental Social Psychology, 3*, 1–24. doi:10.1016/0022-1031(67)90034-0.

Jones, R. M., Vaterlaus, J. M., Jackson, M. A., & Morrill, T. B. (2014). Friendship characteristics, psychosocial development, and adolescent identity formation. *Personal Relationships, 21*(1), 51–67.

Jung, C. G. (1938). *Psychology and religion.* Binghamton, NY: Vail-Ballou Press.

Kahana, E., Ghatta, T., Lovegreen, L., Kahana, B., & Midlarsky, E. (2013). Altruism, helping, and volunteering: Pathways to well-being in late life. *Journal of Aging and Health, 25*(1), 159–87.

Kaniasty, K. (2012). Predicting social psychological well-being following trauma: The role of postdisaster social support. *Psychological Trauma: Theory, Research, Practice, and Policy, 4*(1), 22–33.

Kawano, S. (2014). A sociocultural analysis of childrearing support for mothers of preschoolers living in Tokyo. *Japan Forum, 26*(1), 46–64.

Kim, T. H. M., Connolly, J. A., & Tamim, H. (2014). The effect of social support around pregnancy on postpartum depression among Canadian teen mothers and adult mothers in the maternity experiences survey. *BMC Pregnancy and Childbirth, 14*, 1–15.

Ko, H-J, & Youn, C-H. (2011). Effects of laughter therapy on depression, cognition, and sleep among community-dwelling elderly. *Geriatrics and Gerontology International, 11*(3), 267–74.

Krause, N. (2010). Receiving social support at church when stressful life events arise: Do Catholics and Protestants differ? *Psychology of Religion and Spirituality, 2*(4), 234–46.

Kreider, R. M., & Ellis, R. (2011). Number, Timing, and Duration of Marriages and Divorces: 2009. Current Population Reports, P70-125, U.S. Census Bureau, Washington, DC.

Kuhle, B. X. (2012). It's funny because it's true (Because it evokes our evolved psychology). *Review of General Psychology, 16*(2), 177–86.

Kuttler, A. F., Parker, J. G., & La Greca, A. M. (2002). Developmental and gender differences in preadolescents' judgments of the veracity of gossip. *Merrill-Palmer Quarterly, 48*, 105–32.

Laertius, D. (2009). *The lives and opinions of eminent philosophers.* Charleston, SC: BiblioBazaar.

Lansford, J., & Parker, J. G. (1999). Children's interactions in friendship triads: Effects of gender and relationship intransitivity. *Developmental Psychology, 35*, 80–93.

Lauer, C. S. (2007). A friend in need: Character counts when someone near and dear is ill. *Modern Healthcare, 37*(48), 37.

Layous, K., Chancellor, J., & Lyubomirsky, S. (2014). Positive activities as protective factors against mental health conditions. *Journal of Abnormal Psychology, 123*(1), 3–12.

Le, B. M., Impett, E. A., Kogan, A., Webster, G. D., & Cheng, C. (2013). The personal and interpersonal rewards of communal orientation. *Journal of Social and Personal Relationships, 30*(6), 694–710.

Lemay, E. P., & Clark, M. S. (2008). "Walking on eggshells": How expressing relationship insecurities perpetuates them. *Journal of Personality and Social Psychology, 95*(2), 420–41.

Lemay, Jr., E. P., Overall, N. C., & Clark, M. S. (2012). Experiences and interpersonal consequences of hurt feelings and anger. *Journal of Personality and Social Psychology, 103*(6), 982–1006. doi:10.1037/a0030064.

Letters, *Time*, U.S. edition, September 16, 2000, and Australian edition, October 9, 2000.

Lin, Y., & Forrest, B. (2012). Happiness, fear, and forced struggle. In *Systemic structure behind human organizations*. New York: Springer.

Lindsey, E. W. (2002). Preschool children's friendships and peer acceptance: Links to social competence. *Child Study Journal, 32*, 145–55.

Luthar, S. S., Shoum, K. A., & Brown, P. J. (2006). Extracurricular involvement among affluent youth: A scapegoat for "ubiquitous achievement pressures"? *Developmental Psychology, 42*(3), 583–97.

Lyubomirsky, S., King, L., & Diener, E. (2005). The benefits of frequent positive affect: Does happiness lead to success? *Psychological Bulletin, 131*, 803–55.

Mandell, F., & Jordan, K. (2010). *Becoming a life change artist: 7 creative skills to reinvent yourself at any stage of life*. New York: Penguin.

Maner, J. K., DeWall, C. N., Baumeister, R. F., & Schaller, M. (2007). Does social exclusion motivate interpersonal reconnection? Resolving the "porcupine problem." *Journal of Personality and Social Psychology, 92*(1), 42–55.

Matthews, S. (1986). *Friendships through the life course*. Beverly Hills, CA: Sage.

Maurizi, L. K., Ceballo, R., Epstein-Ngo, Q., & Cortina, K. S. (2013). Does neighborhood belonging matter? Examining school and neighborhood belonging as protective factors for Latino adolescents. *American Journal of Orthopsychiatry, 83*(2, 3), 323–34.

McGrath, D. (2012). Interpersonal contact at work: Consequences for wellbeing. *International Journal of Health, Wellness and Society, 2*(1), 33–47.

Miller, J. G., Bland, C., Kaillberg-Shroff, M., et al. (2014). Culture and role of exchange vs. communal norms in friendship. *Journal of Experimental Social Psychology, 53*, 79–93.

Morry, M. M. (2005). Allocentrism and friendship satisfaction: The mediating roles of disclosure and closeness. *Canadian Journal of Behavioural Science, 37*(3), 211–22.

Myers, D. G. (2000). The funds, friends, and faith of happy people. *American Psychologist, 55*, 56–67.

Nantel-Vivier, A., Kokko, K., Caprara, V., Pastorelli, C., Gerbino, G., Paciello, M., & Tremblay, R. (2009). Prosocial development from childhood to adolescence: A multi-informant perspective with Canadian and Italian longitudinal studies. *Journal of Child Psychology and Psychiatry, 50*, 590–98. doi:10.1111/j.1469-7610.2008.02039.x.

Negron, R., Martin, A., Almog, M., Balbierz, A., & Howell, E. (2013). Social support during the postpartum period: Mothers' views on needs, expectations, and mobilization of support. *Maternal and Child Health Journal, 17*(4), 616–23.

Niffenegger, J., & Willer, L. (1998). Friendship behaviors during early childhood and beyond. *Early Childhood Education Journal, 26*, 95–99.

Ogden, P., Minton, K., & Pain, C. (2006). *Trauma and the body*. New York: W. W. Norton.

Ojanen, T., Sijtsema, J. J., Hawley, P. H., & Little, T. D. (2010). Intrinsic and extrinsic motivation in early adolescent friendship development: Friendship selection, influence, and prospective friendship quality. *Journal of Adolescence, 33*(6), 837–51.

Parker, J. G., Low, C. M., Walker, A. R., & Gamm, B. K. (2005). Friendship jealousy in young adolescents: Individual differences and links to sex, self-esteem, aggression, and social adjustment. *Developmental Psychology, 41*(1), 235–50.

Parks, C. D., & Stone, A. B. (2010). The desire to expel unselfish members from the group. *Journal of Personality and Social Psychology, 99*(2), 303–10.

Pew Research Center. (2013). Internet Project Survey, August 7–September 16, 2013.

Pew Research Center. (September 2013). *Social networking fact sheet*. Retrieved July 14, 2014, from http://www.pewinternet.org/fact-sheets/social-networking-fact-sheet/.

Piehler, T. F., Veronneau, M. H., & Dishion, T. J. (2012). Substance use progression from adolescence to early adulthood: Effortful control in the context of friendship influence and early-onset use. *Journal of Abnormal Child Psychology, 40*(7), 1045–58.

Potenza, G. M., Konukman, F., Yu, J., & Gumusdag, H. (2014). Teaching self-defense to middle school students in physical education. *Journal of Physical Education, Recreation, and Dance, 85*(1), 47–50.

Prezza, M., Amici, M., Roberti, T., & Tedeschi, G. (2001). Sense of community referred to the whole town: Its relations with neighboring, loneliness, life satisfaction, and area of residence. *Journal of Community Psychology, 29*(1), 29–52.

Public Agenda. (2004). *Teaching interrupted: Do discipline policies in today's public schools foster the common good?* New York: Public Agenda.

Ranney, J. D., & Troop-Gordon, W. (2012). Computer-mediated communication with distant friends: Relations with adjustment during students' first semester in college. *Journal of Education Psychology, 104*(3), 848–61.

Reddy, S. (2014). Little children and already acting mean: Children, especially girls, withhold friendship as a weapon. Retrieved June 11, 2014, from http://online.wsj.com/news/articles/SB10001424052702304811190457958633180324524.

Renzaho, A. M., Richardson, B., & Strugnell, C. (2012). Resident well-being, community connections, and neighborhood perceptions, pride, and opportunities among disadvantaged metropolitan and regional communities: Evidence from the Neighborhood Renewal Project. *Journal of Community Psychology, 40*(7), 871–85.

Richards, T. N., & Branch, K. A. (2012). The relationships between social support and adolescent dating violence: A comparison across genders. *Journal of Interpersonal Violence, 27*(11), 1540–61.

Riedl, R., & Javor, A. (2012). The biology of trust: Integrating evidence from genetics, endocrinology, and functional brain imaging. *Journal of Neuroscience, Psychology, and Economics, 5*(2), 63–91.

Robbins, M. L., Focella, E. S., Kasle, S., Lopez, A. M., & Weihs, K. L. (2011). Naturalistically observed swearing, emotional support, and depressive symptoms in women coping with illness. *Health Psychology, 30*(6), 789–92.

Roberto, K. A. (1996). Friendships between older women: Interactions and reactions. *Journal of Women and Aging, 8*(3–4), 55–73.

Rogers, C. R. (1957). The necessary and sufficient conditions of therapeutic personality change. *Journal of Consulting Psychology, 21*, 95–103.

Rose, A. J., Carlson, W., & Waller, E. M. (2007). Prospective associations of co-rumination with friendship and emotional adjustment: Considering the socioemotional trade-offs of co-rumination. *Developmental Psychology, 43*(4), 1019–31.

Rose, A. J., Schwartz-Mette, R. A., Glick, G. C., Smith, R. L., & Luebbe, A. M. (2014). An observational study of co-rumination in adolescent friendships. *Developmental Psychology, 50*(9), 2199–209.

Rosenfeld, A., & Wise, N. (2000). *The overscheduled child: Avoiding the hyper-parenting trap.* New York: St. Martin's Press Griffin.

Ross, C. E., & Jang, S. J. (2000). Neighborhood disorder, fear, and mistrust: The buffering role of social ties with neighbors. *American Journal of Community Psychology, 28*(4), 401–20.

Rubia, K. (2013). Functional brain imaging across development. *European Child & Adolescent Psychiatry, 22*, 719–31.

Satir, V. (1988). *The new peoplemaking.* Palo Alto, CA: Science and Behavior Books.

Schaefer, D. R., Simpkins, S. D., Vest, A. E., & Price, C. D. (2011). The contribution of extracurricular activities to adolescent friendships: New insights through social network analysis. *Developmental Psychology, 47*(4), 1141–52.

Schwartz, S. H., & Bilsky, W. (1987). Toward a psychological structure of human values. *Journal of Personality and Social Psychology, 53*(3), 550–62.

Schwarzwald, J., Moisseiv, O., & Hoffman, M. (1986). Similarity versus social ambition effects in the assessment of interpersonal acceptance in the classroom. *Journal of Educational Psychology, 78*(3), 184–89.

Sedaka, N., & Greenfield, H. (1962). Breaking up is hard to do. RCA.

Selfhout, M., Denissen, J., Branje, S., & Meeus, W. (2009). In the eye of the beholder: Perceived, actual, and peer-related similarity in personality, communication, and friendship intensity during the acquaintanceship process. *Journal of Personality and Social Psychology, 96*(6), 1152–65.

Shallcross, L., Sheehan, M., & Ramsay, S. (2008). Workplace mobbing: Experiences in the public sector. *International Journal of Organisational Behaviour, 13*(2), 56–70.

Sheehy, S. (2000). *Connecting: The enduring power of female friendships.* New York: William Morrow.

Shin, H., & Ryan, A. M. (2012). How do young adolescents cope with social problems? An examination of social goals, coping with friends, and social adjustment. *Journal of Early Adolescence, 32*(6), 851–75.

Shrum, W., & Cheek, N. H. (1987). Social structure during the school years: Onset of the degrouping process. *American Sociological Review, 52*(2), 218–23.

Siegel, D., & Solomon, D. (2003). *Healing trauma: Attachment, mind, body, and brain.* New York: Norton Publishing Group.

Smith, H. M. (2007). Psychological service needs of older women. *Psychological Services, 4*(4), 277–86.

Smithyman, T. F., Fireman, G. D., & Asher, Y. (2014). Long-term psychosocial consequences of peer victimization: From elementary to high school. *School Psychology Quarterly, 29*(1), 64–76.

Sneed, R. S., & Cohen, S. (2014). Negative social interactions and incident hypertension among older adults. *Health Psychology, 33*(6), 554–65.

Snyder, R., Shapiro, S., & Treleaven, D. (2012). Attachment theory and mindfulness. *Journal of Child and Family Studies, 21*(5), 709–17.

Spears, B., Slee, P., Owens, L., & Johnson, B. (2009). Behind the scenes and screens: Insights into the human dimension of covert and cyberbullying. *Journal of Psychology, 217*(4), 189–96.

Spock, B., & Rothenberg, M. B. (1992). *Dr. Spock's baby and child care* (7th ed.). New York: Simon & Schuster.

Stevens, A. (1994). *Jung: A very short introduction.* Oxford: Oxford University Press.

Stone, L. B., Hankin, B. L., Gibb, B. E., & Abela, J. R. Z. (2011). Co-rumination predicts the onset of depressive disorders during adolescence. *Journal of Abnormal Psychology, 120*(3), 752–57.

Strohmaier, H., Murphy, M., & DeMatteo, D. (2014). Youth sexting: Prevalence rates, driving motivations, and the deterrent effect of legal consequences. *Sexuality Research & Social Policy: A Journal of the NSRC,* June 2014, no pagination specified. doi:10.1007/s13178-014-0162-9.

Sullivan, K. T., & Davila, J. (2014). The problem is my partner: Treating couples when one partner wants the other to change. *Journal of Psychotherapy Integration, 24*(1), 1–12.

Swanson, L. (2009). Complicating the "soccer mom": The cultural politics of forming class-based identity, distinction, and necessity. *Research Quarterly for Exercise and Sport, 80*(2), 345–54.

Talwar, V., Gomez-Garibello, C., & Shariff, S. (2014). Adolescents' moral evaluations and ratings of cyberbullying: The effect of veracity and intentionality behind the event. *Computers in Human Behavior, 36*, 122–28.

Taylor, M., Carlson, S. M., Maring, B. L., Gerow, L., & Charley, C. M. (2004). The characteristics and correlates of fantasy in school-age children: Imaginary companions, impersonation, and social understanding. *Developmental Psychology, 40*(6), 1173–87.

Taylor, P., Passel, J. S., Wang, W., & Velasco, G. (2011). *For Millennials, parenthood trumps marriage.* Washington, DC: Pew Social & Demographic Trends. Also available at http://www.pewsocialtrends.org/files/2011/03/millennials-marriage.pdf.

Taylor, S. E., Klein, L. C., Lewis, B. P., Gruenwald, T. L., Gurung, R. A. R., et al. (2000). Biobehavioral responses to stress in females: Tend-and-befriend, not fight-or-flight. *Psychological Review, 107*(3), 411–29.

Taylor, Z. E., Eisenberg, N., Spinrad, T. L., Eggum, N. D., & Sulik, M. J. (2013). The relations of ego-resiliency and emotion socialization to the development of empathy and prosocial behavior across early childhood. *Emotion, 13*(5), 822–31.

Theran, S. A. (2010). Authenticity with authority figures and peers: Girls' friendships, self-esteem, and depressive symptomatology. *Journal of Social and Personal Relationships, 27*, 519–34.

Thompson, K. A. (2010). *On and off the ice: A case study of the involvement of parents in competitive youth hockey.* UMI Dissertations Publishing.

United Nations, Department of Economic and Social Affairs, Population Division (2013). World Fertility Report 2012 (United Nations publication).

U.S. Census Bureau, Current Population Survey, 1975 to 2010 Annual Social and Economic Supplements.

U.S. Department of Health and Human Services. (n.d). Age Trends in the Prevalence of Bullying. Retrieved July 1, 2014, from http://www.prevnet.ca/sites/prevnet.ca/files/fact-sheet/PREVNet-SAMHSA-Factsheet-Age-Trends-in-the-Prevalence-of-Bullying.pdf.

U.S. Youth Soccer. "Key Statistics." Retrieved July 6, 2014, from http://www.usyouthsoccer.org/media_kit/keystatistics/.

Van Lissa, C. J., Hawk, S. T., de Wied, M., Koot, H. M., van Lier, P., et al. (2014). The longitudinal interplay of affective and cognitive empathy within and between adolescents and mothers. *Developmental Psychology, 50*(4), 1219–25.

Weaver, J. J., & Ussher, J. M. (1997). How motherhood changes life: A discourse analytic study with mothers of young children. *Journal of Reproductive and Infant Psychology, 15*(1), 51–69.

Wellman, B., & Wortley, S. (1990). Different strokes from different folks: Community ties and social support. *American Journal of Sociology, 96*(3), 558–88.

Wischniewski, J., Windmann, S., Juckel, G., & Brune, M. (2009). Rules of social exchange: Game theory, individual differences and psychopathology. *Neuroscience and Biobehavioral Reviews, 33*(3), 305–13.

Wiseman, R. (2002). *Queen bees and wannabees: Helping your daughter survive cliques, gossip, boyfriends and other realities of adolescence.* New York: Three River Press.

Yalom, I. (2009). *The gift of therapy.* New York: Harper Perennial.

INDEX

abnormal circumstances, normal reaction to, 71–72, 74

acceptance, 15, 16, 17, 38, 39, 46, 53, 100, 109, 111, 130, 131, 149, 151, 194, 195, 218

acquaintance/acquaintanceship, 33, 39, 43, 44, 46, 52, 54, 194, 205, 228

adolescence/adolescent, 121, 140, 141, 148, 149, 151, 158, 217; identity development, 15, 16–17. *See also* teens and new adults

aggression/aggressive, 14–15, 185; handling, 102; in young girls, 153. *See also* bully/bullying

alliance, 102, 106, 180

anger, 102, 105, 110, 222, 224, 228, 231, 234

anxiety, 158, 225

attachment, early, 6–8

authenticity of self and relationships, 20–21, 31, 38, 42, 46, 47, 63, 67, 79, 97, 103, 115, 120, 169, 190, 203, 229

balance: in friendships, 87–96; relational, 85, 118; in relationship give-and-take, 213–214

"Balancing Act" (exercise), 213–214, 215

belonging/belongingness, 4, 8, 14, 16, 17, 22, 39, 58, 59, 65, 89, 111, 149, 176

best friend, 6, 8, 14, 21–22, 43, 56, 59, 60, 110, 130, 236

best self, 224

betray(al), ix, 10, 27, 28, 30, 34, 100, 101, 105, 112, 148, 190; romantic, 9, 192–193, 207–208

boundaries, in relationships, 10, 14, 30, 33, 57, 68, 105, 114, 116, 141, 149–150, 170, 177, 203, 210–213, 235, 236

breaking point, for a friendship, 45, 48, 82, 124, 190, 192, 193–194

break-up: friendship and emotional gains, 221, 227, 228, 229, 232, 234; romantic relationship, 67, 69, 74, 75; suggestions for, 229–234; truths about, 224–229

bully/bullying: adult, 177, 184–185; electronic, 15, 39, 98–99; in the workplace, 184–185

caring, traits of, 189, 194–198

carpools, 157, 162–165

child-free, 18, 43, 113

church friends, 167–173

colleag-emies, 180–186; the brawler, 185–186; the diva, 180–181; the gossip, 183–184; the outright bully, 184–185; the pleaser, 182–183; the stealth bomber, 181; the whiner, 181–182

communication: confidential, 9, 27–36, 139–141, 183, 184; electronic, 231–232; about friendship conflict, 222–224; openness and honesty, 224; poor practices, 102; using "I" statements, 222–223, 230

companion/companionship, 16, 22, 74, 110, 117, 145, 227, 228; situational, 39, 46–47

compassion, 5, 67, 82, 145, 229

competition, among friends, 51, 130

confidences. *See* communication, confidential

conflict: addressing between friends, 222–224, 227, 234, 235, 236; avoidance and management, 9–10; most frequent subjects between friends, 22–23

conformity, 120, 121, 131, 208

Confucius, 5, 175

congeniality, traits of, 189, 198–200

congruent/congruence, 103, 203, 208

coordination rules, 22

core conditions of counseling, 37

co-ruminate. *See* rumination/co-rumination

criticism: of friends in front of others, 119–127, 150–151; of friends' other relationships, 129–138, 152–153

cyberbullies. *See* bully/bullying, electronic

daughters, coping with friendship rule-breakers, 139–153

degrouping, 100

dependability, 6, 8, 33–34, 189, 190, 191–192

depression, 18, 22, 65, 157–158, 217, 232

Dunn, Irina, 13

"Echo or Silence?" (exercise), 214–216

emotional stability, 63–75; lack of by friend, 71–75

empathy, 5, 8, 19, 23, 37–48, 64, 68, 141–143, 146, 149, 160, 194–195, 197, 198, 203, 216

ending friendships, 221–236

envy. *See* jealous(y)

equality matching framework, 87

Erikson, Erik, 79

"Essential Traits for Quality Friendships" (worksheet), 206

exaggerating technique, in counseling, 182

exchange rules, 22

exclusion/exclusivity, social, 10, 14, 33, 39, 51, 53, 79, 100, 111, 130, 144, 169

expectations: of friends, 203, 211; personal, 94, 95

Facebook, 3, 4, 30, 73–74, 196, 216, 231–232

family relationships, early, 6–8

favors, repayment, 23, 84, 87–96, 147–148, 211, 213

fear of disapproval/rejection, 10, 182, 183

feedback, constructive, 105, 119, 126, 127, 151, 160, 183, 191, 224

finances/financial disparity/issues, 70, 92, 95–96, 112, 136, 170, 211

forgiveness/forgiving, 124, 142, 183, 234

frenemies, xii

friend, types of, 22

friendscape, 8, 21, 22, 52, 56, 58, 101, 201, 205, 220, 226, 228

friendship cliff, 85

friendship credits, 179

friendship ethics, code of, 219, 228, 235, 236

friendship jealousy, 129–138

friendship paradox, 51–52

friendship patterns: between mothers, 18–20; in midlife, 20–21; of older adults, 21–22; of teens and new adults, 15–17; of twenties and thirties, 17–18; of young girls and almost teens, 14–15

friendship rules, list of, 22–23

gossip, effects on relationships, 32, 35, 97–108

gratitude, 60, 135, 136

"Gratitude Review" (exercise), 217–219

ground rules, creating, 164, 220

guilt, 32, 77, 94, 114, 170, 172

heart-to-heart conversation, 59, 140, 183

honesty, 21, 31, 33, 44, 73, 85–86, 100, 102, 104, 107, 115, 118, 120, 127, 169, 189, 190–191, 195, 203, 206, 222, 224, 229, 233, 235

humor, trait of congeniality, 198, 200

hurt, being or causing, 110, 121, 122, 124, 195, 233

identity, 13, 15, 16, 33, 40, 41, 47, 55, 65, 79, 101, 121, 130, 131, 149, 151, 173

independence/being independent, 13, 19, 22, 34, 65, 67, 70, 84, 100, 133, 212
inequity, 83, 95
infant, early development and relationships, 6
insecurity, 38, 52, 119, 121, 122, 124, 130, 137, 143, 151, 181
Instagram, 30, 196, 231
integrity, traits of, 189–194
intimacy rules, 22
intrinsic benefits/rewards/satisfaction, 4, 16, 158, 170

jealous(y), 23, 52, 121, 129–138, 152–153, 198, 217
journal/journaling, 75, 217, 219
joy, bringing to your friends, 109–118, 149–150
Jung, C. G., 20, 113, 173

Lauer, Charles, 82
limits, personal, 33, 70, 80, 210–213, 219
listener, good, 194, 196
Lorde, Audre, 97
loyalty, 28, 34, 42, 66, 71, 89, 97–108, 111, 130, 148–149, 189, 190, 192–193

manipulation, 33, 89, 137, 213
Mean Girls, 149
meditation, 75, 182, 230
midlife: friendship patterns, 20–21; friendship rule expectations, 33–34, 43–44, 57–58, 69–70, 82, 92–93, 103–104, 113–115, 123–124, 133–134
mothers: friendship patterns, 18–20; friendship rule expectations, 31–33, 43, 56–57, 68–69, 81–82, 91–92, 102–103, 113, 122–123, 132–133
mutual friends, 52, 106, 112, 127, 144, 226–227
mutual reliance/mutuality, 4, 6, 7, 16, 22, 31, 38, 47, 92, 115, 142, 179, 196, 208, 213

neediness, 75, 84
neighbors, 175–178
networks, social, ix, 3–4, 22, 52, 54, 55, 64, 100, 102, 113, 121, 134, 216, 226
nonjudgmental, 63, 69, 194, 195

norms, cultural or group, 16, 120, 121, 168, 222, 229

older adults: friendship patterns, 21–22; friendship rule expectations, 34, 45, 58, 70–71, 82–83, 93–94, 104, 115–116, 124–125, 134
"Oreo Cookie" feedback model, 160, 191

parental or caregiver influence, early, 6–8
parenting styles, 19
parents: coordinating with others, 157, 158, 162, 165; helping daughters with friendship conflict, 139–153
passive aggressiveness, 180, 184, 186, 190, 223
patience, 69, 115, 165, 181, 182
personality assessments, 179
"Personal Values Self-Assessment," 208–211
Pittacus, 175
positive regard, xi, 23, 37–48, 141–143, 195, 203
possessiveness, 60, 61, 213

Queen Bees and Wannabees, 79

rebounding friendships, 226
reciprocation/reciprocity, 32, 38, 44, 48, 68, 78, 80, 81, 87, 192
"Reciprocity Review," 217
red flags, in relationships, 47, 57, 138, 229, 233
resentment, 71, 80, 117, 136, 137, 197, 218
respect, of self and others, 36, 94, 100, 124, 141, 150, 177, 179, 181, 190, 208, 229
revenge, 228, 234
ripple effect, 204
role model(ing), 46, 120–121, 126, 150, 159, 165, 203–204
romantic partners, friends' jealousy of, 132, 133
rules of relationship, writing, 203–220
rumination/co-rumination, 65, 234

safety, physical and psychological, 101, 185, 225
secrets, 27–36, 139–141, 183, 192

secure attachment, 7
self-assertion, 33, 102, 106, 107, 122, 123, 182
self-awareness, 8–9, 75, 173
self-confidence, 33, 98, 143–144, 146, 198–199
self-disclosure, 29, 31, 32, 88
self-esteem, 4, 22, 33, 38, 119, 121, 130, 143, 146, 148, 169, 195, 198, 230
self-reflection, xii, 20, 73, 108, 203, 217
self-worth. *See* self-esteem
sexting, 30
sexual harassment, 185
soccer moms, 159–161
social exchange, 5, 6, 29, 92, 96, 110, 168, 212, 221, 234
social pressure, 79, 130, 148, 149, 150
Snapchat, 30, 196, 231
sports, youth, 157–158
sunk loss, 91
support: emotional, xi, 20, 23, 63–75, 77, 86, 144–145, 148, 199; instrumental, 19, 33, 43, 77, 80, 81, 82, 83–86; lack of, 71–75; provision of, 194, 197–198; social, 13, 16, 17, 18, 21, 22, 51, 52, 64, 82, 86, 110, 124; system, 125, 226, 228

teens and new adults: friendship patterns, 15–17; friendship rule expectations, 29–30, 39–41, 53–54, 65–67, 79–80, 89–90, 100–101, 111–112, 120–121, 130–131
tend and befriend behavior, 101, 226
"Testing Your Limits?" (exercise), 212
texting/text messages, 30, 111, 196, 204, 227, 232, 235

third-party rules, 22
traits, of friendship, 189–201
trust/trustworthiness, xi, 5, 6, 8, 22, 23, 27–36, 39, 45, 88, 100, 104, 105, 139–141, 144, 189, 190, 193–194, 230
tween years, 15
twenties and thirties: friendship patterns, 17–18; friendship rule expectations, 30–31, 41–42, 55–56, 67–68, 80, 90–91, 101–102, 112, 121–122, 131–132

unconditional positive regard, 46, 195, 203
unfriending, 54, 130, 232

vaguebooker, 73–74
values, personal, 42, 57, 103–104, 206, 207–208, 226
violence, at the workplace, 185
vulnerable/vulnerability, 31, 46, 48, 105, 142, 193

warmth, emotional, 43, 48, 63, 205
well-being, 22, 34, 44, 58, 75, 82, 98, 110, 114, 124, 137, 167, 172, 173, 178, 186, 195, 198, 225, 229, 230, 231, 234
witching hour, 32
workplace, toxic individuals in the, 178–186

Yalom, Irvin, 126
young girls and almost teens: friendship patterns, 14–15; friendship rule expectations, 28, 38–39, 53, 64–65, 78–79, 88–89, 98, 110–111, 120, 130

ABOUT THE AUTHORS

Suzanne Degges-White, PhD, is a licensed counselor and professor and chair of the Department of Counseling, Adult and Higher Education at Northern Illinois University in DeKalb. Her research interests include women's relationships, including friendship and motherhood. She is also the author of *Friends Forever: How Girls and Women Forge Lasting Relationships* and *Mothers and Daughters: Living, Loving, and Learning over a Lifetime*. Her blog, *Lifetime Connections*, is featured on the *Psychology Today* website (www.psychologytoday.com/blog/lifetime-connections).

Judy Pochel Van Tieghem has over three decades of experience in reporting, writing, and researching for a variety of publications. She is a previous recipient of the Illinois Associated Press Spot News Reporter of the year award and was awarded the Kenan Business Fellowship from the University of North Carolina at Chapel Hill in 1990. She currently resides in the Chicago suburban area, where she works as a freelance reporter.